T0245613

RULES TO WIN BY

Advance Praise for *Rules to Win By*

"*Rules to Win By* offers labor partisans a potent set of battle-tested guidelines for fighting management and winning at the bargaining table and well beyond. In organizing campaigns and contract negotiations—stretching from a Philadelphia hospital to a Los Angeles newsroom, and from a Boston hotel lobby to a New Jersey school house—McAlevey and Lawlor explain how working-class power is built and consciousness transformed. It's hard work but also utterly inspiring. Their book is essential reading."

—Nelson Lichtenstein, author of
State of the Union: A Century of American Labor

"*Rules to Win By* is a well-written and worthy follow-up to *No Shortcuts* and a necessary and overdue addition to the collective bargaining and negotiations literatures. This book could not come at a better time. Read it to win."

—Janice Fine, Professor, Rutgers
School of Management and Labor Relations

"McAlevey and Lawlor explain how and why successful contract negotiations also require the greatest possible participation by workers. The more workers participate in negotiations, the more they understand how capitalism works, the more willing they are to do what's necessary to win—and keep winning. I hope McAlevey and Lawlor's ideas find the widest possible audience among trade unionists, social movement activists, and working people generally."

—Jeff Goodwin, Professor, New York University

RULES TO WIN BY

POWER AND PARTICIPATION IN UNION NEGOTIATIONS

BY JANE F. MCALEVEY AND ABBY LAWLOR

OXFORD
UNIVERSITY PRESS

OXFORD
UNIVERSITY PRESS

Oxford University Press is a department of the University of Oxford. It furthers
the University's objective of excellence in research, scholarship, and education
by publishing worldwide. Oxford is a registered trade mark of Oxford University
Press in the UK and certain other countries.

Published in the United States of America by Oxford University Press
198 Madison Avenue, New York, NY 10016, United States of America.

Library of Congress Cataloging-in-Publication Data
Names: McAlevey, Jane, author. | Lawlor, Abby, author.
Title: Rules to win by : power and participation in union negotiations /
by Jane F. McAlevey and Abby Lawlor.
Description: New York, NY : Oxford University Press, [2023] |
Includes bibliographical references and index.
Identifiers: LCCN 2023000192 (print) | LCCN 2023000193 (ebook) |
ISBN 9780197690468 (hardback) | ISBN 9780197690475 |
ISBN 9780197690482 (epub) | ISBN 9780197690499
Subjects: LCSH: Collective bargaining—United States. |
Labor unions—United States. | Union busting—United States. |
Negotiation—United States.
Classification: LCC HD6508.M229 2023 (print) | LCC HD6508 (ebook) |
DDC 331.890973—dc23/eng/20230109
LC record available at https://lccn.loc.gov/2023000192
LC ebook record available at https://lccn.loc.gov/2023000193

DOI: 10.1093/oso/9780197690468.001.0001

Printed by Sheridan Books, Inc., United States of America

CONTENTS

CHARTS AND FIGURES

Introduction: Negotiations as Democracy Building

MOST DAYS, UNION NEGOTIATIONS DON'T end with assault and battery charges. But I will not forget one that did: May 2, 2006. Instead of winding up the day as usual, writing follow-up notes after sitting down across the negotiations table from the hospital management and their hired guns, I was writing a statement for the police about being assaulted by an infamous professional union buster; his sidekick, a convicted international gunrunner; and seven private security guards. I had been corralled by these men toward an elevator in Desert Spring Hospital in Las Vegas. It wasn't until I entered it and they piled in behind me that I realized I needed to get out of the elevator as quickly as possible. But they wouldn't allow it.

I was positioned at the corner in front of the elevator's controls because I had hit the ground-floor button even before they entered. Once I realized they were all getting into the elevator too, flight-or-fight panic gripped me, and as the doors began to shut, I reached my arm out to stop the doors from closing. But Brent Yessin, the chief union buster, smacked my arm down and turned to pin me against the wall. I was lifting weights in those days, so I was strong enough that he had to grab hard and yank to lower my arm, bruising me and stopping me from moving; that is technically what constitutes assault and battery in police report lingo. As I later testified in legal proceedings, the worst wasn't the

Rules to Win By. Jane F. McAlevey and Abby Lawlor, Oxford University Press. © Oxford University Press 2023.
DOI: 10.1093/oso/9780197690468.003.0001

hit to the arm. What left me shaking for months was an even more mali-
cious, insidious act: pressing his body, with an erect penis, into my body
and holding me there until the doors opened. That elevator ride under
him may have been a minute. It felt like hours.

This was explicit sexual violence. If the Me Too movement had been
more prominent in 2006, surely the incident would have been national
news—had we chosen to publicize it. But we didn't, because to call
any media attention to it would be a win for the employer in a set of
the hardest negotiations I've ever led. Fights with union busters, even
if today's Pinkertons are less likely to use machine guns in the United
States, really are that ugly.

The union buster's goal was only partially to intimidate me directly.
Any fire he could start between me as the workers' chief negotiator and
the negotiating committee—or between the negotiating committee and
the rest of the workforce—would do. Any cloud of suspicion, whatever
sexist nonsense he tried to leverage, could be lethal to my legitimacy
among the workers. This is all par for the course in the repertoire of the
nation's top "union avoidance" consultants, and it meant, as disgusting
as it was, that we had to be extremely disciplined. Thus, our strategy was
to move right past the attack, publicly, and keep focused on the immediate challenge: beating an election to decertify the union that was to
be held forty-eight hours later under the auspices of the National Labor
Relations Board (NLRB).

I had come to that United Health Services (UHS) hospital that fateful
day in May at the behest of several well-respected nurses who had been
in negotiations with me since that morning. The session had been a use-
less slog, since the hospital's negotiators believed that just two days later,
they were going to win the decertification election. In their minds, how
could they lose? They'd been running a terror campaign inside the hospital for several months up to that point, behaving in slightly less offensive but no less intimidating ways than I had experienced in the elevator.
From their vantage point, why bother offering anything at negotiations
on May 2 when, on May 4, they would be done with having to negotiate
with their workers altogether?

During our lunch caucus on May 2, nurses were getting calls that
there were more private security guards and men in suits stationed all

over the facility than they had ever seen. The nurses asked me to go to the hospital after negotiations to do a walk-through to encourage the troops right before the vote. That was how I came to end a long day of negotiations giving a statement to the police.

Two days later, the workers, having built a rock-solid organization, would handily defeat their employer and retain their union. This was no small feat. But they would soon learn that the decertification election was only the opening salvo in management's attempt to destroy their organization, and their hopes for improving patient care outcomes and winning better wages, not to mention a healthcare plan that would allow them to afford the kind of health care that they themselves provided. Over the course of the next nine months, the union busters never gave up. Hospital management swapped out the first lawyer they had hired (apparently he was too polite to the nurses) for a legendarily ruthless lawyer named Larry Arnold. Employers who hired Arnold had one objective only: destroy the union by negotiating them to death. Never arrive at a deal, wait until the contract has expired, declare impasse, and implement their last-best-final offer.

Six months later, by early November, we were still in negotiations. Although we had reached tentative agreements on some minor articles in the contract—for example, drug-testing rules and paid time off for jury duty—practically speaking we were nowhere. It was time for us to put an end to the nonsense the only way we could: by informing the employer that we would be holding a vote among all workers on the current proposal from management. If the workers accepted management's offer on the table, we'd wrap it up. But if they voted it down, the next vote would be a vote to authorize a strike. By early December, the first hospital strikes Las Vegas had ever seen were underway. By the second day, with two important emergency departments in downtown Vegas semi–out of commission, Nevada's governor invoked a little-used part of the state constitution to declare a state of emergency, mandating us to go back to work for a defined sixty-day cooling-off period while the contract would be decided in negotiations with a gubernatorially appointed mediator. That the workers, after months of employer abuse, were strong and strike ready is a reflection of the level of organization they had built.

Never letting a delay go to waste, the employer ratcheted up the sense of futility inside the hospitals, driving a message that the nurses would never win, no matter what. The governor's order afforded that I could pick one person only—not a worker—to join me to go up against Larry Arnold and whoever else Arnold chose for our two-on-two match-up. My choice was Larry Fox, a former leader of District 1199 New England and one of the smartest negotiators alive. The governor's special mediator, however, was to be the longtime and highly respected CEO of the Harrah's casino empire, Phil Satre.[1] Satre gave us a fighting chance because he came with prestige, influence, and power, quite unlike a typical mediator assigned by, say, the Federal Mediation and Conciliation Services (FMCS). We had already been using a good mediator, the best the FMCS had, assigned for many months before the strike; obviously that hadn't helped. Satre was perfect for the case because he understood how to work with a strong union and prove a company could still make boatloads of profit while respecting the basic needs of his employees through collective bargaining, because he had been doing it with the powerful casino workers' union for over a decade.

Satre accepted the formidable task of mediating this dispute on condition that it take place in Reno, where he lived, and he offered some executive meeting space in the basement of Harrah's world headquarters. This put 420-plus miles between me and the workers, the entire basis of our power. I was regularly reporting via videoconferencing with them in big group meetings where they sat together in Vegas, but being locked in a room with two of the most immoral and offensive management types I'd ever encountered was as far from my vision of negotiations as one could imagine. The agreement we achieved on day sixty was historic for our side, but not because I was especially clever in that room. It was because the workers had built real power in the workplace over the course of the negotiations, intensively involved a broad base of workers in hashing out our demands, and made clear that our ability to execute and sustain a supermajority strike was the bedrock of our power in negotiations and beyond. In the end, we won and won big.

Merely winning any contract, and thus the right to save the union and fight another day, was the minimum goal the national union had hoped for, and that alone would have been a success. But after the yearlong war waged by hired consultants with a blank check for spending, we were determined to do justice by these hospital workers, win real material gains, and restore the dignity and respect that the twelve hundred nurses and skilled technicians who had been put through hell deserved. It was historic because it involved the first hospital strikes in Vegas, because we beat one of the most notorious union-busting consultants and one of the most vicious lawyers, and also because the gains were huge, including 100 percent fully employer-paid family healthcare plans, staffing rules the nurses never imagined winning, and eyepopping raises. The ratification votes were overwhelming, and the joy, not just relief, led to days of parties and celebrations inside and outside the hospitals.

Working on a few parallel campaigns in different Nevada hospitals and with some large public sector units that year, I gained a lot of experience with a wide variety of employers, who took some dramatically different approaches to negotiating. Not all of the fights were as brutal as the battle royale at Desert Spring, but across the board I found that certain patterns led to durable success. Because my early observations and experiences of union negotiations were with what is now called SEIU 1199 New England (1199NE)—a division of the national union known colloquially as 1199 in the old days—I had already learned that having more workers in the room was a good idea. It provided efficiencies by enabling real-time fact-checking of management's claims. Having every type of worker and worker classification present allowed for faster, better decision-making. If my early training in 1199NE had predisposed me toward electing representative committees of workers, my experience in a right-to-work-for-less state where union membership and dues are opt-in would quickly dispose me to fully open the negotiations process to all workers whom the contract covered.

My own practice has evolved from opening the negotiations room itself to setting a goal of having every worker show up at negotiations at least once, even if only for one hour at a shift change. I developed tools like Article Committees, which involved loads of workers not formally elected to the negotiations teams but structured into negotiations by becoming resident experts on the issues they cared most about in the contract. The more that workers participate, the more they understand, and the more action they're willing to take to win. With time I learned that, to build maximum power, every single step of the negotiating process—from information requests and member surveys to offering counterproposals and ultimatums at the table—must be made into an opportunity for organizing through intentional, mass participation. The informed, invested, and conscious worker organization built by structured high-participation negotiations is then also ready and willing to exercise that power lying behind its demands, to move a stonewalling employer, to deflate the fiercest union busters, and to turn the words on the page into conditions enforced in practice.

Given how the United States had developed by the time I became a negotiator in the early 2000s, the ideological terrain was and still is such that negotiations must have other goals, including strengthening the workers' organization and the labor movement as a whole. At a minimum, this is because enforcing even the best labor contract relies primarily on the workers themselves. Given the grip that social media and huge misinformation campaigns have on the population at large, workers included, negotiations must also be used as a central tool for mass-scale political education. What scenario could be better for workers to learn which side politicians are on than when delegations of workers themselves seek their active support in trying to reach an agreement against large, intransigent multinational corporations making record profits?

The best advice in print that a union negotiator serious about winning can turn to was written by David Rosenfeld, one of the smartest labor lawyers in the United States. In his 1995 report titled "Offensive Bargaining," he lays out how to turn employers' vicious tactics against them, how to use information requests to avert an impasse, and much more. It is brilliant as a starting guide, but it has long been tough to find. You had to have a mentor like mine who shoves it in your hands and says, "Read this, build power, get to work."

This book is a continuation of the core thesis laid out in *No Shortcuts: Organizing for Power in the New Gilded Age.* In that volume, I argue that the chief factor that scholars overlook and that is absent from the literature on union decline is the one factor that unions and workers can control: our own strategy. Obviously, globalization and automation have had a profound impact, along with an ever more hostile legal climate. This book continues to address the primary and insufficiently addressed question of what to do given the endlessly analyzed structural constraints. Thus, this book is also about changing existing union strategy, but this time the focus is on the collective bargaining process.

The devastating impact of the COVID pandemic—the unequal access to vaccines, needed care, and income supports—is a disgusting reminder of why the working class the world over needs more power. One result of the pandemic, however, is a new upsurge in worker organizing. Forced to labor without basic safety protections while upper management sheltered in place, including on their yachts, workers began to fight back. By the summer of 2022, workers in over two hundred Starbucks stores; Amazon workers in Staten Island, New York; and workers at Apple, Trader Joe's, and REI retail stores, to name a few, succeeded in winning NLRB elections in sectors of the economy previously immune to unions. How they negotiate their first contracts will be crucial to determining the kinds of unions they become: implements that workers actively use to change their lives, or sluggish organizations that settle for much less than can be won. This book is for every worker already in a union, for every worker fighting to get one, and for the many workers who will be in tough negotiations with employers as workers battle for justice on the other end of the pandemic. This book extends the theory and logic of high-participation organizing into high-participation negotiations.

—Jane F. McAlevey

Society and Democracy in Crisis

Civic participation across all types of organizations is decreasing in the United States, including among union members.[2] Corporations have been waging—and mostly winning—a relentless war against workers and their unions before and since the passage of the National Labor Relations Act in 1935. The lopsided class war led by employers has resulted in 11 percent of the workforce overall being unionized, including just 6 percent of workers in the private sector covered by union agreements. Over the last two decades, the federal courts have emerged as a particularly successful avenue for corporate attacks on unions. In 2012, the US Supreme Court began delivering one antiworker, anti-union ruling after another.[3] Given the considerably more conservative nature of the Court today and of the federal judiciary overall due to the court packing between 2016 and 2020, we can expect the courts to continue to take a battering-ram offensive against unions as an institution, much as they have with abortion and other rights many people presumed were settled law. The court's open hostility to workers in turn threatens what even the most pro-worker Congress or well-funded and functioning NLRB might achieve.

In a legal context slanting more and more steeply against them, workers need to rely on themselves as the fundamental source of their own power to force bosses into negotiations and to actually win them. This is why the remaining unions—and especially newly forming unions such as the Amazon Labor Union and Starbucks Workers United rightfully celebrating their heroic election wins—need to be extremely serious when considering how they will conduct negotiations. Successor negotiations, that is, negotiations of unionized workers who've already won a contract, are likewise crucial opportunities to revitalize worker organization using a high-participation approach. This is particularly important since most workers in unions today were not involved in the original organizing that produced the first contract covering the terms and conditions of their employment. In order to exercise these solidarity muscles, we need to build them at every opportunity. This concern is equally urgent for tenant unions, debtor unions, racial justice campaigners, and the climate movement—for anyone seeking to use the immense power of ordinary people to shift the scales toward justice.

The labor movement presents some of the best insights for other social movements into how to negotiate effectively, because negotiations are a regular feature of union life. Sadly, very few social movements ever build enough power to pull up to serious negotiations—the kind that result in a written, enforceable agreement. Social movements, when they do win, often fail to secure good enforcement language. To this day, most provisions of the Clean Air Act and the Clean Water Act, achieved some fifty years ago, have never been implemented. Not only can social movements learn from strong unions what it takes to build strong enforcement into an agreement, but also what it means to keep your organization strong enough to hold the inevitable opposition in check. This is true any time there are real stakes to a settlement, whatever the field.

Take, for example, the recent turns in the fight for dignified housing. Faced with the pandemic eviction crisis, more and more tenants have organized and formed tenant unions. Some are already taking lessons from the high-participation labor union approach. In San Francisco, the Housing Rights Coalition helped lead an effort that won the nation's first ordinance granting collective bargaining rights to tenants once a majority become members in their building. These tenants are planning to adapt the high-participation negotiations approach to their now legally guaranteed right to negotiate with big corporate landlords. Farther down the coast, a tenants' association supported by the LA Tenants Union forced a landlord to sit across the table from every single tenant remaining in their twenty-four-unit building following a months-long, all-out rent strike. The association won effective rent stabilization, forty-two-month leases, guaranteed repairs, and the right to renegotiate collectively.[4] As with labor legislation, how legal protections will work out in practice—and how tenants can avoid giving up fundamental tools like the right to strike in the process—will depend on power built through methodical organizing and mass ownership of the project by members in these negotiations. Once workers win a good contract, the employer immediately sets out to undermine it. The only way to enforce the contract is to use an organizing approach to dispute resolution. Anyone fighting in any social movement will find something similar: their ability to enforce agreements depends on what they do with the power they built to win the agreements in the first place. Grievance mill unions, or complaint-lodging nonprofits, are the death of the working class.

Most negotiations today function a bit like our mangled democracy: people believe that voting every four years in the presidential election cycle is all they must do to live in a democracy. Similarly, unionized workers are told that their role in negotiations is to vote to ratify or reject a contract presented to them at the end of lengthy, opaque contract negotiations. When workers haven't been deeply engaged in the process, turnout for the ratification votes is minimal and apathy becomes the norm. The forces lined up against the working class take note. As more and more people in the United States who care about safeguarding democracy have learned quickly, what we do between presidential elections matters as much as, if not more than, simply voting once every four years. Union leaders should have learned long ago that simply allowing members to ratify or reject a contract settlement offer inside a unionized workplace is equally inadequate to safeguard workplace democracy, but they'll learn it pretty quickly once the boss really goes on the offensive. Progressive politicians should take note as well, given the recent series of disastrously failed negotiations with opponents who are as determined to cede nothing and destroy their opposition as the ugliest union busters loosed on the workplace. An electorate, like a union, kept out of the substantive democratic process will be barely equipped to defend it, as we're seeing. It's well past time to change tack.

Wisconsin governor Scott Walker was a clear example of this kind of politician and employer, bragging about his war-on-terror-style union busting as he floated a presidential run in 2015. After the state's teachers' union and its allies fought valiantly against his move to gut many public employees' right to collectively bargain in 2011, Walker bragged, "I want a commander in chief who will do everything in their power to ensure that the threat from radical Islamic terrorists does not wash up on American soil. . . . We need a leader with that kind of confidence. If I can take on 100,000 protesters, I can do the same across the world."[5] If we joke that he's a bit of a monster, it's clear public school teachers are, to him, something much worse. We need an approach to negotiations that's ready to build power to meet and overpower this level of well-organized contempt.

The twin crises in democracy and labor are in so many ways the same problem. In today's extremely hostile climate many workers are somehow not even considered to be workers—like some in Silicon Valley and so-called platform or gig workers—and thus are effectively exempt from the limited worker protections that do exist. There's also been a narrowing in some states about what's on the table in public sector negotiations. Wisconsin's Act 10 stripped most public service workers of the right to negotiate over basically everything except an annual cost-of-living adjustment. In New Jersey, teachers and other public employees were forced to contend with state legislation backed by Governor Chris Christie that revoked their ability to bargain over employer-paid health insurance (see chapter 3 for how teachers fought back). Given that working conditions in the public sector essentially determine the quality and quantity of public services the working class receives as a whole, strong unions ready to effectively win public-interest demands can help fill the enforcement gap, protecting hard-won rights in the years between increasingly gerrymandered elections. As Congressional policymaking has now entered a stage in which one party shows up with the intent of destroying the other side's objectives—making a mockery of what was once the give-and-take of compromise—many of the insights in this book are directly relevant to how the working class can still win state and national policy battles.

How Unions Negotiate Is a Strategic Choice

Unions negotiate or renegotiate contracts every few years. For the most part, negotiations between employers and unionized workers are shrouded in secrecy. Seldom do union members experience the actual process of collective negotiations over the issues that are crucial, urgent, and relevant to their own lives. The purpose of this book is to discuss how negotiations can be different—significantly different—from what has become the norm. Our hope is to start a robust conversation about how workers can still win big, even when their employer hires the top union busters whose only interest in negotiations is as a weapon to decertify the union, and how the act and process of negotiations relate to power, union governance, and the practice of democracy as a whole. The typical collective bargaining process in the United States involves a small committee of mid- to lower-level management and their lawyers, negotiating with an equally small committee of workers who are selected to represent the majority. The members of these union committees are typically paid, and they negotiate during the hours they'd normally be clocked in and working. The lead negotiators for the union are either negotiation specialists within the union (worker members or union staff) or, quite commonly, lawyers hired to lead the negotiations with the small committee. Most union committees are not elected, except in the sense that they involve elected union officials or position holders who, per the union's constitution or bylaws, are ex-officio members of the negotiations team. The mechanics of collective bargaining are typically governed by ground rules that both parties legally negotiated. These rules often dictate confidentiality—gag rules for talking with media or even workers themselves—throughout negotiations.

No uniform rules govern the length of contracts, although there are many specifics at the federal, state, and local levels in the public sector, as well as various rules in the private sector. Generally, unions directly negotiate not just the contents but the duration of their contracts, and, though many don't know this, the very rules for their own negotiations, like those participation-killing gag orders. Despite the ongoing degradation of workplace and civic democracy, most unions can still choose to transform the negotiations process from a closed one with little worker involvement into a process that serves as a key lever for rebuilding robust worker participation and power. The approach to negotiations laid out in this book builds the kind of collective bargaining that can serve as a dynamic classroom for workers' political education, where they learn about power, politics, and change.

One key overarching rule that covers all negotiations is that each side chooses its own team. That's right. Unions decide whom to send to negotiations for the union. Moreover, because most workers care deeply about what is in their union contract—not just how much they are paid or what recourses they have for when they are treated unfairly by management, but a wide range of other issues, such as health and safety, schedules and hours, whether and when they may retire, and everything in between—union contract negotiations offer a cornucopia of opportunities to develop and build deep and broad solidarity. The depth of engagement provided by real high-participation negotiation raises worker power to the level required to win and to sustain unionization despite the busters often brought to destroy unions during successor contract negotiations.

The reason that union-busting firms often surface close to a contract's expiration with a hostile employer is the hostile nature of US labor law. Even after workers win their first union contract, the employer can still try to get rid of the union by initiating a decertification election, as described in the opening of this introduction. Under US labor law, a special thirty-day period occurs prior to a union's contract expiration. The most ideologically antiworker employers understand that this window provides their best, unofficial chance to get rid of a union. Theoretically, the employer is legally prohibited from initiating a decertification petition, in which at least 30 percent of the workers represented by a union sign a petition to hold an election to decertify (unelect) their union. But in practice, this happens when an anti-union workers' committee is formed, generally with expert, covert coaching by a union-busting firm in how to initiate a petition, spread anti-union talking points, and gather signatures. This is why it is so important to build mass participation in the workplace through preparations for negotiations because a supermajority that understands and has fought for a contract won't fall for divide-and-conquer campaigns nearly so easily.

Less dramatic than a decertification attempt, but no less dangerous, employers involved in the long game of undermining worker solidarity often propose two-tiering many of the best provisions of a contract. In such a scheme, workers currently covered by the contract will keep all aspects of what they've won, but employees hired after the contract is ratified will be forced to accept cheaper, lesser standards. This practice is deeply corrosive and quickly pits new, often younger workers against the more senior or tenured employees. Two-tiering should never be accepted, as it decertifies the union in all but name for the new employees, which itself helps to undermine the base of longtime workers who thought the move would protect them. Avoiding a two-tier contract requires power, and also requires starting the political education about how bad two-tiering is before the contract talks start so that workers won't ever agree.

Today's extreme climate of animus and ideological warfare, combined with outdated and dysfunctional labor law, means that what might have been a garden-variety union-contract renegotiation can become a war in itself.

Power in Negotiations Flows from Active Participation at *and* away from the Table

This book hopes to build on labor lawyer David Rosenfeld's tradition of offensive bargaining by explicitly outlining a high-participation, high-powered organizing approach to big, transparent, and open negotiations. In laying out the fundamentals of this approach, and showing them in action across a variety of situations, we seek to provide usable insights into the new directions many unions are taking to winning transformative contracts. Building on the model for organizing and winning unions outlined in *No Shortcuts*,[6] and for changing society by reinvigorating the labor movement in *A Collective Bargain*,[7] this book details how these principles work in contract negotiations, a process that is often treated as secondary to winning a union election, even among those who take a deep organizing approach to the certification process.

This book seeks to remedy that and prevent as many mistakes as possible, rookie or otherwise, along the way. The text should be helpful for anyone interested or involved in extremely tough negotiations in any context. For workers and the working class—whose only real option to win is how much power ordinary people can build to effectively withdraw their labor; or their rent if in a tenant union; or their cooperation with the norms of society as up against the climate crisis, a bungled response to a global pandemic, or a corrupt or sadistically motivated government.[8] Whether the working class is fighting for climate justice, more affordable and better housing, or dignified workplace agreements, if our side can't materialize the only effective weapon we have—durable mass participation and structured unity—we can't sit down to any negotiations of any kind and win real improvements, whether in the United States, the United Kingdom, Tanzania, Argentina, or Germany. All serious negotiations involving the redistribution of money, such as public expenditures or so-called private wages, are about power. And our approach to negotiations has to start and end with an approach that builds power before and through the negotiations themselves.

The literature on how to adopt an organizing approach to the *mechanics* of negotiations simply doesn't exist. While some important academic journal articles and a handful of books describe comprehensive campaigns where negotiations are a piece of a larger story,[9] most lack the focus and detail required for those who seek to transform negotiations, to better align the negotiations process with an overall transformative power-building approach that makes the workers themselves the key actors. The books that do focus on the mechanisms of the collective bargaining process can mostly be divvied into two piles: business books like *Getting to Yes*[10] and academic textbooks used to teach industrial relations.

Business books on negotiating can be a bit bewildering to those who have spent time in contract talks where the employer's only goal was to utterly destroy the union and salt the earth where it once grew. The classic in this field, the book on learning how to succeed at negotiations, has long been *Getting to Yes*, written by Robert Fisher in 1981 (with William Ury in subsequent editions). At its core, the book advances a theory called interest-based bargaining (IBB). Fisher simply and eloquently laid out four central concepts: focus on each party's interests in the negotiations, and not their positions; separate the people or emotions from the process or sides; work cooperatively toward finding and achieving common interests; and agree up front to create systems that both sides can use to assess if the parties are reaching their common interests. Sounds reasonable enough.

Getting to Yes also coined the best-known acronym in almost any negotiations discussion, a negotiator's BATNA (Best Alternative to Negotiated Agreement). That is, if negotiations fail altogether, what alternative course of action can a negotiating party take, and how would that outcome compare to a compromise settlement? In short, is risking an overshot worth it? This stuff is all crucial to have in mind, and the book has a lot of tactically useful material. But for a labor negotiator, its advice presumes a particular reality: the employer is not only willing to settle but is willing to allow the other party to continue to exist. Of course, not every employer hires the Brent Yessins of the world. In fact, one of the healthcare corporations in the 2006 Nevada campaign, Catholic Healthcare West, was pragmatic and nonideological enough to meet the union on IBB-based grounds. Compared with the UHS war, these negotiations were constructive, as both parties could agree that they shared a common interest, with such goals as improving patient care outcomes. Even there, however, the workers needed to back our version of the resolution to those goals with supermajority public actions, even if the employer's relative willingness to "get to yes" allowed workers to keep a decidedly high-road tone. Each side must have power to check the other and to advance the cooperative approach to finding and negotiating a common interest. Corporations simply have too much power for workers not to demonstrate visibly that they are ready to use the only power they have: a real supermajority strike.

Most negotiations in the United States today fall somewhere on the spectrum toward UHS's Nevada smackdown. *Getting to Yes* and its sequel, *Getting Past No*, simply don't prepare negotiating workers for an employer bent on an ideological crusade to wipe out unions altogether. In 2010, Fisher's and Ury's protégé, Robert Mnookin, published *Bargaining with the Devil: When to Negotiate and When to Fight.*[11] Mnookin does indeed take up a case involving unions: a set of unpleasant labor-management negotiations, where management's tense relations with the union at the San Francisco Symphony often resulted in strikes, bad public relations, and bad feelings. But Mnookin's devil, the symphony's CEO, believed in unions, and he even believed they had a right to strike to get what they thought they deserved. While the attention to workers and a union conflict is an improvement over the glaring absence of unions in this team's earlier books, people negotiating with much more devilish employers and union busters will need much tougher advice.

In 2016 Chris Voss released another blockbuster book on negotiations with a title that seemed to match the stakes that today's unions face: *Never Split the Difference: Negotiating as If Your Life Depended on It.*[12] Voss had spent decades as the FBI's top hostage negotiator. As he explains, his strategies weren't hatched in Ivy League towers but on the streets with bank robbers taking hostages and with international terrorists. Being held hostage comes considerably closer to what UHS had put the nurses through in 2006 in Las Vegas. Voss's book highlights an important limitation about BATNAs: they could lead to lowering your side's expectations by allowing you to achieve your "best alternative," as opposed to setting higher expectations and developing the strategy to build the power required to win them. Now, in Voss's case, as he explains, the best alternative would be something like letting half the hostages die and settling to save the other half—a preposterous proposition. Like the above books, Voss's *Never Split the Difference* offered plenty of good tactical ideas, like carefully framing and reframing questions to help the other side realize that yours simply couldn't make their demands work from a logistical or practical perspective, and this kind of method has long been in the toolbox of a good union organizer or negotiator. His focus on emotions and tactical empathy sounds just right for hostage negotiations, and may come in handy on a micro level for social movements. But when we zoom out, as a good union negotiator should, to the future of the union and of the entire working class, workers need something more.

Unions in negotiations need to prepare themselves for a different kind of fight. Often enough, it's one where your opponent flat-out wishes you didn't exist, and the law and the pressure of time are slanted hard against you. This book seeks to fill that gap, reminding union negotiating committees to build and bring in the ultimate basis of their negotiating power—workers themselves.

Workers and union staff looking for something more immediately relevant than these general books on negotiations—which mainly focus on deals between companies or 1-percenter married couples doing battle in drama-filled divorces—might turn to the many industrial relations textbooks in circulation, as they indeed focus specifically on the collective bargaining process between unions and employers. These books can provide some solid introductions to aspects of the process (though their direct relevance can lean more toward management), and often enough contain a few cases from real negotiations, or provide helpful and exhaustive glossaries of legal decisions affecting labor law.[13] Some of the best help place labor strategy in a global context,[14] but in most cases, they are written for a market of upper-level undergraduates and professional-level graduate students seeking to wrap their heads around the social phenomenon rather than trying to engage directly in it.[15] Those that do give prescriptive advice often promote concessions, like gag orders and promises to not "negotiate in the press," that high-participation experience warns against.[16]

Coming as many of the classics do from another era in the employing class's counteroffensive, these books tend to assume an almost quaint good faith on the part of the employer, very narrowly focusing on the hypothetical mechanisms of at-the-table give-and-take. This book seeks to show workers how deep organizing across workplaces and communities can help ensure that the employer is meaningfully and lastingly cornered into giving a lot more give and taking a lot less take. Indeed, in union negotiations with forward-thinking unions, deal-making or signing a

CHART 1. Three Core Concepts of High-Participation Negotiations[a]

TYPICAL UNION		
TRANSPARENT?	**BIG?**	**OPEN?**
Ground Rules Agrees with employer to negotiate "ground rules" before negotiations start, or as first item. **Gag Orders** These are a key element of many ground rules. Gag orders include a prohibition on members of the union negotiating committee discussing negotiations with the media and members/workers. Thus, the first chance workers learn about the proposed agreement is during the ratification process. **Permissive Not Mandatory** Most union workers, if they know anything about their negotiations, assume these ground rules are mandatory, and the gag rules are too. They are not. Under the NLRA, ground rules are a permissive subject of negotiations and need not be discussed at all.[1]	**Small** Committees commonly consist of 5 to 10 workers, plus an attorney or paid professional union representative. **Appointed** These committees are selected by language in a union constitution stating that the officers are ex-officio, and/or that the local president appoints the committee, or some similar variation. **Paid** This generally applies to successor negotiations, and the language agreed to in a previous contract will specify that the committee stays in paid status while attending negotiations.	**Completely Closed** Closed to anyone but the negotiations committee. Union position holders believe and often state some version of "their workers" will be "uncontrollable" and disruptive, and not understand the complex process.

[a] Because government workers at the local and state level are governed by state law, some states require discussing ground rules, but not their content. Democratic unions in these cases could simply agree to things like, for example, the start time of negotiations, being respectful to each other, and that's it. There are also subtle nuances for federal government employees and those covered by the Railway Labor Act. But these *concepts* can be applied in all cases.

BOTTOM-UP / GRASSROOTS		
TRANSPARENT?	**BIG?**	**OPEN?**
No Ground Rules Period. Certainly, no gag orders. **Constant Communications** Regularly communicate in detail to the membership/workers within 12–24 hours of the conclusion of each negotiation session.	**Big** Every classification of worker is represented on the negotiations team, giving the workers with the knowledge of their position the right to inform the negotiations process directly. **Elected** Workers are elected by their peers to serve as negotiators, best done by department/unit and shift. These positions only exist for the duration of the contract negotiations. **Voluntary** To choose a large, representative committee requires surrendering a demand that the employer keep everyone in paid status for the contract talks. A positive side impact of an unpaid committee is that workers who are passionate about the cause run for election to represent their area and want the negotiations to proceed much faster (efficiently) because they are volunteering. This might accompany a demand for negotiations after hours, or in the case of 24-hour facilities, electing alternates for each position so that each area is represented by at team member in the event one has to be at work during negotiations.	**Open** Open to all workers covered by the contract, but not open to anyone else, unless invited as special guests for a specific session, in agreement with the employer. **Legal Equals** Formal negotiations sessions are the only place workers serve as legal equals to their managers and employers. Why deny workers this experience? **Try to Get Every Worker Once** If only for an hour coming off shift, going onto shift, on their lunch break, etc. Even the most skeptical worker will often be positively transformed by spending as little as one hour in the negotiations room.

good, final contract is just one component in a larger, self-reinforcing strategy to place the empowered and democratized union at the command of the workers who created it.

For students of industrial relations and for workers, who both can become experts on their own industry in the process of negotiations, these pages present the building blocks of a high-participation organizing approach to negotiations. We take readers through the process of opening up the collective bargaining process, featuring both the fundamental principles of the approach and its application in case studies across a variety of winning campaigns for contracts in different industries and sectors. In reading about this approach in theory and real life, practitioners can learn how to apply it, and observers can see how its components snowball into an extremely powerful force at the negotiations table and beyond.

High-Participation, High-Power Negotiations

When workers who have low trust in their own organization—as many do in today's typical do-nothing-or-do-too-little unions—are invited to take part in the very process at the heart of every union, they can quickly shift to having immense trust in and effective ownership of the organization. This can happen during one negotiation session, if not just one hour in a session, when the union goes out of its way to ensure that all workers understand the process and dynamics of negotiations, especially when previously skeptical workers see their employer's often disrespectful behavior in negotiations. The old union saying that "The boss is the best organizer" comes to life when workers can witness, firsthand, management lawyers resolutely rejecting reasonable demands, leading skeptical workers to come to the conclusion that their active participation in a collective project is the only way to win changes that meet their pressing needs.

A crucial goal of the approach to negotiations we lay out in this book—transparent, big, and open negotiations, the high-participation approach—is something else urgently needed around the globe: the democratization of unions. The political theorist Robert Michels warned us over a century ago in his discussions of the "iron law of oligarchy" that unions, political parties, and all organizations made up of everyday people have to build in guard rails against reproducing hierarchies.[17] The sad and enraging story at the United Auto Workers, where a corruption scandal has revealed a disgusting and entrenched culture that has not served union members for decades, is only the most recent example of what mass union democracy can help preempt. Involving workers in the most important decisions removes the possibility of top union officials getting too cozy with top bosses. The mechanism is designed to keep position-holders accountable and has an important bonus: the approach also develops many more leaders, who build a much stronger union that is more firmly in the workers' hands (see Chart 1).

Notes on Methodology

This book began as a report for the University of California, Berkeley Labor Center. It grew out of an interest in studying how a high-participation approach to negotiations—particularly big, transparent, and open contract campaigns—transformed the balance of power at the bargaining table and strength of the unions involved.

Surveying the terrain of recent contract struggles in the United States, we first created a survey interview tool that aimed to dissect each aspect of the collective bargaining process. (The survey interview tool is included in the appendix.) After reworking this core document several times, based on feedback from practitioners and academic researchers alike, we used the survey to identify cases that could meet most if not all the criteria we deemed vital to a high-participation negotiations process. It was challenging to find many cases that met our minimum threshold to exemplify high-participation campaigns, which reflects the paucity of worker involvement in today's union negotiations. We explicitly set out to include a mix of types of workers by sector, geography, gender, race, and ethnicity, though fully representative coverage was not possible, given the limited number of cases in which this approach has been applied.

Then we conducted semistructured interviews with fifty-eight rank-and-file workers and current lead strategists in the contract campaigns selected, identifying their strategic decisions and their evaluations of the nature of and reasons for their success. This was complemented with archival research on each case's strategic planning documents to develop a concrete timeline, and to evaluate the turning points in the campaigns as participants identified them. Analysis of this data identified the mechanisms of their wins, examining how high levels of participation were built, and the effect of such participation on the process of negotiations.

This book covers public sector and private sector workplaces in small towns, big cities, and two countries. It covers single-employer and multiemployer negotiations. It spans workforces that have high levels of ethnic, racial, and gender diversity, and others that are less diverse. Some of the unions are wall-to-wall units, meaning all the workers are in the union except those in management (referred to as an *industrial approach*), and some of the unions involve only a portion of the workforce, such as nurses or teachers (known as *craft unionism*). In these case studies, some workers struck to win contract demands; others took strike votes and won their demands on the power of a credible strike threat. In all of these cases, the application of high-participation methods to contract negotiations, in different combinations, were the key to a transformative settlement.

In selecting our cases, we sought radical transparency as the starting point for the negotiations process: this foundational practice can kick off the transformation of a union and lead to greater overall worker participation in the life of the organization, but transparency absent robust organizing is insufficient. From the baseline of transparency, we then added other criteria and elements that enhance workers' understanding of what it means to be unionized. We sought unions that hold elections for their negotiations teams. We looked for unions that have big bargaining teams, as opposed to the typical small ones. We searched for unions that practice open negotiations, by which we mean open to all workers covered by the collective bargaining agreement. The nine sets of negotiations discussed in this book were conducted between 2016 and 2021; they involve six unions in which workers achieved breakthroughs of all sorts and in some negotiations achieved the best standards in their industry in their country. These case studies show that even among a smaller set of unions practicing a quite different approach to the closed, top-down version of negotiations, significant variation exists.

Our work is in the tradition of scholar-activist action research, where skills from academic training are put to use to produce actionable knowledge, in collaboration with practitioners in the field, about how to make change happen.[18] Central to this methodology—as much as to the book's core argument—is the recognition that people in their day-to-day working lives are developing knowledge about how their workplace, employer, and

CHART 2. Negotiations Discussed in This Book

Workforce & Sector	Union	Employer/Location	Year
Nurses *Private*	PASNAP	Albert Einstein Medical Center, Philadelphia	2016–2017
Education *Public*	NJEA	Readington Township School District, Readington, New Jersey	2017–2018
Education *Public*	NJEA	Mercer County Special Services School District, Mercer County, New Jersey	2017–2018
Education *Public*	NJEA	Watchung Hills Regional High School, Warren, New Jersey	2018–2019
Journalism *Private*	NewsGuild-CWA	*Los Angeles Times*, Los Angeles	2018–2019
Journalism *Private*	NewsGuild-CWA	Law360, New York City	2017–2018
Nurses *Private*	MNA	Baystate Franklin Medical Center, Greenfield, Massachusetts	2016–2018
Hotel/Hospitality *Private*	UNITE HERE	Marriott, Boston	2018
Hospital Workers *Public and Private*	ver.di	Charité, Vivantes, Vivantes subsidiaries, Berlin	2021

community all operate. The role of the researcher, like the role of an organizer in the high-participation approach, is to help workers systematize that knowledge, sharing specialized experience and methods learned in years of studying and testing approaches to change on the ground.

Funnily enough, most of the action research around workplaces focuses on scholars assisting management in accomplishing their goals.[19] The little that is focused on action research in collaboration with unions concentrates more tightly on studying work processes and working conditions—important research, but different from the goal of this book.[20] This book applies the methodology to the efforts workers undertake to change those conditions, in organizing themselves through their unions into structures capable of negotiating with their employers in a highly unfavorable legal environment. In doing so, it examines how the mechanisms for creating a high-participation union transform the negotiations process in the workers' favor.

It is crucial to recognize that each of these cases features intelligent people—workers—adapting the methods indicated by the high-participation theory of change to their own circumstances, and thus a great deal of the testing of the theory in the process takes place by the actors themselves. By engaging in detailed process tracing in each of these diverse cases, the most striking thing we noted was the similarity of outcomes and of worker leaders' explanations for *why* they succeeded. Presenting these cases in narrative form, then, allows for broader readership for the worker leaders' insights, which is consistent with our goal to make the knowledge generated by the researchers and the worker leaders relevant to workers in a variety of settings trying to see how they can build power to win, as much as to researchers seeking to understand how these processes can work.

This research is, of course, partisan. We aren't interested in hiding that we want the workers to win—and win big. By presenting in detail how each of these successful unions' high-participation activities helped propel them toward transformative victories in contract negotiations across very different industrial, political, and legal terrains, we hope to show the myriad ways that people in these campaigns turned their diverse starting situations into durable victories by applying a series of principles to the work.

Anyone studying society is part of the very thing they're studying. In action research, this situation is not only unavoidable but serves as an enabling condition for work as a scholar-activist.[21] As a longtime practitioner in the field, who has also trained many organizers on the basis of practical theory-testing in the field, the influence of the approach McAlevey has been refining can be documented even in cases in which she was not directly involved. This is another difference in action research: the workers are made aware of the theory of change and are actively applying and revising it. We see this as an asset to the relevance of this kind of writing to researchers as well, even if it may come in an unfamiliar format.

This kind of study naturally produces a different form of knowledge from a controlled set of case studies. There is indeed no official control group here, other than the obvious background of decades of concessionary contracts and declining union power, which McAlevey has argued elsewhere has more to do with a no- to low-participation strategy rather than simply a hostile legal climate, globalization, or automation.[22] Even critics of this approach agree that these campaigns— where McAlevey has worked as organizer, negotiator, or coach—stand out against a widespread norm of failure and compromise.[23]

Certainly, we need more data, more research, and more future evidence. We hope this book expands the use of the high-participation approach in the field and sharpens reflection on how workers can win big in negotiations. So far, the earlier report from which this book was hatched, as well as national and international online discussion groups around it, have already begun to have an impact in the field. We hope more will join the conversation and, more importantly, join in winning.

The Chapters

The book is structured as follows. In chapter 1, we lay out the playbook, element by element, of the kind of approach to negotiations this book discusses. From experience and from close study of our cases of successful contract negotiations where masses of workers took the central role, we distill the principal components into a kind of ideal type of a *maximal and comprehensive* high-participation, transparent, big, and open approach to negotiations.

In the following chapters, we present in narrative form our findings about how the process of winning unfolded in each case, highlighting the high-participation factors workers whom we interviewed and we agree most contributed to worker power at the negotiating table. The cases we profile each demonstrate key components of the approach we are studying, testing in practice, and improving.

The first and final cases (chapters 2 and 7), in which McAlevey was a central participant, show a self-consciously maximalist application of the high-participation model, as close as it gets to methodically reproducing an ideal type in the messiness and rapidly shifting timelines of actually existing fights (see Chart 2).

Chapter 2 features negotiations McAlevey led in 2016 among nurses at a large and prestigious safety net hospital in Philadelphia. Faced with world-class union-busting consultants intent on destroying the unionization effort, a complex high-participation, strike-readiness approach succeeded in negotiating an end to legalistic stonewalling and a resounding victory in the final contract. A key component of chapter 2 helps readers understand how to defeat the too common practice of an employer filing legal objections to derail the effort after workers manage to win an NLRB election.

Chapter 3 walks the reader through a dramatic example of a very traditional teachers' union throwing caution to the wind, breaking from established practice, and going overnight from top down and closed to fully open, in a pitched battle against a legislated attack on their healthcare benefits. These locals of the New Jersey Education Association (NJEA) demonstrate a powerful effort to apply all the methods at once.

Chapter 4 captures the new momentum among journalists, who won the two featured unions while building dynamic new leadership at the NewsGuild, a division of the Communications Workers of America. The chapter chronicles the amazing unionization at the *Los Angeles Times* and also shows the potential reach of the rebuilt union in the digital era, unpacking how journalists at born-digital Law360 won their union and first contract by using transparency and a big committee.

Chapter 5 involves nurses in the Massachusetts Nurses Association (MNA). In a rural western Massachusetts community with a long industrial union history, the association used mass participation to drive a community-based campaign linking the nurses' demands with the fight against the shuttering of local services. This case is particularly notable because it lay in a more rural labor market dominated by one major, mostly non-union, hospital system, far outside of the union's comfort zone of more liberal-blue Boston—where the association is used to winning based on preexisting power and its history of successful strikes where hospitals and healthcare are a significant player in the city's life and economy.

Chapter 6 involves hotel workers and their union, UNITE HERE, waging and winning a historic strike against the largest hotel chain in the world, the Marriott Corporation. This case involved cracking a giant corporation's union-free strategy after their acquisition of another company through coordination of mass-participation negotiations committees across employers in a labor market, eventually setting the sectoral standard even at hotels that did not themselves strike.

Chapter 7 also involves a massive and open-ended strike, this time in Berlin, Germany, during the depths of the COVID crisis. The pace of the transition here away from small, closed, top-down negotiation parallels the NJEA's pace of change in chapter 3. For both unions, a significant internal culture had to be overcome to unleash the creativity of, in this case, thirty thousand workers, including nurses, service workers, and contract labor, to negotiate together—all of whom previously negotiated separately. This unprecedented campaign links the methodical work of transforming longstanding union practices with an accelerated path to winning high standards. This chapter challenges the narrative of Germany as a workers' paradise, showing how workers developed creative ways to massively open up negotiations despite legal and cultural limitations, and emphasizing how high-participation methods can be just as transformative in legal regimes apparently much more labor-friendly than those in the United States.

The conclusion discusses contemporary debates about the future of collective bargaining, locating the debate in the context of the very real crises facing democracy in the United States, and in industrial democracies broadly speaking.

The final section, "Handy Terms and Explanations," is, we hope, more than a mere glossary. It gives a short description of often-used words and phrases in union negotiations parlance, but is distinct from other such glossaries in the industrial relations literature because it's designed to be used practically. For practitioners, these descriptions will prove essential for optimizing the book for your efforts.

There's no book like the one in your hands. No laws have to be changed to implement any strategy in it: all of the tactics are readily available, if we choose to implement them. This book is about what to do *now*—not tomorrow, not in some fictional future in which the laws have been improved and the courts remade. Academics writing about reforming labor and other laws may provide some insight, but faced with the legal terrain we're navigating on this portion of the planet now, passing even their most modest propositions would take a backing of massive worker power.[24] This book is grounded in the reality of the present, in which conditions are worsening, not improving, even as we write these pages. These strategies work in countries and states with less hostile legal regimes, and extra-hostile ones such as most of the United States, because workers everywhere are smart enough and strong enough to negotiate and win, against their bosses and against the people broiling our planet. Let's get to it.

I

Twenty Key Elements of High-Participation Negotiations

This is a very funny contract. It's very different than a contract that you will sign for anything else. If you sign a contract to buy furniture, a car, a house, or anything else, and if the contract isn't lived up to, you go to court and you ask a judge to enforce it. This contract is enforced by somebody else. It is enforced by you.
—Bernie Mintor, *1199 Handbook*, Members Basic Information (undated, about 1973)

WHEN MANAGING TO OVERCOME THE scare tactics and divide-and-conquer efforts of their employers and win National Labor Relations Board (NLRB) elections, or their Railway Labor Act or public sector equivalent, the workers' fight has only begun. Union-busting firms immediately advise corporate management to pivot from kitchen-sink efforts of sowing distrust to kitchen-sink legal challenges to the election results. This means filing objections with the NLRB on every imaginable point—from the arguable, like a ballot or two being ambiguously filled out, to the completely absurd, like a union organizer personally and individually using unknown and unstated powers to compel each and every worker to vote yes for the union against their will. Even when everyone can plainly see that the workers won their election fair and square, the goal of these challenges is to kill the workers' organizing with a thousand delays. The employers have already ensured that even this first step, hearings on the objections, will cause huge setbacks to the campaign, because employers as a class have been using their considerable lobbying muscle for decades to defund the agency that oversees them. The NLRB by the twenty-first century has grown anemic, with too few staff and too many cases to move much faster than a plodding turtle crossing a busy street.[1]

Rules to Win By. Jane F. McAlevey and Abby Lawlor, Oxford University Press. © Oxford University Press 2023.
DOI: 10.1093/oso/9780197690468.003.0002

The National Labor Relations Board is now responsible for far more workers than it was a decade ago

Number of private-sector workers per NLRB full-time employee, 2006–2019

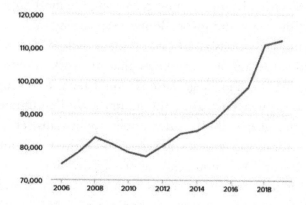

While NLRB courts have upheld some of the ridiculous complaints employers have filed, even when the tribunal dismisses the objections as without warrant, workers are often still kept waiting to start their negotiations. Corporate management immediately appeals the first ruling, pouring more creative writing into a new and longer legal brief explaining why the administrative law judge was wrong, and starting the next round of their delay tactics. This lawfare strategy works its ugly magic either way, as the delays can take the wind out of the sails of rank-and-file momentum. That's the entire point.

If this sounds familiar from Donald Trump's Big Lie following the 2020 election, know that highly paid lawyers and union avoidance firms have deployed it for well over fifty years.[2] But just as when Trump set out to sow confusion and division in the period as ballots were counted and recounted and recounted, the period following a union election is crucial to the outcome of the union effort. In a fight like this, the actual vote count becomes less and less relevant than the will of the parties involved to fight to defend or overturn it. In order to succeed, workers need to turn the power they built winning the election into an even stronger tool capable of winning a first contract—not to mention forcing the employer to give up stalling and recognize the election and the workers' right to negotiate.

Even before Trump, Cold Warrior Ronald Reagan, president of the Screen Actors Guild from 1947 to 1952, learned this game from General Electric's Lemuel Boulware, among the most creative union busters of the 1940s and 1950s. Boulware, planning to destroy powerfully established unions at GE, had to fight their existence indirectly in collective bargaining—and knew that his work undermining the basic premises of labor negotiations would require turning a whole host of constituencies against the union, including union-skeptical workers, the media, the broader public, politicians, civil servants, and more. Enter pre-politics Reagan, who starred in Boulware's famous series of TV commercials aimed at dividing consumers and the above-referenced audiences from unions. So successful was this advertising campaign, so perfect was Reagan—a former union president, after all—that it led to GE later promoting him to other corporations as the perfect man to run for California governor and eventually president, to do to unions nationally what he had done at GE.[3] A year into his presidency, Reagan let people know what he thought of a union's right to strike when he fired and replaced every single striking air traffic controller in the United States. Like at GE, the boss was using contract talks as an opportunity to decimate the workers and their well-established union, the Professional Air Traffic Controllers Organization, not to mention to strike fear into the heart of the labor movement as a whole by firing over eleven thousand highly skilled workers.[4] These are the kinds of brutal, no-holds-barred fights for which so much of the negotiations literature does not prepare workers.

If the NLRB rules again in its second opinion that an election was fair, after the first appeal of the decision that found the workers in fact legitimately won the election, contemporary union busters often advise that the employer must continue to appeal the ruling through all the various understaffed stages within the NLRB and then begin the appeal all over again from the ground up, but now in a strategically chosen local or federal district court (depending on the employer), where legal moves can take years, even decades.

This entire charade has become textbook. From the perspective of organizing, most unions in the United States make a crucial error in these situations: they spend huge sums of money hiring the best union-side law firms to fight management's best lawyers. Equally problematic, the workers themselves spend too much time focusing on the trials rather than on continuing to organize in the face of the employer's challenge-delay-destroy strategy, which can drag on endlessly. Even unions committed to an organizing approach for winning the election can retreat into a lawyer-driven approach at this point, corralling motivated workers onto the sidelines to wait for smart lawyers to win for them. This learned reflex, familiar to the staff-and-counsel-driven approach many take to contract negotiations as well, stakes an awful lot on processes over which the union's main source of power—the workers—has the least influence, while allowing the very power of the organization that won the election to atrophy.

Often, the process is designed to take so long that if a revote is ordered, or if an outside court deems the union legitimate and finally legally certifies it, many if not most of the workers who formed the union are gone. Typically, the activists who endured to win hard-fought elections become targets of management harassment in subtle ways: they may have their once-reliable shifts changed, their vacation requests retroactively denied at the last minute after plane fare and tickets to Disneyland have already been purchased, and their assignments mysteriously switched to the most onerous ones. Management will try to make them miserable and get them to resign, retire, or—best of all—renounce the union as ineffective.

The alternative to this litigate-a-budding-union-to-death strategy is for the organized workers to immediately begin planning for their negotiations, because they *did* win their election, and an organizing and power-building strategy offers their best chance both to outmaneuver a protracted legal strategy in a hostile arena like the courts *and* to win the kind of transformative first contract that solidifies the union's legitimate presence. Whatever the outcome of the legal challenges—an employer's more likely to give them up if it's clear the union is already operating de facto in the workplace—workers are more prepared for tough negotiations or another election if they've continued organizing and laying the foundation for negotiations that, like the election, rely on every single worker's commitment, intelligence, and action. It will also mean a union better able to enforce its contract in practice, assuming the workers can win one.

In this chapter, we present a set of fundamental elements of a high-participation, high-powered approach to negotiations, distilled from our study and from our own participatory-action work in the field. While only one of the unions in the cases we present employed all twenty elements we discuss, each featured union employed many of these elements, and all relied on majority—and eventually supermajority—participation by the workers. In theoretical terms, what follows is an ideal type of this method: bringing these power-building elements together into one comprehensive approach in order to encourage thinking on how these elements can interact and reinforce each other within a single campaign. These principles all share that they turn routine activities into opportunities to build maximal power for the workers' side, and see their fundamental source of strength as existing within the demonstrable and verifiable power of workers to move each other to action. This kind of power has proven decisive in overcoming whatever challenges, legal or otherwise, a union may face in its fight to win.[5] Given our commitment to using research and reflection in action in the field, we have tested and refined these in campaigns where we've worked, and we hope that some of our readers will consider doing the same, using this ideal type in order to imagine and propose a maximally worker-driven, power-building organizing approach to negotiations.

For people trying to understand—or better yet, prepare for—other forms of social movement action that will culminate in hard-fought negotiations in an unfavorable environment, it takes only a small amount of creativity to see the relevance of these principles to building mass-based power and to adapt them to another context. Students striking against tuition increases, tenants striking over skyrocketing rents and deteriorating homes, people uniting to fight against climate injustice, the list goes on. Union organizing in the United States is extremely hard, structure-based work. While no NLRB equivalent may exist in many other fights, building a bedrock of deeply informed high participation among those organizing for an outcome will no doubt bring many closer to winning their own transformative "contracts."[6]

Just as the most advanced and durable methods for organizing unions in a right-to-work state—where the law offers only impediments to the right of workers to organize—form a methodological bedrock for effective organizing in less intensely labor-hostile states,[7] these methods also strengthen workers in any successor negotiations. As unions seek to consolidate their election win in a transformative contract, and their contract in its day-to-day enforcement, the power they build at each phase—and the methods they use to build it—forms the basis of winning at the next. Unions that take these steps as methodically as possible from the beginning often find themselves best positioned to act decisively when the

---

20 Key Elements of High-Participation, High-Powered Negotiations

1. Conducting a power structure analysis
2. The information request
3. Majority contract survey as organizing/reorganizing tool
4. A big, representative committee
5. Electing committees (not appointing)
6. A volunteer, not paid committee
7. Ratify contract proposals before negotiations
8. Creating article committees
9. Three rules of the room when management is present
10. No ground rules (if state law requires, surrender-no-power-ones)
11. Location, where to negotiate
12. When and how often to conduct negotiations sessions
13. Avoid employer and lawyer communication between sessions
14. Training, role-playing, and the opening session
15. The article checklist: make it easy for workers to follow
16. The role of the union caucus
17. Negotiations bulletins, simple and published before the employers'
18. Comprehensive charting and the community campaign
19. Contract action teams
20. Ratification of the contract

stormy waters of a campaign force a deadline or opportunity well before it would otherwise be comfortable.

1. Conducting a Power Structure Analysis

Contract talks don't happen in a vacuum. They are embedded in the real world, in communities big and small, with some workers considered harder to replace and others considered easier to replace. For unions to win in any setting, against any employer, the most successful ones chart the interconnections between the institutions dominating the local labor market and the two negotiating sides. This kind of preparatory work is called a *power structure analysis* of the employer, and it moves well beyond a traditional union's narrower corporate analysis that examines profit and loss statements, reports to shareholders, supply chains, and other financial and potential legal liabilities. This kind of power structure analysis aims toward something more robust, which specifically helps workers understand the employer's relationship to the labor market in which the negotiations take place. It asks: Who holds power in the area, including other corporations, corporate trade associations, media institutions, politicians, large nonprofits, houses of faith, and so on? Which of these are the employer connected to, and how? What are the mechanisms of influence being wielded by as well as over the corporation? Which institutions are the workers connected to, and how? Once these unions find that their workers' internal worksite structure (i.e., level of organization) is strong and a majority are engaged, which is happening concurrent to the first phase—the second phase of the power structure analysis— the power analysis expands to a third phase: direct engagement with workers about all the people they know in the community. That process, an element called *comprehensive charting*, comes later in the contract campaign and is discussed near the end of this chapter (element 18).

The kind of power structure analysis that locates power in local labor markets is too often overlooked by most researchers on union staff, who prefer to target shareholders, seek resolutions from pension board members whose pension funds are invested in the corporation, blow up or at least slow down mergers and acquisitions important to the company, search for wrongdoing that can be brought to light in the media, and undertake a kind of tactical warfare called the *air war*. While these approaches meet with some success, they lack an engagement with the power of workers themselves, in the workplace and in their community. Experience shows that those community relations are still decisive, even with financialization disguising ownership and complicating how a corporation expresses itself in a local labor market. The kind of power structure analysis we found in our cases is one that supplements the more traditional approach by asking what the employer needs from the local labor market. Does it seek tax relief for construction or expansion, a good image to compete more effectively with competitors in the same labor market, procurement deals with local or state governments, seats on a local quasi-public–quasi-private economic development board to grease some of these wheels? These questions bring into view the social and political context of consent and public expenditure that subsidizes and underwrites the employer's operations, opening up all manner of specific ways that workers themselves can build power in the community to make employers feel the pinch, and to sustainably raise the cost to the employer of not meeting workers' demands.[8]

The method for conducting such power structure analyses can range widely, but we present here the most systematic three-phase model.

In phase one, the union measures the strength of the employer on two key scales: (1) the firm's own power, internally built and in relation to other institutions; and (2) the broader power structure that governs and greases the labor market where the employer is embedded. The first, depicted in the list later in this section, attempts to relatively quantify, as a ranking, the employer's power on several axes. The research aspect of the power structure process described here, what we refer to as phase one, was originally conceived of by groundbreaking community organizer and thinker Anthony Thigpenn. To do this, some qualitative work will be necessary, usually between fifty and one hundred semistructured interviews with a range of actors in the market, from journalists on the beat to competitors to elected decision-makers, and more. Meanwhile, some explicitly quantitative measures can be generated by things like media database searches to assess coverage over time, numbers of followers on social media, number and value of demonstrated policy successes, and so on. Local newspapers and their archives are rich resources for this work as well. Information from this analysis can then also assist in parallel work on the local power structure in general, identifying key actors within the labor market (politicians, houses of faith, ethno-cultural organizations), their relative power over each other and over the employer, and their relative disposition toward the outcome (strongly or weakly pro-union, strongly or weakly pro-employer). This two-pronged preliminary analysis helps set the stage for strategic work in the community, but also always develops over the course of a fight, as powerful actors, surprising allies, and fresh realignments reveal themselves. Tools for visualizing this work appear in Figure 1.

Then in phase two, staff, along with worker leaders, chart the work-place unit by unit, shift by shift, and identify the informal power structures within the workplace: the relationships that make work happen, the people each worker turns to when something goes wrong, the people who have shown an ability to make others take risks, the other relationships that structure who talks to and convinces whom. This is related to organic leader identification but also extends into charting other relationships. This portion of the power structure analysis forms the basis for the systematic work of the organizing committees, espe-cially in big wall charting, quantifying how many workers in each unit are on board for each collective action taken, identifying holdouts and respected workers, and focusing attention on areas that are trailing. This captures the "structure" being tested in structure tests.

Phase three links these components together, as the maximum number of workers possible receive a detailed presentation of the power structure, and work with a dedicated team to chart all of the potential intersections between their own lives and relationships in the community and key actors and institutions in the power structure. Do they, or their cousin, attend a key religious leader's services? Who else in the power structure is that key religious leader connected to, and how? Do any of the workers have unique relationships with area politicians? Which ones, and how?

These are types of power for phase one of a power structure analysis:

• Mobilize base / disruptive power: Can the company sustain a strike? Can the workers sustain a strike, and for how long, based on what

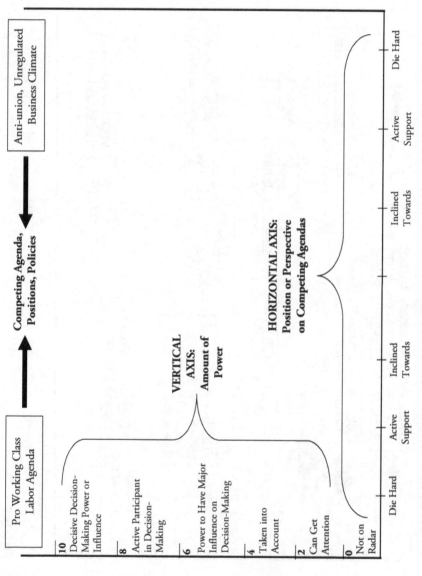

FIGURE 1. Tools used to visualize the initial power structure analysis.[13] Anthony Thigpenn created and developed this PSA in the early 1990s.

STEPS TO DEVELOP A STRATEGIC POLITICAL LANDSCAPE POWER ANALYSIS

STEP 2: Sketch the **Competing Agendas.** The agenda of those who are causing or perpetuating the problems, and your agenda (the conditions you want to bring about)

STEP 1: Define the major **Problems or Conditions** which are negatively impacting primary constituencies

STEP 3: Sketch the major centers of **Decision-Makers** over the problem conditions

Board of Supes

City Council

STEP 4: Sketch major **Issue/Policy Battles** related to problem conditions which are going on

Automated Solar Farm

STEP 5: Sketch major organized **Opposition**

PINK

Lack of Good Union jobs

STEP 8: Analyze the picture, develop strategies for changing the equation

STEP 6: Sketch Organized **Progressive Groups**

GREEN

STEP 7: Sketch key **Unorganized** social sectors

YELLOW

10	Decisive Decision-Making Power or Influence
8	Active Participant in Decision-Making
6	Power to Have Major Influence on Decision-Making
4	Taken into Account
2	Can Get Attention
0	Not on Radar

| Die Hard | Active Support | Inclined Towards | Inclined Towards | Active Support | Die Hard |

FIGURE 1. Continued

history and present conditions? Are other forms of disruptive power aside from a strike (particularly relevant in many public sector battles) such as civil disobedience available to the union that might shut down a meeting, preventing approvals or denials an employer seeks (e.g., blocking entrances to buildings, occupying public offices, signing up five hundred people to speak for their three minutes each during typical local open meeting laws covering governmental agencies.

- Electoral power: How does the employer contribute to elections locally to entities where it seeks policy gains? How deep into the local electoral system is the employer, and how does this express itself (financial contributions, endorsements, hiring third-party firms to support their candidates of choice)? What electoral allies do the workers have, and what power do they hold? What is the union's real and perceived ability to get out the vote for candidates it donates to or endorses?

- Media/public perception: How is the employer viewed in the media and related power structures, including in the union leading the contract campaign, as well as among other unions and potential allies in the area? Does the employer appear on the front pages or at the top of the hour on local news, are they only getting a fifteen-second blip late in local TV coverage, or a small mention in the business section buried near the end of it? Do they have one million or one hundred social media followers? What is the union's public profile like in all of these arenas?

- Expertise: Do policymakers regularly consult the employer or the workers' organization on how to understand issues like jobs, safety and health, public budgeting, and more? Are they invited to speak at forums and panels covering these related topics?

- Relationships: What kind of local relationships does the employer need to do business, and does it possess many? With key people directly? With less key players who might have access to the key ones? If the customer picks up the phone to call the mayor's or governor's office, is the caller patched right through or told the elected official is busy for weeks? Does the employer's staff have the direct cell phone number of the many power holders they need? How fast will a meeting materialize if they request one? What do these relationships and forms of access look like on the union side?

- Financial resources: Is the employer sitting on massive reserves, ranked high by credit rating agencies, or in dire straits? What do they report to shareholders or board members, as opposed to what they might tell the employees heading into negotiations? Does the union have access to reserves, like a strike or solidarity fund?

- Demonstrated success: In any given labor market, has the employer weighed in on local policy fights directly or indirectly through trade associations? Have they been consistently on the winning or losing side of these recent policy fights? For example, Amazon has now twice been defeated in the greater New York City labor market—in their attempt to build a new second headquarters in Queens, and then to expand their cargo holding terminal at Newark Airport. Both efforts against them were led by unions and community-based organizations.

This research effort is most comprehensive when it involves the workers. At a bare minimum, it is shared with them, something rarely ever done between big union research departments and the workers at the center of the given effort. In those settings, the voluminous corporate research conducted by typical unions is seen only by the researchers and most senior full-time strategists. The points of labor market power structure analysis in the high-participation model are both to educate the workers *and* to tap into their many connections to challenge and win over the power holders to their cause. For more on the thinking behind the whole-worker organizing community campaigns this kind of power structure analysis makes possible, see the chapters 1 and 2 of *No Shortcuts: Organizing for Power in the New Gilded Age.*[9]

2. The Information Request

Information requests are a formal, legal part of the negotiations process. Workers who have formed a union that has been legally certified have the statutory right to information that will help them prepare for negotiations, the very information their employer has on just about any topic or issue area that is related to conditions of work. Unionized workers can request that the employer provide spreadsheets that show what every worker in the bargaining unit—the workers covered by the collective agreement—is paid, their date of hire, the experience they brought to the job, years of service with their current employer, what benefits or bonuses they are being paid, how many hours of overtime they are asked to work, how many of their work shifts are being cancelled, and much more. The employer is required by law to provide this information as part of the contract negotiations process.

If the employer fails to provide this information, crucial to constructing the demands the workers will put forward, it constitutes an unfair labor practice (ULP) under the National Labor Relations Act (NLRA) or other applicable labor law. While no negotiations committee would release or publish this sensitive data in their raw form, a committee can quickly develop a database that allows each worker to see, for example, whether they are being paid under, over, or the same as workers with the same experience and years on the job. This is a key tool used to confront gender-, age-, race-, and ethnicity-based discrimination in the salary structure, as workers at the *Los Angeles Times* (chapter 4) were able to do, using data from information requests to call out five-figure pay disparities. Wage and benefits transparency is fundamental to a negotiations process with mass participation. This is especially true in first contracts, such as at Einstein (chapter 2) where, prior to unionization, the employer paid individual workers whatever the manager felt like, creating huge and often staggeringly discriminatory disparities.

Discussing and explaining the information request with workers before sending it to the employer is one way unions can illustrate a right they have relative to not-yet-unionized workers. (See the appendix for the Einstein information request.) The union is not limited to only one request: they can submit additional requests throughout the negotiations as topics arise where information is needed. For example, a debate about security needs for a hospital emergency room might not emerge until an actual incident happens during negotiations that prompts a need for data on how many other times said incident might have occurred. Employers often delay handing over this information, especially when they are aware that it will reveal management behavior that workers will then challenge. When employers unreasonably delay, the union can file a ULP charge against the employer. This can be an effective weapon with the public, to show how management is hiding something, and it can also give workers the right to hold a ULP strike. In the United States, workers cannot be permanently replaced when striking over ULPs, whereas they can be replaced in economic strikes.

In the end, sharing information requests with a large negotiations committee helps inform workers of the larger picture they're negotiating within, and thus develop strategic ideas a smaller committee with less coverage would likely miss. There are reasons management keeps this information secret when they can: putting it directly in front of workers allows them to take rightful ownership of their working conditions with fuller knowledge of what those working conditions are.

3. Majority Contract Survey as Organizing/Reorganizing Tool

Most unions have handed out, mailed, or emailed an anonymous survey to the workers about contract priorities, while some have gone so far as to post the anonymous survey on social media or even send a reminder email.[10] While a higher response rate would clearly be preferred by most unions, the process tends to be a relatively low priority, without concrete high-participation benchmarks or explicit strategies to get there. In New Jersey, as we discuss in chapter 3, organizers with the teachers' union found that most members didn't even remember filling out the union's traditional bargaining survey—a clear indication that the negotiations team or even the workers themselves didn't take it very seriously. By contrast, in a contract process truly aimed at reaching supermajority worker participation and strike readiness, the contract survey is not merely a straw poll for setting priorities, but itself represents a tool for organizing: the first of what will likely be many "structure tests" in the contract campaign. The most effective approach unions took to this phase of negotiations preparation entailed taking every opportunity—even apparently simple ones like opinion gathering—to continue building a documented structure of workplace relationships, the foundation of the workers' own power structure.

A structure test is a mini-campaign that helps workers identify where their internal structure is strong, middling, weak, or nonexistent. In other words, it allows workers to gauge their current capacity to convince other workers to take risks together. Based on the results of each best attempt at a structure test, workers know where to focus their organizing energy in order to build toward maximum power. Each structure test seeks to engage 100 percent of the workers who work for the employer, with the aim of achieving an ultimate participation rate of no less than 90 percent—the amount needed to deliver a credible strike threat under difficult conditions. Since the strike is the underlying basis of worker power,[11] structure tests measure progress toward the level of commitment required to confidently demonstrate that structure with a supermajority strike vote—hopefully at 90 percent participation—and, if necessary, that strike's execution. In any hard fight, the employers are assessing whether a strike threat is real or a bluff; the latter leads to winning a little; the former, considerably more.

To make a contract survey function as a structure test, worker leaders themselves are responsible for holding conversations, one on one or in small groups, with workers in their own work area (department, unit, shift, classification, etc.). Each worker activist is responsible for carefully tracking who filled in the contract survey, as they methodically meet with their coworkers so that they know whether, or when, they have achieved majority or supermajority participation in their work area. Setting the intention of getting to majority or a supermajority, or 90 percent, or some other specific goal is a crucial differentiating step, up front. Hardly any unions establish a numeric percentage goal of how many workers need to fill in the contract survey for it to be credible, and even fewer stick to that goal. But both are fundamental to taking the process seriously, for purposes of information gathering and for building the union. As we discuss in chapter 2, PASNAP set an objective of 60 percent in each hospital unit, then carefully analyzed the data and presented it to management at the opening session, legitimately claiming these demands represented a majority of workers' opinions. In chapter 4, the negotiations committee at the *Los Angeles Times* carefully tracked who had completed the contract survey and did repeated follow-ups until they were able to reach supermajority completion. At a minimum, the higher the percentage of workers, the more credible the demands presented to management are during negotiations. Meanwhile, the union's sense of its own reach and power becomes more accurate and thus more open to targeted improvement.

While one of our cases did still pursue an anonymous survey, for unions that use the survey process as an effective structure test to make the union structure stronger—that is, strong enough to *win* the many demands workers will prioritize in their surveys—having workers put their name, unit, and shift on the survey has proven essential. This turns the survey into an organizing tool that explicitly encourages relationship building among the workers. Structure tests foster trust and solidarity building by how they are conducted. They build in permanent two-way conversations between the workers and what becomes the central negotiations team. If a person's name is on the survey, it allows for later engagement with each worker, tapping into their specific interests and recruiting them to help play a role in winning on the article in the contract that addresses their issue (see the section later in the chapter on article committees). Contract negotiations, starting with a well-executed majority survey, are an opportune time for unions to engage the hard-to-recruit workers and those who have been hired after the union election (or since the last negotiations if the union is already established). The process of persuasion among workers, central to recruitment, can best—if not only—be executed by the recruiting worker first listening to and hearing what the engaged coworker wants to change about their workplace. Careful listening can happen only if the survey is a conversation tool, a document that one worker fills in while listening to the issues that matter most to their coworker. The recruitment then happens once the worker activist knows the coworker's top issues and can walk them through the steps of how their concerns will be raised in the negotiations process, connecting worker participation to the outcomes that can be achieved in the contract campaign. Anonymity prevents the ability to persuade and stops negotiations committees from better understanding each worker's specific issues, making it impossible to go back to individual workers and solicit their active involvement on the issues that motivate them as negotiations are heating up.

4. A Big, Representative Committee

There are interwoven elements that matter when it comes to applying the word "big" to negotiations. The first is that negotiations should be open to all workers covered by the contract. In the public sector, where the US Supreme Court's *Janus v. AFSCME* decision means the entire public sector functions much like previously state-based right-to-work laws, where union membership and dues are voluntary, we do mean open to all workers, not just members, provided any worker abide by the three rules of the room when management is present. It's their contract, which is generally the most important reason workers form and sustain unions: to fight for and win fair working conditions. Naturally, it is not realistic that all workers attend all negotiation sessions, and in no union of considerable size we have encountered does that occur. But successful unions using this approach go out of their way to invite as many workers as want to and can attend. See "Three Rules of the Room When Management Is Present" later in this chapter for more discussion on how such mass participation is combined with high-level discipline to enable maximal power in open negotiations.

The second element is that negotiations committees should also be "big." Aside from encouraging workers in large numbers to drop in from time to time, it is essential to first establish a well-informed standing negotiations committee that adequately represents the workforce.

The size of the official negotiations team in this approach depends in part on the size of the workforce, and whether the negotiations are for a master contract that covers multiple facilities or an entire sector, or, more commonly in the United States, enterprise-level, meaning covering a single facility (which can be large, like the Amazon warehouse in Staten Island with over eight thousand workers in a single fulfillment center, or small, say twenty-five workers in a coffee shop). The rule of thumb in this approach starts with ensuring that every type of worker, in every classification category, is directly represented on the committee. If a facility has more than one shift, then it ensures representation for each classification *by shift*, as different shifts can have almost completely different work environments. In a hospital or nursing home, for example, the night shifts tend to have far fewer staff, as management's assumption is that most patients are sleeping (a notion with which most overnight shift workers strenuously disagree). In addition to types of workers and shifts, representation by department can likewise be important, as the same kinds of skill sets and even job titles might be put to work differently by the employer depending on the department or unit. Unions that put this level of thought into their central negotiations committee achieve the most success, as we shall see.

Strong teams also ensure there is an alternate team member, or two, per classification, department, and shift, in case one can't attend. Typically, these alternate team members share one negotiations binder, which houses every document relating to the negotiations process: from the proposed language to counterproposals by management to negotiations notes from each session to the various supporting documents like financial data, and so on. The sharing of one binder between the alternates helps ensure that when they pass along the binder to their colleague, they also have a conversation alerting their colleague to nuances that might have taken place at the previous session but that would not be found in a negotiations binder (like places where the workers' committee might be stuck or in disagreement, and why). Teams constructed this way have proven to be incredibly efficient: having every type of worker across shifts in the room means the negotiations committee doesn't have to wait to respond to a management proposal by checking with workers on how things function in a particular work area, as workers with that knowledge are already present.

Further, having every type of worker present means the workers can easily, and often, correct the management team on things managers say that are innocently wrong, willfully deceitful, or outright lies. A common case of this kind of correction is when, while discussing staffing needs, managers act as if the scheduled number of staff per shift represents the actual number of staff present on any given day. If twelve workers are on a posted schedule, but two or three call in sick, and management fails to follow protocols to get their replacements, then the actual number of staff wasn't twelve, it was nine, creating huge stress on the remaining too-few staff. Often enough, this kind of short-staffing may be the norm in practice. This kind of knowledge, even in smaller workplaces, is almost impossible for even the most brilliant negotiator or union executive council to know in detail. The methodical construction of this kind of large formal negotiations committee helps to combine the knowledge workers have of every aspect of the work into a powerful collective strategic operation.

At UNITE HERE Local 26, the focus of chapter 6, the union assembled a negotiations committee that included not only Marriott workers—who would be directly covered by the contract being negotiated—but workers from other unionized Boston hotels, because the union planned to extend the agreement to other employers. Workers from every union hotel, regardless of which company owned it, could and did attend Marriott negotiations. This concept can easily be extended to workers in the same geographic area who do the same kind of work, and are employed by the same or related employers, but have not yet formed a union, giving not-yet-unionized workers a feel for the difference between personnel policies handed down to them from human resources and the bottom-up creation of workplace rules.

5. Electing Committees (Not Appointed)

Across the diversity of unions and hundreds of thousands of different contracts across the United States, it's hard to ascertain how many of their negotiations committees are directly elected by the broad membership to negotiate the specific contract, rather than appointed by union executives or elected to standing positions. In our research, we can say that many unions do not specifically elect their negotiations teams. The most typical scenarios involve small committees with the elected union position-holders (president, vice presidents for this and that, secretary-treasurers, recording secretaries, and the like), serving as ex-officio members of the negotiations team. In addition, they often then appoint a few additional members as they see fit.

While it is absolutely true that having elected union officials serve as the committee is far more democratic than how the management team is selected, it is a far cry from the union choosing to have a big team, as just discussed, and actually having a big team elected each contract cycle by their own peers in their own departments and shifts. This approach emphasizes how workers who toil together, side by side, day in and day out, know best whom they trust to represent them on the official negotiations committee. It also avoids favoritism and loyalty as the criteria for selection, which happens as frequently in unions as in political appointments, with similar effects of eroding trust. Unions seeking to avoid this outcome, and build a more democratic organization in the process, trust workers to elect their own representatives at the table. These unions take these elections seriously, both to gain legitimate representation *and* to use the election as an opportunity for organizing and conducting a structure test, with candidates needing a set and significant percentage of workers to sign onto a form for their nomination. The duties of an elected negotiations team member are put down in writing in a short job description that all candidates must sign, acknowledging that they know what is expected of them when they choose to stand for election. This avoids later confusion and disagreements about things like attendance, two-way reporting structures between negotiations team members and their colleagues in their work area, and expectations of how much time is required to get the job done well.

Unions pursuing deeper democratization through organization at this phase require a department or unit to achieve at least a simple majority participation on their nonanonymous contract surveys before they can elect their negotiators. From the get-go, using this approach strongly reinforces for workers the understanding that power is what wins in union negotiations, and that in a democracy, participation equates to power—be it to hold a supermajority strike or to elect politicians who will solve problems to the benefit of the working class. Because most unions practice such a top-down negotiation process, workers are rarely educated that getting what they want is directly tied to their active participation in the fight for a good or great contract. Establishing majority participation on the input into the contract—building on the organizing of the previous prenegotiations phase—helps workers understand that it will also take majority participation to win. Likewise, it helps generate a bigger pool of workers who will then seek election to represent their coworkers as part of the standing negotiations team. Ideally, elections for these seats should be meaningfully contested and not simply acclaimed, so that coworkers have to concretely articulate their vision for how they will engage their work area in an ongoing way throughout the negotiations. These processes of thinking through strategy in collective conversation helps bring workers, including those voting to elect representatives, to this expanded committee, where they can be most effective, which is at the heart of the bargaining process.

6. A Volunteer, Not Paid Committee

For workers who have just won union recognition and are constructing a new first contract, there is normally no expectation that they will be paid to attend their negotiations. But in many workplaces where a union has existed for years and the workers have negotiated and renegotiated their contract multiple times, the workers will often have language written into the contract that states they will be in paid status at their regular rate of pay (i.e., not overtime) and be "released" from their job duties to attend negotiations. Public sector labor law may also provide for paid time. For workers, overworked at work and at home, the impulse is understandable, and this approach can work if the committee is small. Employers, of course, prefer no union and no contract negotiations, but if they're forced to deal with both, they too prefer a small, paid committee. If workers want a big committee, they will have to decide to forfeit pay and be willing to volunteer, as it would be an unreasonable demand that 60, 90, 120, or even more workers will all be paid to negotiate. This presents a challenge and often a barrier when longtime and entrenched position-holders inside unions often side with the employer and favor keeping the committee small and paid. Why? Many workers don't like their day jobs—for good reason—so anything that gets them released from their regular duties while they are still paid is a better day at work for the handful of workers who are on a small committee.

But the paid-to-negotiate-during-the-day approach often, though not always, presents challenges to other workers participating as they too will be at work, but doing their regular duties. Given the vastly different structures of employment schedules across different workforces, generalizations about this can only go so far. The difference between a private sector hospital that operates 24/7/365 and a Department of Motor Vehicles (DMV) office with strictly regulated hours in which all workers start and end at the same time represent merely two of the many varied workplace schedules out there. If the workplace schedule is set to daytime hours, as in the DMV example, or for teachers and most education workers, the simple solution for such unions is to demand that all negotiations take place after the workday ends. That way, any worker can conceivably attend. Employers, of course, resist this, because when their day ends, they want to go home. But particularly in the public sector, demanding that negotiations take place not on the taxpayer's dime is an issue unions have won. It also motivates the management team to take the sessions more seriously, to move more efficiently, and disincentivizes their favorite tactic: delay.

In 24/7/365 workplaces, whether in negotiations for a first or successor contract, a high-participation approach requires that management agree to release people from their shifts. This is where unions with elected alternates have an advantage: management struggles to argue against having a big committee when there are always other workers who can step into a shift to cover an elected worker negotiator who needs to miss work in order to attend negotiations. In big, complex workforces with lots of types of workers, some paid a lot less and some paid a lot more based on skill designations, many lower-wage workers find the prospect of missing a shift to be too financially difficult and genuinely need to be compensated. To bridge this gap, successful unions have forced management to agree to a set number of paid hours that the workers' committee gets to allocate as needed to ensure that lower-wage workers can attend. This worker-controlled bank of hours that the committee itself votes to allocate to workers who need compensation to participate is an important priority in setting terms for negotiations for unions working with multiple classifications of workers on staggered schedules in a big, unpaid committee. If this can't be won, the other alternative that unions we have studied have employed is to exercise sensitivity in setting negotiation dates when the lower-wage-worker committee members are not on shift.

In almost all the examples in this book, and based on decades of negotiations experience, a volunteer committee results in the most committed workers standing for election. They are not there to avoid an unpleasant day at work on paid time. They are there to make every day more pleasant for everyone by winning far better working conditions for all.

7. Ratify Contract Proposals before Negotiations

A high-participation approach to transparent, big, and open negotiations requires a union to hold many meetings, involving many workers, to draft either a proposed first contract or to amend an existing one. As stated, the first step is achieving at least a simple majority of all workers filling in their contract surveys. Once a majority of a unit has done so, they then begin to meet as departmental teams to establish their work area's goals for the contract. If the departments that have hit their majorities on their contract surveys have elected their negotiations team member and alternate team member, those leaders can facilitate the collective process of sifting through the survey results by the department's team members to determine priorities. These meetings occasionally take place at one big weekly meeting, where all workers interested in the contract process can show up, divide into their departmental teams, and then regroup for a check-in across departments to see how much commonality or difference is emerging from the various work areas. In other unions, meetings take place independently, sending their negotiators to the bigger weekly meetings to narrow down collective proposals.

Once workers draw up a draft contract proposal, the negotiations committee moves to hold a ratification vote for the draft contract. This is crucial to the approach for two reasons, at least. First, it sends a powerful message to workers that they themselves will decide which proposals will be negotiated. Second, the ratification vote itself can serve as the next structure test to assess where participation is growing, shrinking, staying the same, anemic and in need of serious attention, and so on. To be sure, this process can be laborious. But for this kind of democracy to function well, high-participation unions have sought maximum participation at every turn, not merely nominal representation. This approach helps build governing power in the workplace, that is, the ability to enforce the contract the workers later win, because considerably more workers understand, and will later defend, the language when they help draft it. Finally, a high-turnout vote, *at least* a majority vote to ratify the proposals, sends a very clear message to management that workers are ready to fight for their contract.

8. Creating Article Committees

An organizing approach to a contract campaign sets worker leaders to the task of tirelessly looking for ways to have an increasing number of workers involved in the negotiations process. Creating "article committees" presents yet another opportunity for workers to focus on and engage in the issue or issues that matter to them the most. In this approach, a standing, elected negotiations committee member serves as the chair of each article committee. This ensures direct and consistent dialogue between the official negotiators and the larger group of workers who are engaging on one issue in the contract. These article committees can meet anytime, but trying to streamline both article committee meetings and departmental team meetings into regular weekly meetings creates a structure that often simplifies this process.

Once the negotiations are underway, these committees lay the groundwork for an almost dizzying level of efficiency in the actual ne-gotiation sessions. When the employer provides counterproposals all at once, workers on the article committees can quickly meet during a union caucus and review the changes the management team is proposing. A dozen article committees can work simultaneously to read through the union's proposal, compare it with the employer's counterproposal, and then have the article committee members themselves stand up in the larger union-only caucus, one article committee at a time, to present their committee's recommendation to the full negotiations team about what to accept, reject, or counter.

When the lead negotiators plan which contract articles they will take up at the next negotiation session prior to ending the session they are in, it allows for the article committees to be notified that their issue is up at the next session. This helps build turnout to negotiations, partic-ularly from workers who are already experts on their topic, from how overtime works, to actual staffing levels, to what the workflow should be in their area, to childcare needs, and so on. As with these elements, building meaningful participation at every step strengthens and expands the negotiations committee's knowledge base, while likewise allowing workers to understand their ownership of the contract fight.

9. The Three Rules of the Room When Management Is Present

Crucial to a big—and especially a big and open—negotiations process is reaching an upfront agreement for how everyone on the union side will conduct themselves when the management team is in the room and negotiations are taking place. Big, open negotiations committees have various approaches, but for the most part have settled on three simple rules to keep the union side on strategy, assuming all workers agree to abide by them. Getting all workers on board starts with the standing, elected negotiations team first discussing and debating these rules themselves. Perhaps they come up with additional ones, but in our observation, these three work: (1) workers maintain a poker face at all times, (2) no one speaks except the chief negotiator unless it is planned, and (3) workers can write and pass notes to the negotiator anytime they want to talk, or let the negotiator know something such as a fact-check on something untrue a manager just said, or ask to take a break, requiring the management team to leave the room (known as a "caucus" in labor negotiations). A fourth rule matters, too, which became relevant once cell phones were ubiquitous: absolutely no pictures, no recording, and no phone use when the employer is in the room. This is because the workers' committee would not want management to do this, as it could easily be

3 RULES OF THE ROOM
When Management Is Present

1. POKER FACE AT ALL TIMES

2. No one speaks except our negotiator *unless planned*

3. Send notes to the negotiator *anytime* if you want to talk or let her know something or request we take a "Caucus" (a break where we can ask management to leave the room for private conversation time)

And of course, absolutely NO cell phones, photos, or recording.

FIGURE 2. Three rules of the room

a form of intimidation. Even the most confrontational and open unions in our observation agree neither party has the right to record anything during the official negotiations.

The workers themselves enforce the three rules. The negotiations room stays so silent you can hear a pin drop, because workers understand the responsibility they are taking on in big and open negotiations. A simple system many unions following this approach use has worker activists volunteer to be stationed near the room entrances. When the door opens, if during actual negotiations, the volunteer will step outside the room with those wishing to enter. They explain the three rules voted on by the negotiations committee and ask each worker to print and sign their name on a sign-in sheet stating that they agree to abide by the rules. A worker who can't agree to sign is instead invited to attend planning or update sessions, but not the negotiations. Peer-to-peer enforcement enables this system to work.

The third rule, allowing for notes to be passed at any time from any worker to the chief negotiator, is absolutely key to this highly disciplined outcome. Workers have an immediate outlet to express their concerns, even if they cannot speak aloud at that exact moment. To show how seriously the chief negotiator takes the need for workers to express themselves in reaction to either something the union negotiator said, or something the management-side negotiator said, the team places blank three-by-five-inch index cards and small golf pencils on every seat in the negotiations room. This doesn't just allow for but actively encourages instant communication, helping people who urgently want to speak out to instead write out and relay their thoughts into a note to the negotiator. At that juncture, the negotiator could either invite the worker to make the point they are raising, to directly call out management for something it said that was false, or to ask for a formal break—a caucus. During the caucus, a debate or issue that is emerging among workers in the room can be quickly resolved without management's presence.

10. No Ground Rules, (If State Law Requires, Surrender-No-Power-Ones)

While establishing the committee's rules for the room when management is present is vitally important, the opposite is true when it comes to ground rules often sought by management for the negotiations process it-self. Generally, management kicks off negotiations by presenting proposed ground rules. They usually introduce them as if workers would automatically agree to them. Moreover, most workers who have been in negotiations before believe they have to discuss and agree to some form of ground rules. In the private sector, this is not true. Under the NLRA, which governs private sector labor law, there are three types of subjects in negotiations: mandatory, permissive, and prohibited. Agreeing to even discuss ground rules for negotiations is a permissive subject of bargaining in the private sector.

In practice, ground rules have essentially been weaponized by management to create confidentiality and gag rules; to prevent discussions about negotiations with other workers, the media, and the community; and to build in a seemingly infinite list of other repressive measures from mandatory employer sign-in sheets, aimed at intimidating workers in the room from showing up, to penalizing the workers' committee if they start negotiations late, even if they have a good reason. Half the negotiations committees discussed in this book rejected ground rules outright. Public sector labor law is governed state by state, and in some states ground rules are considered a mandatory subject. When this happens, a clever committee can simply agree to discuss them and only accept something as plain as a statement that they plan to show up on time when they've agreed to negotiate, or that both parties agree to be polite to one another, or some other simple ground rule. In some cases, workers' committees do suggest a ground rule saying that management and the union agree to be on time and not needlessly cancel pre-agreed-to negotiation sessions, particularly when the management team has a history of abusive behavior. The main salience of this element of the approach is to prevent the expanded negotiations committee from being bullied by default into unnecessarily accepting anything against the committee's interests, particularly items that would make worker participation more difficult, by means of a seemingly innocent or mandatory ground rules process.

11. Location, Where to Negotiate

Per labor law, both parties must agree on where negotiations take place. If the employer has a space big enough to accommodate a large committee's size and the negotiations involve a single facility or single employer, conducting the negotiations on site works well and provides several advantages. Many workers visit the negotiations room on work breaks, be it having lunch there (while they adhere to the three rules) or using a fifteen-minute break when it is important for a particular worker to join the session—for example, if the employer had earlier brought up or misrepresented an issue that the on-break worker knows about and can address. Most employers facing big and open negotiations will try to make negotiations as inconvenient as possible for the workers. Obviously, if workers want many coworkers to participate, getting the negotiations as close to the facility, or as central or convenient as possible for multisite negotiations, is key for unions using this approach.

Management often proposes cushy and expensive hotels for negotiations. For a hotel workers' union, this can be great. But for most unions, spending lavish funds on negotiations is a questionable use of the members' dues money. Unions pushing for big, open negotiations look to community centers and places like nearby houses of faith, which often have lots of empty space on weekdays. Any facility chosen will have to offer a separate, secure space for the management team to hold their own private caucuses—a big and open negotiations committee naturally uses the big room or main negotiating room as its caucus location. To minimize the possibility of rejection of the space by management, unions have found it essential to get management a space that is comfortable for them to meet in for their private sessions.

12. When and How Often to Conduct Negotiations Sessions

Many employers—especially if they've hired lawyers who fly in from another state to lead the management side—seek to schedule a series of negotiations on back-to-back days and to schedule a few months of dates all at once for their own travel and planning convenience. For workers, especially at the beginning of the negotiations process, this can pose a few problems. They need time to process and discuss with their coworkers what happens at the negotiation sessions. When scheduling, high-participation unions work to understand management's strategy and do whatever is best schedule-wise for the workers, not the employer or their hired guns. There are times when back-to-back meetings work best for the workers' committee, but that tends to happen later in the contract talks, when real progress at the table has begun.

13. Avoid Employer and Lawyer Communication between Sessions

The first thing a smart management-side attorney who is serving as chief negotiator will do is begin to communicate with the union's chief negotiator. This is even more prevalent since email and texts became ubiquitous. When adopting a transparent approach to negotiations, it is important to train the management-side negotiator early and often that the negotiations room is the place to have conversations, rather than in private chit-chats. It can be a perilously slippery slope when union negotiators or officials engage with the other side without the workers present. The last thing most management wants to do, even in negotiations with workers' representatives, is to be required to act as if the workers matter. They often do everything they can to open a line of "informal" communication. Even if this seems innocent— especially if they want to "discuss" an idea that might be one the workers would like—one principle of this approach is for union-side negotiators to make management learn to respect the workers, meaning that conversations happen with all the workers, not the ne-gotiator or a top union official.

There will, however, come a time in nearly every negotiations when the employer asks for an off-the-record meeting (sometimes called a *sidebar* when it happens during a negotiations day). This is usually when the worker power is so strong, the pressure is so intense, that man-agement is finally trying to sort out how they can get to settlement. These calls are different than the ones mentioned earlier. They are spe-cific and a clear indication to the union negotiators that the workers are on the verge of winning. The ask is generally some version of, "We believe we have a comprehensive settlement offer to wrap things up. Are you able to meet and discuss it?" According to this approach, there is a right way and a wrong way to handle these crucial moments, and under principled terms, the union side should absolutely agree to this kind of between-session meeting. The difference here is subtle, but many high-participation negotiators have learned it is crucial.

Under labor law, every conversation that takes place in the *official* negotiations room is something that could be brought forward later in an arbitration process or dispute about interpreting the contract. Because of this, management arguably has a legitimate need to try out ideas that they might not yet have full authority to offer, say, from their own higher-ups. Before they risk their hide with a top CEO, they need some indication that if they go ask for more funds to settle the dispute, it will be worth it, as the "comprehensive offer of settlement" is one the union will accept. They at least want to know if they are moving in the correct direction, if they are getting close enough to the workers' demands to possibly settle. For the cases we've studied, this happens several times when negotiations are nearing the endgame.

The principled provisos to conduct these kinds of off-the-formal-record meetings start with educating the management-side attorney or company representative that the union negotiator doesn't do "secret" off-the-record meetings. What can work, the union negotiator then explains, is that they will inform the workers' committee that the request has come, and if the committee is comfortable with the idea, the union negotiator will conduct such a meeting. Additionally, the negotiator makes clear to the management attorney that any proposals floated will be informally and confidentially discussed with the workers' committee. Finally, the union negotiator insists that they will not come alone and will be bringing at least one member of the workers' committee. Essentially, the negotiator does not have a mandate to meet off the record without all the above conditions being met.

Some management negotiators balk immediately at such requests and refuse to meet with the union side unless it is a "secret" meeting. This is largely because so many unions following less democratic approaches will happily meet seemingly endlessly in such off-the-record meetings, and so it can shock a management-side negotiator when they have to deal with a union negotiator who states clearly and politely that there is no condition under which they will be met with secretly. If the union negotiator understands how much power the worker side has built at that point and is confident that they are supermajority-strike-ready, it is with calm and confidence that they can simply reply, "Have a nice day," and hang up politely.[12] If the union side's assessment is correct—see the first element: the power structure analysis—it is only a matter of hours, maybe one day, before the management side calls again and agrees to the union's terms for an off-the-record meeting. And now all indicators are that victory is imminent. It is important not to minimize this decision, as rejecting an offer for a secret off-the-record is definitely high stakes. But making such calls is essential in negotiations where the demands are substantive, rather than piecemeal.

Informing the workers' committee, or minimally the top leaders on the committee—and they will be obvious, as they are the workers leading the negotiations team with the negotiator—is crucial for a chief negotiator following this approach. They seek worker leaders' counsel about asking for permission from the full committee, and perhaps convene a quick conference call deemed "urgent," because timing usually is of the essence. When the committee gives the negotiator their blessing and their mandate, this kind of meeting affords each side the ability to frame close-to-end-game settlements without yet having them on the record in the official negotiations. Being sure management understands that the union-side negotiator will report back to the committee on the discussions, although not publicize them, is fundamental. Two of our cases offer strong illustrations of this tense dynamic, first in the Einstein hospital union (chapter 2), in what became the endpoint of the negotiations to get to the negotiations, and in UNITE HERE (chapter 6), where the hotel workers followed these protocols and began to have small team meetings in the office of Boston's mayor to try to settle a strike that was disrupting the entire city. In that scenario, a powerful actor played the role of informal mediator, one with far more power than government-appointed professional mediators, and a stronger incentive to try to end the crisis gripping their city or state. That mayor, incidentally, was Marty Walsh, who had previously been an elected leader of the building and construction trades unions, understood negotiations himself, and would go on to be President Joe Biden's labor secretary.

14. Training, Role-Playing, and the Opening Session

Whether unions choose traditional small committees or big ones—but especially if undertaking big and open negotiations—ongoing trainings in negotiations basics for members, starting with the three rules, is essential. Many successful committees role-play each aspect of what might happen in the negotiations room and practice these scenarios repeatedly. Even in the earlier discussion of the off-the-record scenario, if the workers are informed early in the process that at some point that phone call will come—if and when they have built the power to win their demands—they will be ready for the conversation, and they will trust from the beginning that their negotiator will not hold secret meetings over their heads. Strong committees hold mock negotiation sessions, where some workers are asked to play people on the management team and behave in utterly charming ways, trying to get workers to break their poker face with funny jokes, and then in outrageously rude ways, trying to get the committee to break any of the three rules. Just as worker organizers should practice one-on-one structured organizing conversations, it's crucial for workers to practice putting these tactical responses to predictable scenarios in motion, so that these operating principles become more than words written on butcher paper during orientation.

In big and open negotiations, the entire negotiations team and even key worker leaders who are not formally on the committee make an opening presentation to the management team on all the subjects they will address in negotiations. This presentation can include areas in which the workers believe there is a *common interest* with management, setting the tone that, if the management side wants to take negotiations seriously and arrive at win-win solutions that improve their business practice and the lives of the workers, the union is ready and able to approach negotiations in such a manner. The presentation can include the results of the majority contract survey, with data and statistics about the key issues that workers will bring to the negotiations themselves. These presentations can also be role-played and practiced in front of coworkers, to get some of the nervous jitters out of the way. Having the committee plan this presentation by having a PowerPoint slide for each topic or issue, and having workers plan who will do the presenting and in what order, can get negotiations off to a roaring start. In our cases, it sent a strong signal to management that workers were in control of the negotiations.

15. The Article Checklist: Make It Easy for Workers to Follow

Most union committees, especially the small and closed kind, have a binder or folder of some sort that helps them keep the contract proposals in order. This record keeping becomes immensely important when negotiating with a big committee with alternates for the formally elected committee, as they have to hand off their binder to each other and be well organized to keep track of what happened at the session they missed (see the earlier discussion, "Big Committees"). This tracking becomes essential, however, with negotiations open to all workers covered by the contract. In order for workers to be able to actually engage in the complex back-and-forth of negotiations, and even more to want to show up again, experience shows that they need to know the context of what's happening in the room when they arrive. If they are simply sitting passively as confused observers, they can get bored quickly.

One practice to ensure that each worker knows what is taking place is to create, use, and constantly and meticulously update an article checklist. This is a simple table that tracks which negotiating side made what proposal; what date it was made (sometimes what time it was made during a long session, as it might pass back and forth more than once); and whether the other side presented a counterproposal, when, and whether it was accepted, rejected, amended, and so on. In short, the article checklist contains a simple summation of the status of each article, created for each negotiation's session. In practice, nothing is secretive about the checklist: it has no, "It will take xyz to get us to agree," or any such language, and thus it is not a problem for the committee for workers who are not on the committee to visit a session, leave with it, and hopefully show it to their coworkers with interest and excitement. (See Einstein checklist.)

Article	Nurse Proposal	Management Counter	Name If Interested
Article 10 Holidays	8-17-16 (I) 10-13-16 (c)	10-6-16(c) 10-19-16 (c)	Trish ▮▮ (PACU), Keryy, Jane ▮▮▮▮ (MB), Pam ▮▮▮▮ (L&D), Stephanie▮▮▮ (L&D), Rhonda▮▮▮(PCU), Darlene ▮▮▮ (PCU); Patty▮▮▮ (NPED)
Article 11 Vacation Scheduling	8-17-16 (I)	10-13-16(c)	Carolyn▮▮▮ (ED), Pam▮▮▮ (L&D), Cathy▮▮▮ (SICU), Christine▮▮▮(MB), James ▮▮▮ (ED), Karen ▮▮▮ (ED), Jen ▮▮▮▮ (CM
Article 12 Health, Welfare and Pension	9-28-16 (I)		Pat▮▮ (MICU), Jerri▮▮▮(NICU), Pam ▮▮▮ (L&D), Cathy▮▮▮ (SICU), Trish ▮▮ (PACU), Dorthea▮▮▮(OR), Adrienne▮▮(SPU), Judy▮▮▮(CCU), Patsy▮▮ (NICU), Angela▮▮(NICU), James ▮▮▮ (ED)

FIGURE 3. Einstein article checklist

16. The Role of the Union Caucus

In formal negotiations, each side has the right to request what's called a caucus. It is a more formal way—because negotiations in fact are legal and official—of requesting a break for a private discussion among one's own side. Neither party can refuse them. As mentioned in the discussion of the rules for the room, caucuses are crucial for committees seeking a structured way to harness the knowledge and strategic thinking of both formal members and attending workers not on the committee.

One can imagine, given these rules, that either side can abuse this practice. The primary reason for sides to call a caucus is to respond to a proposal or counterproposal that one party has just offered across the table in negotiations. When a union is dealing with a union-busting consultant advising management, it is extremely common for management to abuse caucuses, calling for them often and staying outside the room for hours, sometimes the entire day, just to delay the negotiations process while avoiding getting hit with what is called a "bad faith bargaining" ULP charge. In these cases, management agrees to a negotiation date and shows up, but actually spends the entire day in another room either doing nothing, doing other work on their phones, eating high-quality takeout food, or going out to a local steakhouse for a long meal with martinis.

An organizer's approach to negotiations, building high participation and high power, thus means planning meaningful work that needs to get done during long caucuses called by management. Otherwise, this can lead to huge frustration—a union buster's objective—boring the committee, provoking infighting, and inducing a sense of futility in the entire process. To defeat the effect of demoralization, the union side working with a large committee needs to turn this time into organizing time—just as this approach has done with every step of the process. If bargaining near the workplace, the union side can send a team of workers into the facility to gather signatures or pictures for a structure test petition they might be developing. If this is a first contract, they may send delegations of workers into the facility to get workers who have yet to sign a union membership card to fill one out. If most have already signed a card, they can send in a team to sign up workers on a different card, a political-action dues card whereby they agree to donate an additional sum of their paycheck to the political program. If negotiations are far from the facility, committees can have an alternative task ready, such as phone banking with workers in a negotiations committee member's area who have not been sufficiently engaged.

If the worker organization is already strong, committees can have a plan to send workers to visit city hall or the CEO's office to demand their fat-cat lawyers return to the negotiations room. They can send delegations to meet with other workers who are employed by the same employer but not yet unionized to start worker-to-worker discussions about what they will be able to win for themselves, their families, and their communities once they all form a united front together against the employer. In short, a high-participation, high-power union will always be ready with meaningful work that the committee and any visiting workers can do in order to advance the worker-power agenda and diminish the power of the bosses' delay–bore–drag out tactic. These unions never let a caucus—even one called by the boss—go to waste.

17. Negotiations Bulletins: Simple and Published before the Employers'

When a big committee is present and many additional workers are attending negotiations, unions have a vast, built-in volunteer corps filled with the talents needed not only to negotiate, as we've seen, but also to do such things as writing simple negotiations bulletins—even while the negotiations are taking place. Worker volunteers can take key notes and capture the energy by taking photos during caucus time of one another and workers who showed up to present, witness, or participate in any other way. Committees can turn these materials into a flyer within minutes of negotiations wrapping up for the day.

With a big team, some members volunteer to go to a nearby copy shop and duplicate the fliers, while others wait at the facilities, ready to post the news in the breakrooms, hand them to workers at work, and immediately get the word out with visuals of what just took place in negotiations. Surely social media can help, but its reach is limited to pro-union activists who already follow the union. Paper still matters, as there are inevitably workers who remain on the fence, not terribly interested, maybe resisting, and thus are not following negotiations on any social media channel. In a high-participation approach, the committee's top job is to recruit the holdouts—to actually focus on them—which means a face-to-face walk-through with a flyer and a quick conversation. In this way, the workers frame the events of the day before the management team has even had a chance to sort through their often-legalistic approach to communications.

18. Comprehensive Charting and the Community Campaign

This chapter began by discussing the need to conduct a power structure analysis before a contract fight begins. In the third element, we elaborated on the contract survey as a majority structure test, the mechanism of learning to understand the power structure among and between the workers—each structure test deepening the understanding of the workers' own power structure, a key to building high participation and thus high power. The final step in a power structure analysis is called *comprehensive charting*. This refers to charting the workers' connections to their own community, to their houses of faith if they attend one, to their kids' schools and Parent Teacher Associations, to the Little League teams their kids play on together, to book clubs, parents' sports leagues, knitting circles, and any and all ways that a worker in a contract fight is connected to their broader community. In order to succeed in appropriate depth, this phase of power building has to come later in the process of the contract fight, as workers need to be in high-trust mode with each other, fully understanding the purpose of why they might be asked questions about their lives outside of the workplace.

As should be clear from the other steps in the process, this kind of work can't be done by a survey left in a worker's locker or mailbox, or an online tool asking them to fill in who they know. These approaches do bring back some results, but usually only from the most hardcore pro-union activists, and not at the level or volume required to find the intersections needed between the bosses' ties to the external power structure, and the volume and location of workers' own connections in their lives in the community. Comprehensive charting is most effectively done after a presentation to a mass meeting of the workers where the committee presents the external power structure analysis. When workers see for themselves who and what institutions have power in their labor market, they can begin to envision their own role and their own points of influence in that power structure.

By directly engaging the workers in the process of charting their own connections to local power structures, they can collectively bring those connections into the collective-bargaining process for maximum worker power and public-interest outcomes. According to this approach, there's simply no way to bring the broader community's interests to bear in negotiations unless and until the workers' power itself is at the highest possible level. This dynamic in negotiations—the interplay between workers, their community, and the power structure, and then the eventual checkmating of the employer—produces the kinds of gains that lead more workers in other workplaces to be willing to overcome the employer's often brutal tactics in unionization campaigns.

19. Contract Action Teams

Contract action teams, called "CAT teams," are an additional layer of workers who help ensure two-way dialogue between the negotiations committee and each work area, worksite, and worker classification. Historically,

CAT teams have been an important part of bottom-up contract campaigns. Interestingly, in a big and open negotiations process, where a large team of negotiators and alternates are elected, committees find less need for a formal CAT team than in unions with small committees and a more closed process. Negotiations that are big and open create structures that engage every unit and type of worker in direct and indirect ways. If, however, unions are managing multisite negotiations or very large workplaces, the CAT teams can serve as a supplement to the big negotiations team. When all workers are being encouraged to attend negotiations to listen, watch, and participate when planned, the work of the CAT team is functionally replaced by a big negotiations team with representatives from each classification and work area. There's certainly no harm in having CAT teams supplement the work, but it is simply a less important function when a union is practicing transparent, big, and open negotiations.

20. Ratification of the Contract

For many workers in traditional negotiations, the first time they hear about or see the newly negotiated contract, or encounter the new language in a successor agreement, is during the ratification process—which is still a requirement in most, but not even all, unions. When the negotiations have been closed, with a small committee operating under gag rules of some sort that they agreed to, the contract can indeed be voted down, but there are few other ways for workers to be involved in shaping the outcome—not only as a list of demands but also as a list of wins. Typical unions offer a few meetings to brief the members on what's in the contract and call an up-or-down vote on the entire proposal. Worker frustration with lack of engagement in the process can lead to a no vote on ratification as a protest against their exclusion. More commonly, in a poorly functioning union, an unsatisfactory contract proposal will lead to low-turnout ratification votes rather than outright rejection. For a union that hasn't prepared an action plan, and the structure tests necessary to know they can execute it, workers aren't wrong to worry about what will happen should they say no, and so a rejection seems like too risky a proposition. In this manner, the controlled demolition of working conditions—and of the movement that could transform them—continues.

When a union practices transparent, big, and open negotiations, the entire workforce is apprised of the progress being made throughout the process. There's no final surprise, bad or good. Masses of workers are fully informed. When the proposal is put to the membership, most unions using this approach still consider it good practice to hold meetings where the members of the negotiations committee can answer and address any questions the workers have about specifics, giving at least twenty-four hours, if not forty-eight hours, between formally sharing the tentative agreement and running the ratification vote. In high-powered, hard negotiations—the kind settled in a mayor's or mediator's office, or at the end of a supermajority strike where negotiations are going round the clock as the strike is on—management will sometimes demand an immediate vote or threaten to call off their agreement, as odd as it may sound. Contemporary unions have been schooled by the mighty Chicago Teachers Union strike of 2012 to not let the employer force fast settlements despite threats to take the deal off the table—even when pressure mounts to end the disruption the union has managed to impose on their employer. Workers in a democratic, bottom-up union need time to digest and understand the settlement offer before being asked to vote it up or down. Even if leadership believes there will be a yes vote, the lingering effects of not giving workers the time to digest a settlement can damage the trust between leadership and the ranks.

———

These process mechanisms are tools that transform a union from low participation to high participation by way of contract negotiations. High participation influences everything: winning better contracts, building or maintaining high membership, unionizing more workers in a union's industry or across a labor market, and developing a robust political mobilization structure so that workers can get more from elected politicians than does the corporate class. Because negotiations are about power, many successful unionists often correctly express that winning at negotiations is decided by what you do *away* from the bargaining tables. But that assumes the typical small-committee approach. The processes described in this chapter and throughout this book suggest that a high-participation approach to negotiations translates to directly helping skeptical workers overcome their doubts about collective action, to helping workers see through "the big lie" their boss is pushing at work, and to sharpen workers' understanding of their employer. This approach, bringing the vast but organized "away" directly into negotiations, serves as an important mechanism that connects the power of the workers directly to the negotiations—and their outcome. It brings the power of strong shop-floor organization into the strategy room and to the negotiations table, and uses the process of negotiations to strengthen that organization—something a union needs both to win and to enforce a transformative contract.

2

Legal Rope-a-Dope (PASNAP)

IN EARLY 2016, SEVEN MONTHS after completing my PhD, I received an email request to be the keynote speaker at the annual convention of a union for which I had been doing staff and leader trainings during the first two years of my graduate studies. The union writing me was the Pennsylvania Association of Staff Nurses and Allied Professionals (PASNAP), an independent state-based union that had been racking up some big victories for healthcare workers in Philadelphia. At the time, I was busy putting the finishing touches on my first written Harvard Case Method for a course I was teaching as part of a postdoctoral fellowship at Harvard's law school. That case distilled the lessons for how to win a labor-market-wide, multiyear, multi-union campaign, an experiment I directed for the national AFL-CIO in Connecticut from 1998 to 2001.[1] My PhD dissertation was in the final stages of production for what would become *No Shortcuts: Organizing for Power in the New Gilded Age*, published in November 2016. My twin lives as organizer, negotiator, and academic researcher were crisscrossing regularly, but I was pretty ensconced in teaching when I received the email request in early January.

A call quickly followed from the executive director of PASNAP, and my noncommittal response earned me a second call straight from the union's president. She admitted upfront that, though they hoped I would come to Pennsylvania to give the keynote, they were plotting to convince me to move to Philadelphia to help them with their own burgeoning

Rules to Win By. Jane F. McAlevey and Abby Lawlor, Oxford University Press. © Oxford University Press 2023.
DOI: 10.1093/oso/9780197690468.003.0003

labor-market-wide campaign, which was well underway, creating a whirlwind of unionization wins in America's fifth-largest city. I told her I could do the speech, but my academic obligations meant there was no way I could move to Philly. Three months later, they outorganized me. After their convention, they rented me a furnished apartment near the 30th Street train station so that I could commute between Cambridge, where I taught, NYC, where I lived, and Philadelphia, where I would soon be consumed in an all-out organizing war.

This chapter tells a particular kind of story as a case study. Bringing together as it does my own application of principles in the field, alongside my prior research and reflective documentation of the campaign, this piece is written in the first person by me, Jane McAlevey, and can be understood in a tradition of practitioner action research. Though the strategies we deployed in the PASNAP fight were learned in the decades of hard unionization and contract campaigns prior to my PhD, the meticulous approach I took to documenting the campaign was informed by my dissertation research, having just completed several years deeply analyzing many other cases of hard-won organizing victories from which I could learn.

One case from my dissertation in particular sharpened my thinking about this fight: Smithfield Foods in North Carolina, where the employer dragged out the unionization struggle of thousands of meatpacking workers at the United States' largest slaughterhouse for sixteen years. This now-notorious North Carolina case saw union busters throwing every conceivable legal challenge to a series of United Food and Commercial Workers (UFCW) union elections conducted by the National Labor Relations Board (NLRB), hoping that delays, disillusionment, and breakneck turnover in a state with already rock-bottom unionization would drain the union drive's momentum to zero. Even favorable rulings by the drastically underfunded and understaffed NLRB were a long time in coming, and once the employer exhausted the internal NLRB judicial process, it then pursued an even longer delay in the outside courts. Multiple legal strategies siphon precious energy into a courtroom drama workers have as much power over as the ones on TV. If the Smithfield case's eventual victory seared one thing into my brain, it was to immediately act as the union workers voted to form, rather than waiting for the go-ahead from the courts.

A key thing you learn through high-participation negotiations is that people learn how to take effective actions in all sorts of ways. Training, study, and mentorship matter deeply, but learning to take control, strategize, test, revise, and execute a winning collective-action campaign happens when workers are actually made to do it themselves—when workers understand that they and their coworkers are the ones who are making this change. When we lock workers out of these roles—out of the strategy room and out of negotiations—and rely on smart lawyers in front of the NLRB tribunal or at the negotiations table, we're losing the main tool we have for offense (winning powerful new contracts) *and* defense (beating back spurious legal claims and contract violations). The organized, mass-participation union we should be building all along is the main tool we have to really force the boss to give up the stalling legal shenanigans and meet us at the table on our terms, as both the UFCW and PASNAP cases show.

While all of the cases detailed in this book demonstrate how key aspects of this approach fit together to build impressive power in negotiations, PASNAP is different. As action research, it comes closest to the ideal type of the approach we outlined in the previous chapter, insofar as the theory was being implemented, tested, and improved on the ground by one of the authors herself, in collaboration with worker leaders, over the course of the campaign. I've described aspects of the PASNAP fight at the Albert Einstein Medical Center before from the perspective of taking an organizing approach to starting a union, identifying leaders, and winning an election.[2] This chapter examines the same fight from a complementary but different angle: how a high-participation, high-power organizing approach can maintain strength and momentum in first contract negotiations, even as union-busting tactics of delay encourage us to dump our energy elsewhere—and eventually fizzle out.

The Union We Wanted Didn't Exist, So We Created Our Own

Those words are the first you see under the "About Us" section of the union's website. PASNAP was birthed by nurses at Temple University Hospital who were trying to build an organization that could arrest the long-run decline in their working conditions. They broke away from a management-dominated nursing association in the mid-1990s, and then again from a professionalism-focused federation that was returning them weaker and weaker contracts, eventually establishing their own independent union in 2000, joined shortly thereafter by nurses at Butler Hospital. As profit-driven healthcare has exploded, building a union that was ready to fight was crucial for the nurses, since CEOs had begun cutting the largest expense lines on their ledgers—staff nurses—exponentially increasing the strain on remaining nurses and severely compromising patient care.

PASNAP nurses worked hard to build an organization that could actually win, and they understood that the ultimate source of their power, even in the highly regulated legal framework of labor in healthcare, was the supermajority strike. Not only did they believe it, but with time they proved it in practice, earning a reputation for being a democratic union ready to strike to win, even as their membership grew incrementally. Most healthcare worker strikes in recent decades are planned, single-day strikes, a shot across the bow letting management know that the workers are capable of more if their action doesn't lead to a satisfactory contract. But in the spring of 2010, the hospital workers who founded PASNAP walked off the job in a strike that was unprecedented in the new millennium: they waged an open-ended strike that sustained 97 percent unity for a month.

The Temple strike wasn't over money—though it did result in the highest wage standards in the labor market, making the union wages the envy of area nurses and certified professionals. The strike was prompted by management proposing writing a gag order into their contract intended to silence nurses from ever speaking out against declining patient care standards. Specifically, the contract proposal read (p. 176), "The Association [PASNAP], its officers, agents, representatives and members shall not publicly criticize, ridicule or make any statement which disparages Temple, or any of its affiliates or any of their respective management officers or medical staff members."[3] Given the whole reason PASNAP nurses went independent, they knew this infringement on their ability to advocate to improve the conditions they share with their patients would be make-or-break for their future.

CHART 3. PASNAP Strikes between Their Founding and Einstein Certification

Hospital and Unit	Date of Strike	Duration of Strike	Unit Size	Date of Contract
Wilkes Barre	January 30–February 18, 2003	21 days	475	February 2003
Temple	April 1–28, 2010	28 days	1000 RNs, 600 techs; 97%	May 2010
Wilkes Barre	December 23, 2010	1-day strike, 2-day lockout	450	May 3, 2010
Wilkes Barre	December 3–5, 2013	1-day strike, 2-day lockout	500	September 5, 2014
Wilkes Barre	July 4–9, 2014	5-day strike	500	September 5, 2014
Crozer	September 21–25, 2014	2-day strike, 3-day lockout	570; 100%	June 15, 2015
Armstrong Techs	March 31–April 2, 2015	1-day strike, 2-day lockout	125; 90%	June 8, 2016

Employers typically lock workers out when they declare a one-day strike, arguing that to get a contract with a temp nursing agency, they have to pay the strike breakers for at least three days. Additionally, all strikes were at least 90 percent out for the duration, but researchers could only produce actual counts for the three strikes noted.

By 2015, PASNAP's methodical growth exploded into a nurses' movement, more than doubling their size over the next year. Contrary to the long-dominant narrative espoused by many unions, haunted by Reagan's firing of over eleven thousand air traffic controllers in 1981—that strikes give unions a bad image—PASNAP's success is directly correlated to its ability to win strong contracts with impressive standards through supermajority strikes. As PASNAP grew, they were faced with the challenge of managing rapidly increasing numbers while maintaining the same methodical, high-participation, high-results organizing approach that won them these new members—an overwhelming prospect. And so they looked for someone who shared their vision for worker power, was a negotiator, and had experience running contract campaigns and scaling them up region-wide. That's when I got the call.

Kitchen-Sink Union Busting

PASNAP hired me as a consultant for two different but related assignments. One involved creating a bottom-up worker structure to coordinate citywide negotiations involving thousands of nurses across the newly unionizing hospitals (seven in all). The second, and more pressing, assignment was to focus hard on a key battle in their labor market: getting the prestigious and massive Albert Einstein Medical Center to drop their relentless union-avoidance legal strategy, filing objections to the election the workers won, and if we could win against this lawfare, then lead what were sure to be tough first contract negotiations.

Einstein's management had hired an A-level union buster, one who would stop at nothing to defeat the workers. They had been dumping truckloads of cash into the effort, as later investigative reporting made clear.[4] While unions have to regularly file forests worth of paperwork documenting how many paper clips they purchase, employers— many of them recipients of huge sums of taxpayer money, including hospitals through Medicare and Medicaid—can spend lavishly on union busters and delay for months if not years with no punishment under the miniscule reporting requirements that do exist. And often enough in the United States, it succeeds, nipping in the bud workers' efforts to unionize. For many union-frightened employers, it's a million well spent.

Not always, though. Despite the union busters' tactics—including a fancy anti-union website, constant mandatory captive-audience meetings, and seemingly endless one-on-ones to intimidate every nurse at Einstein—on April 8, 2016, the nurses voted to unionize. The effect of the union busters' tactics were evident, though, since the Einstein vote was much closer than several of the recent pro-union blowout elections sweeping hospitals across the city. Nurses saw a 516-117 victory in January at nearby Hahnemann University Hospital, and a whopping 311-49 vote weeks later at St. Christopher's. At Einstein, out of 925 nurses who were eligible to vote, 463 cast a yes to 343 nos. An additional 55 votes were never counted, called "challenged ballots," as the number of challenges was not sufficient to change the outcome of the election.[5] Compared to a presidential election, the margin may seem wide, but for PASNAP nurses it was a clear sign the union busters were successfully disorganizing people, making for a harder path ahead. This kind of vote split, where abstentions plus challenges plus no votes could be rephrased as "over 50 percent did not vote yes," gave Einstein management the opportunity to hammer away at the legitimacy of the decision workers had taken, even though the higher than 90 percent turnout represents a threshold almost no modern US election could meet.

More immediately, the employer took their high-paid consultants' advice and filed legal objections to the union election within the legally mandated period of seven days. Einstein used some extra-creative thinking about their spurious legal arguments and spent heaps of money and time trying to make up some grounds that sounded plausible to overturn the election. In fact, in a strategy later repeated by Amazon in challenging the first successful unionization election in Staten Island, New York, in April 2022, Einstein filed charges against the union *and* against Region 4 of the NLRB itself, accusing the labor board of somehow aiding and abetting the nurses and rigging the election. (For anyone who lived through November 2020, this should sound eerily familiar.) This resulted, like the Amazon JFK8 unionization case, in the national NLRB removing the election case from Region 4 and shifting the case to another region, in this case Region 22, in Newark, New Jersey.

In boxing, rope-a-dope is a strategy where a boxer lays back on the ropes of the ring, encouraging their opponent to burn out their energy in ineffective punches, until eventually the boxer doing the fake-out can take down their now-exhausted opponent. One can't say for certain what Einstein's strategy was here, but it's hard not to notice how this extra challenge on the legitimacy of the local NLRB office would generally slow things down even more, making the trial itself harder to access for the workers and union-side Philadelphia-based labor lawyers, and preserving the right to use their attack on the agency itself to give them more flexibility in where they could appeal the case once they had exhausted the internal agency appeals. In any case, this form of legal rope-a-dope meant that, although the workers had voted to unionize, the NLRB could not yet legally certify the election. Without the certification, it was the employer's position that there was no union and thus there would be no union negotiations. To give a sense of the intensity of this one campaign, Chart 4, from a report highlighting the crisis of union busting in the United States, shows the resources Einstein brought to bear against overworked registered nurses for daring to think they should have a say in how to improve patient care.

Meanwhile, the union busters continued their usual divide-and-conquer, scorched-earth approach inside the hospital and among the

CHART 4. Union Busting at Einstein[11]

Employer	Amount reported	Years
Laboratory Corporation of America	$4,300,000	2014–2018
Mission Foods	$2,900,000	2016–2017
Albert Einstein Medical Center	$1,100,000	2014–2017
Simmons Bedding Co.	$848,000	2015–2017
FedEx	$837,000	2014–2018
Trump International Hotel Las Vegas	$569,000	2015–2016
Nestle, USQ	$566,000	2014–2018
Bed Bath & Beyond	$506,000	2014, 2018
J.B. Hunt Transport	$354,000	2016–2018
Hilton Grand Vacations	$340,000	2014–2015
Owens Corning	$340,000	2014–2017

SOURCE: Juliana Feliciano Reyes, "Report: Philly's Einstein Medical Center Spent $1.1 Million on 'Union Avoidance.' It Isn't Alone," Philadelphia Inquirer, updated December 11, 2019, https://www.inquirer.com/news/anti-union-busting-employers-report-20191211.html; Celine McNicholas, Margaret Poydock, Julia Wolfe, Ben Zipperer, Gordon Lafer, and Lola Loustaunau, "U.S. Employers Are Charged with Violating Federal Law in 41.5% of All Union Election Campaigns," Economic Policy Institute, December 11, 2019, https://www.epi.org/publication/unlawful-employer-opposition-to-union-election-campaigns/.

workforce. Management strategy at this stage of union busting is known as futility: "Nothing will change just because you voted to unionize," and "There will not be a union here despite the election." While of course union-side lawyers fought the election cases in the relocated NLRB hearing, unionizing workers had to keep their eyes on the prize, building the organization they could wield to discourage further dirty tricks, bring their bosses to the table, and win a standard-setting contract.

To maintain momentum and faith among the workers who had chosen to unionize, we had to launch a counteroffensive, to act as if the union *was* certified and continue organizing and strengthening the worker organization by preparing for negotiations, regardless of the ongoing legal battle. If the employer was going to ignore an election won fair and square, our position was that we'd ignore their legal objections and keep moving forward, demanding they start negotiations. PASNAP's experience winning hard contracts made it clear that they couldn't afford to retreat into the low-participation approach typical unions fall into in the face of a legal challenge. If PASNAP's leadership, particularly the nascent one at Einstein, became consumed with lawyers, testimony, brief writing, and the blow-by-blows of the legal process, this case would likely have resulted in the union still waging a court case in some appellate court years later, as in Smithfield's stonewalling, rather than producing the story of defeating vicious employer campaigns captured in this chapter.

Forward Motion Beats Futility

We'd clearly have to bring every lever of power to the contract talks, assuming we could even get to the negotiations. This meant we had to simultaneously be building our knowledge of the terrain we were fighting in, in the form of a power structure analysis conducted at warp speed, while also staying laser-focused on continuing to organize the nurses into the force we would win with. In the process, we had to make preparations for negotiations the centerpiece of our organizing.

A three-phase power structure analysis (PSA) is a ton of work to conduct at the best of times, and even tougher in a union with no extra staff to spare—and next to no money, since dues don't usually come in until after workers win their first contracts. Nevertheless, if we were going to force Einstein to the table, we needed to know how they fit into how the city works, and who could make them grow up and start negotiating. Always trying to think of how to combine concrete training in organizing with getting each step of the work done, it occurred to me to drag in representatives of some Canadian unions, whom I had been booked to train in power structure analysis before I had to cancel in order to dive headfirst into this campaign. Within weeks, two very smart Canadian trade unionists were on the ground in Philadelphia learning the method by apprenticing. Additionally, a Harvard university student who was from Philadelphia and home for the summer was loaned to the effort to quickly help us understand with maximum precision the landscape of potential points of leverage.

Phase one of the PSA had thus begun, and phase two was also underway: charting the relationships (and thus power structures) among and between the nurses' base. The indispensable third phase, bringing the workers' own knowledge to the process, would come five months later. With close to no resources, we were forced to look under every rock for how to make things happen that needed to happen.

Meanwhile, we had to keep building our operations on the ground. We concurrently launched the second majority structure test, a comprehensive contract survey allowing nurses to specify in detail the changes they voted for on April 8. We set a goal of getting responses from at least 60 percent of all the workers *in each unit*—not just a hospital-wide majority—to be sure that we had real input from a supermajority of workers by work area and type of nursing. The crucial aspect of the unit-by-unit approach from a power-building perspective is that it serves as an opportunity to actively teach worker leaders how to develop a strong site structure, the kind they will need in any escalation capable of winning the policy changes they desire. In the process, the nurses learned how to use a tool called "big wall charting," where they would together discuss which nurse was best positioned, based on shift and relationships, to engage which other nurse in the survey process. They would put a yellow sticker on the name of each nurse in their unit- and shift-based chart as each nurse completed a survey. They also tracked who got the nurse to do the survey. This is the process of leader identification, the cornerstone of doing power structure analysis among the workers. Often, they filled them in together in their break rooms or came to our regular weekly meetings at shift change and sat together while they debated priorities.

We set up a headquarters at out-of-sight nearby locations, a small church and the basement of a nearby restaurant, where we held end-of-shift meetings—complete with donuts, dinner, and decaf coffee—at 7 a.m. for night shift workers and 7 p.m. for those on the day shift. The 7 p.m. meetings allowed the nurses to order full dinners and an occasional beer. A beehive of activity happened, with nurses placing their unit charts on the walls, debating why they had holdouts, who would approach particular holdout workers next, and with what strategy, so that the nurses in that unit could hit their majority and start electing their representatives.

With the legal process sputtering along in the background, by the week of May 20, nurses in eleven units had achieved their majorities and began the next step of building their structure while preparing for negotiations. They held very publicly announced elections for negotiations committee representatives inside their breakrooms and at shift changes. On Monday, May 23, we distributed a two-page flyer filled with pictures of the first members elected to represent their department. Under each photo, the nurse stated why she was excited to represent the nurses in her unit. Peg Lawson, a highly skilled nurse who carried huge respect in the single largest unit, the ninety-nine-person emergency department, was easily the choice of her unit. She said, "I am looking forward to tackling the issues that, for far too long, have weighed heavy on the hearts and minds of the incredible nurses that I work with and represent as part of the negotiating team." Jenny Dussek, a leader chosen by her peers in the Medical Intensive Care Unit, said, "I am excited to be moving forward and representing my coworkers. Let's put our minds together here at Einstein and accomplish greatness!" Some, like Adrian Flint, a Special Procedures Unit nurse, spoke directly to management's anti-union campaign, stating, "The majority of Einstein nurses voted yes for a union. Why does Einstein continue refusing to listen to our voices by failing to accept the final results of the vote?"

The announcement of the rolling negotiations elections at Einstein created a buzz of excitement, and a friendly but competitive environment. In areas or units where worker activists were struggling to reach majority participation in the survey process, being able to show their coworkers the flyers from other units—demonstrating through visuals that others were achieving the 60 percent threshold—created a healthy motivation for those units to catch up. They realized that without participation, their unit and their specific issues would fail to have representatives on the negotiations committee. Within days, three more units would elect their negotiations team members.

And then that very week, on May 26, the Administrative Law Judge in Region 22's Newark office published his findings, recommending that the NLRB dismiss all six of Einstein's objections to the election, and recognize the union.[6] The news spread throughout the hospital like wildfire: finally, the nurses had validation that they won their election. No sooner than the next day, management issued every nurse a lengthy memo, stating their intent to appeal the ALJ's ruling to the next level, more artillery meant to douse a bucket of water on the previous day's joy. Without giving workers something more durable to hang onto, like the increasingly tangible organization they're building with their coworkers, the brittle wins in the courts can really dash workers' hopes on appeal— the strategy of futility at work. For several weeks, there was a drop-off in the weekly shift-change meetings, and some nurses were thinking they'd never win. But that wouldn't last long.

Make Einstein More Than Medicine

Payoff from the first phase of the power structure analysis landed quickly. We knew the hospital was marking its 150th anniversary in 2016—that did not require PSA researchers as it was plastered on billboards all over the city. The celebrations highlighted Einstein's history as an institution founded by Jewish doctors to serve injured Union soldiers during the Civil War, alongside all other patients, regardless of ability to pay, race, ethnicity, or faith. With the creation of Medicare and Medicaid, the hospital (which had Albert Einstein's personal blessing to use his name) was designated as a "safety net" hospital.[7]

Given the profound structural racism of the United States, manifesting here as inequitable access to resources and care, Einstein has long been a central service provider for Philadelphia's Black community, with this ethos of fairness and justice being a source of pride for the nurses themselves. As the hospital branded a year of celebrations with a new motto, "Einstein: More Than Medicine," nurses saw a bitter irony. The profit-driven move to intentional short-staffing the very same management was introducing was eroding the parts of the job nurses love the most: caring for people.

What we didn't yet know came in an urgent June 14 email from PSA researcher Jeff Rousset, on loan from Harvard, who had been tasked with daily poring over the *Philadelphia Inquirer* and *Philadelphia Business Journal*, scouring the legal notices in the classifieds for anything that could be useful. In addition to the more obvious search for stories relevant to the power structure the employer's embedded in, things like lawsuits, proposed site expansions, and a plethora of legally mandated items help sustain the income of what remains of print media, so these papers are a crucial resource.

What he found was an absolute gem of an opportunity, on no one's radar screen: "Seems like this might be important, there's a legal notice of meeting buried in the paid classified ads in the back of the paper today stating that tomorrow is the annual public meeting of the hospital's board of directors, mandated by PA law to be open to the public." Holy crap! Even with almost no notice, there was simply no way we could miss crashing a meeting like that, despite having next to no time to mobilize or prepare for it. But that's the zig-and-zag of real-world organizing—if you start organizing early, you'll be as ready as you'll ever be when these things fall in your lap.

The nurses went to work immediately trying to put together a team who could attend the meeting on such short notice. Had we not been building the kinds of trusting relationships that allow people to drag others into boring and potentially uncomfortable actions, we would not have been able to turn on a dime like this. While the nurses had been busy recruiting and prepping, the staff of the union had worked overnight to produce glossy packets with the legal ruling from May 26, and the employer's filled-with-more-fiction legal appeal, a copy of a letter ten state senators had written in response to the NLRB ruling calling on management to drop the legal appeal, nurse flyers about their negotiations committee elections, and more, as we were certain the union busters and management had been briefing the trustees on the battle going on around the unionization. We had to hit them with everything we had.

Our plan was simple: we'd show up and ask to be put on the agenda during the mandated open comment period at the end, and the nurses would lay out their case to the hospital's trustees—a mix of business types, but also a few top doctors—about why they believed the hospital should withdraw their legal objections to the union election and get on with negotiations. To say the trustees were shocked when we entered the room would be an understatement. No one ever showed up at these meetings because, in fact, they weren't publicized except for the legally mandated paid ad in the papers—the tiny room they held them in only had enough seats for trustees and management staff, and the meeting's chair seemed completely baffled as to why the nurses were in attendance. Uncomfortable watching us stand silently all around them lining the walls of the room until the mandated comment period, he quickly revised the agenda so that we presented first.

Of the nurses who showed up, six of them nervously made brief remarks, and they were all fabulous. But one nurse leader, Pat Kelly, who was the first nurse to contact PASNAP about forming a union back in early 2015, delivered the closing remarks. He broke the poker faces on most trustees when he opened with, "We are here because we are the people who make Einstein 'more than medicine.'" According to Kelly, "I described to the trustees some very real patient-care issues happening in our unit and then explained that patient care is the reason we voted to form our new union. I asked the trustees to direct management to stop spending precious patient-care dollars on fighting us and instead spend this money on fixing staffing issues."

We put out a flyer with pictures from the meeting and a summary of the statements, and the collective rush of enthusiasm we had lost from the employer's appeal returned. The subsequent shift-change meeting had nurses back in high numbers, charts on the wall, driving to complete their third hospital-wide structure test, a majority petition demanding the employer drop their legal fight and start negotiations. The symbol for this structure test on their big unit wall charts was a red dot, and some units were already at majority. One of many values of the big wall charts is that all the nurses would mill around, looking at each other's units before the meeting began, with those from departments that were lagging taking motivation—and getting ideas from the nurses in the departments where majorities were being achieved more quickly and consistently.

By late June, energized by the direct action at the trustee meeting, the nurses had achieved their first hand-signed public majority petition. It's a monumental achievement as it requires workers to take, and embrace, a higher level of risk, because the intention is to *publish* the petition. This distinguishes it from the first two majority structure tests: the private act of signing the cards authorizing the election, which are only seen by the NLRB officers who would call the election; and the second test, which was the contract survey. In the escalation of structure tests, part of the science is increasing the risk factor—given that the ultimate test of workers' structure, a strike, requires a tremendous amount of risk for the workers who engage in it together. On June 27, a team of nurse activists assembled near the elevators that go up to the CEO's office, carrying a large five-foot-by-three-foot copy of their now poster-sized hand-signature petition, and unfurling it as they boarded the elevator to deliver it directly to the CEO's office. Talk about risk.

FIGURE 4. Einstein majority petition

The next day, we produced more of these giant posters, so nurses could show them to other nurses in their breakrooms. Once a first public majority petition is actually published, a special dynamic sets in: nurses who were previously holding out begin to shift. Einstein management's union-busting message was that "a majority hadn't voted to unionize," recalling management's intentionally fuzzy math. Any confusion among onlookers was put to rest once the majority petition appeared, with 60 percent of nurses' hand-signed signatures on it, proving the boss wrong by showing the majority in black-and-white. This demonstration of worker power and commitment came just in time for the next phase of the campaign to force the employer to drop the legal appeal, as we found ourselves thrust into another opportunity we just couldn't pass up.

Jiu-Jitsu: The 2016 Democratic National Convention Was Coming to Town

We kept plowing ahead on our two primary tracks, with the PSA growing in detail about how big things get done in Philly, by whom and how, and with preparation for contract negotiations never missing an opportunity to shore up our own structure in the workplace. The two came together as nurses were busy doing nearly daily delegations to the places of work of every member of the board of trustees, walking in, asking to see the trustee, and delivering the big-size version of the majority petition. About half the time, they'd leave it with a secretary. But on a few occasions, the trustee being visited was there to accept their petition, resulting in some excellent impromptu meetings. The ask was always the same: please call the CEO and tell him to start negotiating and drop the legal appeal. The nurses were feeling great about this process, and keeping them engaged in meaningful work mattered as the legal process chugged along.

By then, we had completed negotiations-team elections in nearly every unit. We had also come up with another way to raise the nurses' expectations of a new and better working life by having them begin to actually draft their proposed first contract. To get nurses' imaginations going, particularly for a workforce that had never had a union contract, we distributed one thousand copies of the best contract PASNAP had to every nurse in Einstein: the Temple contract won through the massive 2010 strike mentioned earlier. We enclosed with the contract a form for nurses to fill in with article-by-article information about which clauses in the Temple contract the Einstein nurses liked, and which ones they wanted to amend in small or big ways. Each unit's elected negotiators would then gather these and begin to develop contract language proposals, combined with earlier survey responses, to meet that unit's most pressing needs.

Management hated this, putting out memos saying how ridiculous it was that nurses were drawing up a contract when they didn't even have a union. The more management said it, the more the nurses took pleasure in announcing what parts of the Temple contract they wanted at Einstein. We held a well-attended meeting where we invited the Temple nurses to join the Einstein nurses to discuss the language in the contract and how it worked. It was super energizing.

Meanwhile, our PSA researchers had plenty on their plates: when it comes to revenue-generating events for a city, the two major political parties' every-four-year conventions rank almost as big as the Super Bowl. Hotel rooms are filled, restaurants booked, museums packed, concerts abound. The state's official host committee is a reflection of its most powerful players, gearing up to showcase their city and state, and they all have a ton of interest in everything going off without a hitch. By early July, they were often in the news, announcing another entry on the list of public and private events leading up to the convention. One PSA researcher did nothing but compile and analyze these players and events. The other stayed focused on deeper work, looking for leverage that we would need after the convention.

The Democrats' entire strategy to win the crucial swing state of Pennsylvania was to drive a massive turnout in the city of Philadelphia, targeting the huge and loyal base in the Black community, as well as generating a much higher turnout than in 2012 among white women in Philly's suburbs. And who were our one thousand nurses? Basically, the exact demographics the party leadership had decided would win the swing state. In a Democratic machine city, every scale of the party, and the power players they depended on, would be in a position to tell Einstein to clean up their mess, and do it fast.

Then, on July 11, the second NLRB decision hit, and it could not have been better. The director of Region 22, David E. Leach III, affirmed every recommendation of the previous findings from May, rebutting every single assertion the union busters had packed into their legal brief. The decision by the regional director stated,

> IT IS HEREBY CERTIFIED that a majority of the valid ballots have been cast for Pennsylvania Association of Staff Nurses and Allied Professionals (PASNAP), and that it is the exclusive representative of all the employees in the following bargaining unit: INCLUDED: All full-time, regular part-time and per-diem Registered Nurses (RNs) and Nurse Practitioners (NPs) employed by the Employer at its acute-care hospital located at 5501 Old York Road, Philadelphia, Pennsylvania.

His eighteen-page ruling gave Einstein a deadline for a further appeal, to the full board of the national NLRB, of July 25.

July 25. What a gift. The official DNC was July 24–26, with the nomination of the first woman as presidential candidate of a major party at its center. There is some luck in this field, mixed in with a hell of a lot of skill, strategy, and hard work. To deny the good fortune of the timing of the ruling, and the date for the appeal, would be silly. It put our campaign on steroids. Thankfully, we had been building, which to underscore, was key. Had we not continued acting like the union, organizing nurses throughout the months of management's futility messages, we could not have pulled off what had to happen next.

There was no way in hell Einstein wasn't planning to take this chance to raise their failed appeal *again*; the union busters had been on the ground to preempt PASNAP's move since at least a year before workers went public with their intent to unionize, and were clearly in it for the long haul. Even if this ruling was so clearly on the workers' side, and another one likely would be too, these workers needed management at the negotiations table, and soon, or they could lose everything. We had to use what we had built while the appeals were raging in court to drag management away from their affidavits and into our contract fight.

The PSA helped us identify key targets in the local and national terrain who could make Einstein feel the heat, and the structure-building approach we'd taken to negotiations preparations, regardless of the employers' feigned ignorance, gave us the beginnings of the power to act. Even having hit the ground running despite the rope-a-dope at the NLRB, we were much further from the kind of supermajority structure we needed than I would have liked. But national party strategy depended directly on our base, raising the potential disruption costs we could place on Einstein, and the due date for the employer's appeal fell smack-dab in the middle of the dates of the convention, kicking us into high gear.

We had thirteen days to win or blow our biggest point of leverage. The ongoing organizing and contract drafting that we drove hard during the legal process, combined with tons of points of attack from the PSA, made the thirteen-day countdown doable, but not a guaranteed coup. If that didn't sound tight enough, in the healthcare sector, workers calling a strike—and nearly any job action possibly misconstrued as one, like official picketing where you can hold a picket sign—are legally bound to provide an official notice of intent to strike, or to picket, ten days in advance to the employer. This meant that to have the maximum-power threat in hand at our moment of maximum leverage, we would have to hold the vote in a crazily tight two days.

Popular consciousness in the United States, atrophied by a shrinkingly timid labor movement over the last few decades, easily confuses any official picketing with a strike, despite the vast difference between the two. Union busters make the most of this, both sowing the same level of apprehension among workers that a decision to take strike action would, and threatening even more legal action if anything even looks like an unannounced strike. The union busters' flyers almost write themselves: "The UNION will MAKE YOU abandon your patients and STRIKE, it will cost you money and patients their lives." Whether we liked it or not, we had to make leaps and bounds to prepare the nurses' structure for this kind of action.

The alignment of these dates was good for our public campaign, but it was actually incredibly challenging internally. Honestly, the nurses were not yet ready to take a vote for legally sanctioned picketing, precisely because the union busters would confuse them enough given the short timeline by telling them they were taking a strike vote, versus voting to authorize a ten-day legal notice for picketing! The organizing had been going great, but we were only one successful public majority structure test in, at a 60 percent threshold, not the 90 percent we'd need for a real strike. From the science side of organizing, to go from a 60 percent majority petition to a strike vote with no steps in between is way, way fast—in organizing, going from 60 to 90 is a lot harder than on the highway, and you might overheat your engine.

Our first act, on the day after the legal decision dropped, was to immediately write the legal information request for financial and other key data, including staffing levels per shift, injury reports, and more, and fax it to the CEO. The request lifted the NLRB decision language, asserted we were certified, demanded they start providing information required for collective bargaining, and closed by requesting we commence negotiations August 3. The committee loved the letter, and again, deepened their understanding of the power of unionizing. Seeing just how much information unionized workers get access to helped raise expectations among these core worker leaders, which was going to prove crucial as we stared down the coming structure test.

Top worker leaders then came together to strategize how to move on the deadlines imposed by our golden opportunity. Organizers worked to inoculate leaders about the coming management strategy of painting any picketing as a strike (untrue) abandoning patients (also untrue about a strike). Then we framed the hard choice: it's now or maybe never. This was when cases from my PhD research came in handy: I reminded them about the Smithfield fight, where it took serious worker power and decisive action to end sixteen years of legal delays to UFCW workers' certification, and the leaders agreed to call for emergency meetings to be held the next day, July 13. We had no choice, in order to meet the letter of the law—if you fail the letter of the law, even for simple picketing, workers can be fired. It's serious stuff. The shift-change meetings the next day were hard, which we expected, and long, with tons of questions from nurses who had not expected to take such a vote. We made a decision to keep organizers and worker leaders awake all night, driving the night shift's turnout to the 7 a.m. meeting especially hard. We had a bigger base of militants on the night shift and calculated that, if they came out the next morning in impressive numbers, and they voted yes, their vote would help carry us in the much bigger and more risk-averse evening meeting of the day shift. It all worked.

10 REASONS FOR SENDING THE 10 DAY NOTICE

10 — Number of State Senators who sent a letter to the CEO urging him to stop appealing your election, respect your decision to form a union, and start negotiations with you

9 — As in 90.2% of you participated in a high-turn out free and fair election where you chose to form a union

8 — The Tower where management is proposing to place high risk OBGYN patients interspersed with radiation and chemotherapy patients (and drugs)

7 — The article in the Crozer PASNAP contract that guarantees self-scheduling by nurses

6 — The number of patients no nurse should have alone

5 — Years of experience guarantees a nurse $42.58 in the Temple nurses PASNAP contract

4 — The number of months since our election without management agreeing to respect our decision and start negotiations

3 — Because it is past time for the proper 3:1 patient-to-nurse ratio to be implemented in the emergency department

2 — The number of times so far that the NLRB has dismissed management's objections to the free and fair nurse election at Einstein

1 — RESPECT and A REAL VOICE in PATIENT CARE in our hospital

On Tuesday, July 26, evening shift change, let management know we are serious about getting to negotiations! Contact your elected negotiations committee member and sign-up yourself, your family, your faith leader and your friends to demand high quality patient care. Should management offer to drop their delays and appeals and negotiate before July 26, we'll put our energy into problem solving and negotiations instead!

RESPECT OUR VOICE, RESPECT OUR PROFESSIONALISM, START NEGOTIATIONS!

For more information, call 610-567-2907
PENNSYLVANIA ASSOCIATION OF STAFF NURSES AND ALLIED PROFESSIONALS

FIGURE 5. 10 Reasons for Sending the 10-Day Notice

With the vote to send a legal ten-day notice to picket, we were immediately in violation of a "labor peace accord" signed by the local Central Labor Council (CLC) of the AFL-CIO with the host committee of the DNC a year earlier. These kinds of negotiated agreements, way too common, see the unions agree to surrender the right to disrupt at their biggest points of leverage, like a national convention of the political party that is supposed to represent workers, in exchange for narrow, temporary gains, things like overtime pay for the convention workers such as stagehands and guards and construction workers. The fact that PASNAP was an independent union meant they weren't bound by this power-killing accord. And because of PASNAP's history of strong strikes, everyone took the ten-day picketing notice completely seriously, even as we quietly panicked about what would happen if the chess moves failed. Our ability to wield power right then rested on the majority petition, which we had already been giving out to the power structure as noted, the strike history of the union, and the Democratic Party flipping out that their first female candidate was about to be picketed by the demographics she needed to win.

On July 14, armed with the workers' vote to send the ten-day notice stating we'd be picketing on the day of the nomination, PASNAP's able president, Patty Eakin, went to work with the president of the CLC, with whom she had very friendly relations over the years. She explained our strategy to them: our vote to authorize the picketing had a proviso built in that, if the employer agreed in writing to drop the appeal before the July 25 NLRB deadline, we'd call off the action. The president of the CLC was a decent guy and immediately understood his mission. He got authorization to send a letter to Einstein's CEO stating that the CLC unequivocally supported the nurses' demands. In this way, he wasn't technically violating the labor peace accord, but he was signaling to the host committee that the shit was about to hit the fan, from a union known for effective strikes. A team of people made sure the letter from the CLC to the CEO was quickly faxed to the leaders of the DNC host committee as a CC.

These are moments in a campaign that put intense pressure on the whole team, and everyone's commitment to the power of transparent, big, and open operations. Every temptation emerges to take a shortcut, funny enough often right as a settlement is on the horizon. We faxed the official legal notice to the CEO on July 15, and I boarded a plane to England, nerves fraying, to do a training for the one union that refused to let me cancel for the campaign. Sitting in my hotel room, my phone rang, and it was Buzz Satinsky, then a partner with Fox Rothschild LLP representing Einstein, calling to politely ask for a private meeting with me to "work something out from the letter you sent over." With as polite, clear, and unambiguous a tone as I could muster to disguise the nearly audible heartbeats pumping loudly in my chest, I explained I could not and would not agree to a secret off-the-record. He shifted from friendly to angry in seconds, yelled that under no circumstance would they meet if I was going to inform the workers, and hung up.

My commitment as an organizer and negotiator to the approach I had learned and been practicing and teaching for years was being tested. Had I just blown our one shot? Hyperventilating, I called Jerry Brown, one of my most important union mentors from 1199 New England. No sooner had Jerry told me that it actually sounded like we had Einstein management "by the balls," that familiar sound of call waiting hit my ear. It was Buzz. I set my terms: workers would be notified, two would come with me, and the entirety of the nurses would approve anything we agreed to. Another click. Another Buzz. In exchange for a ban on sharing the meeting through flyers and the media, alongside no Einstein workers in the room, the lawyer agreed to one of my demands, to have the CEO present, instead of the usual HR lackeys, and to allow me to bring the union's executive director. This was still far from the ideal situation, but it was finally worth putting before some worker leaders for their approval. No secret meetings, ever, and especially when a negotiator has developed high trust with the workers. We set a tentative date for July 17, pending worker-leader approval—and my overnight flight back from London, unbeknownst to Buzz.

I chose the two top leaders to call first, Pat Kelly and Peg Lawson. They were, predictably, incredibly happy to hear the news. Together we discussed how many workers to consult, and who in particular. By

Saturday, July 16, Kelly called to give me the all-clear to get the deal done to drop the damn legal appeal! Over the course of two days of negotiations in the lawyers' offices, complete with each side storming out at various moments, fists pounding on the table, shouting, and just about any scene you've seen in a movie, we did come to agreement. And Jerry was right: our work had paid off, and we had them by the balls. Conscious of the power we had built, we didn't just settle for them agreeing to drop the appeal. We knew they could use that to get us off their back and then proceed to waste our time surface bargaining, delaying giving us negotiation dates, and stifling our momentum. No, we hammered out an agreement for a two-and-a-half-month period of expedited negotiations, with all dates preselected, before shaking hands on the deal.

They, of course, had a laundry list of demands, which we whittled down to two we were willing to accept. PASNAP had to agree to surrender the right to organize a position called CRNAs (nurse anesthetists), a new highest-level nonmanagement nurse position, and a role the industry was just phasing in to take work away from even higher-priced doctors. There weren't many of them, and the CRNAs had been overwhelmingly anti-union during the organizing drive. A tougher decision was a temporary agreement to not organize nurses at the three new, smaller suburban hospitals in the larger Einstein Health Network. This was a harder pill to swallow, but we ultimately understood, and discussed with the nurse leaders at Einstein, that if we failed to get an agreement with management to drop the appeal charges and didn't win a great contract at the big hospital, our chances of ever organizing the smaller ones would be near zero anyway. Winning good standards within the network would form the bedrock for later organizing success once this agreement expired; being dragged into a multiyear legal fight before anyone saw a win would most certainly not.

On July 19, we held a second round of emergency meetings for all the nurses to come, hear and discuss the proposed agreement, and vote it up or down. The attendance was high, and so was the energy. There was little disagreement and a ton of celebrating. Worker power had won the day. They had done something virtually unheard of, which few people thought we could do, including our side's lawyers: nurses had forced an employer to break with their hired union busters, and withdraw from what was clearly a plan to drag the appeal process out for a decade until the workers' organization withered on the vine.

Big and Open Builds to Supermajority Unity

Even with the bosses dragged kicking and screaming to the table, we were still having to move fast. The nurses had a little under one month to get ready to finally pull up to their own negotiations table. We had done so much preparation work on the contract itself, partly to keep positive momentum going, that it was practically ready by the time we won the agreement for expedited negotiations. If we hadn't, we would've been either scrambling to build collective ownership over demands, or abandoning the strength of the high-participation approach entirely, and winning a lot less. The nurse leaders in most units were now seasoned at hashing out contract language, and they just needed to come to agreement across units on priorities. That allowed my focus, and the full-time organizers, to return to uniting the remaining anti-union units. There was a smattering of smaller units still to persuade. KB Brower and Amanda Shimko ably took on the smaller holdout units. I turned my attention to cracking what's called the "biggest worst" in organizing lingo: the one large unit of nurses where, functionally, nothing had been happening since the April 8 election. That unit was Telemetry, the beachhead of the professional union busters. None of the existing nurse leadership had any hope we'd succeed in winning over Telemetry. But from experience, I was confident it could be done if we were methodical.

Once the union buster's empty threats that "there will never be a union here" were destroyed, the leaders in the holdout units would be posed a simple, direct question: are you prepared to let all the other nurses, from every department other than yours, make the decisions about your priorities for you? This advantage of the unit-by-unit big committee structure, and our very public negotiations team elections, meant the holdout units were aware that the other nurses were ready to go. But because of the diabolical union busters, happy to rip apart any friendship or family and create huge tensions between nurses, one has to pay careful attention to bring the previous holdout units, the anti-union units, into the union in a particularly respectful way. They knew they had been on the wrong side, but telling them that or making them feel ostracized will not help, even though some militantly pro-union workers will be understandably tempted to do so unless we explain this dynamic. And it is hard for the pro-union nurses to accept suddenly cozying up with the anti-union nurses who've been calling them all sorts of names as they fight for their coworkers. But what we had to do in very clear terms was explain to the pro-union nurses that it was even harder for the anti-union nurses, who had been completely committed, with a very public identity as anti-union, to themselves enter the process. And we framed the hard choice to the pro-union nurses most likely to be negative with the anti-union nurses: do you want to achieve what you've been writing in the contract drafting process? Because if so, you need to unite together to the tune of at least 90 percent to stand a chance of winning the contract. Some of that 90 percent will be people who've made the effort extra hard for us, but who've come around.

For workers who have been in pitched public battles with pro-union nurses for months on Facebook and in the hallways, the usual good sense that those in the ranks are always best at organizing their peers can stand a slight exception. With Telemetry, we strategically put this mission on two members of union staff: me as lead negotiator and a more recently hired organizer named Candace Chewing, who had come from the hospitality workers' union UNITE HERE.

With the agreement in hand that negotiations would commence on August 17, we set out to win over the long-identified organic leader of the Telemetry unit, Marne Payne. To give you a sense of the power of organic leaders, Payne had literally instructed every nurse in her unit to not talk to anyone—not a nurse, and certainly not union staff—since just before the April 8 election. And they listened to her, with one exception, a night-shift nurse named Liz Miller. Miller was an activist, by textbook definition. She was an enthusiastic supporter of the union, no matter what Payne said. The problem was, the other nurses didn't listen to Miller, they listened to Payne.

After a round of phone banking through the unit by the PASNAP president herself, a few nurses agreed it was a problem that they were being left out and they committed to persuade Payne to come to a meeting. I instructed Chewing to bring a full draft copy of the contract proposal to hand to her, and suggest Payne read through it to see what she liked, didn't like, and so on. Some of the leaders were quite nervous about this, telling me Payne would immediately give their draft contract to the employer. My response was straightforward: You are all about to give it to the employer, it's not a trade secret, and if it moves Payne to get on board, who cares if management gets a sneak preview? The leaders got it, and the plan worked. Except Payne didn't commit yet, and Chewing decided to suggest that she should meet the chief negotiator in person.

Two days later, I walked into the hospital for the tête-à-tête with our most intransigent and important leader. I was ready for her, as there were many like Payne in other campaigns I had already led. Anywhere you have an A-level union buster, they will create hard-to-overcome divisions. They are mercenaries; that's their job. I knew to be as tough with her as she was going to be with me—firm and polite, but not trying to be her friend. There's nothing worse than organizers thinking that what a leader wants is a friend. What they want is to be convinced that the person they are talking to has a credible plan to address their issues.

Across the board, units had identified staffing levels as *the* problem degrading both nurses' working lives and the standard of care they can provide to patients. Telemetry is a unit where the nurses don't interact much directly with individual patients, but operate sophisticated computer systems while training their eyes to every monitor on every patient throughout the hospital. It's life-and-death work as much as any other worker, but it's more like being in a control tower than doing the hands-on bedside work of their colleagues. This structure of work seemed to separate the concerns of Telemetry from those of other units, and the staffing conversation just did not land the same way in their unit.

Within minutes of our meeting's start, Payne began to finally discuss her unit's issues, and the biggest one she identified was how often they were being mandated to stay on-call. Being on-call means you have to be able to report back to the hospital within thirty minutes of being paged, no matter what you were doing. For Payne, a young nurse who had a social life and was dating and all the things young, smart people do, the fact that most of the time she left the hospital she couldn't have a glass of wine or a cocktail, or settle into a relaxing night out, was her biggest issue with work. It was interesting because the Telemetry nurses didn't discuss this as a staffing issue, but of course fundamentally it was. The stress of low staffing just took a different shape for them. Rather than having to walk away from a frightened patient in one room to respond to another patient whose call button was buzzing, the Telemetry nurses couldn't have a social life. When I echoed this back to her, and linked it to the demonstrated campaign to win on staffing that her coworkers had been building, something clicked.

By the next morning, Payne agreed to sign up with the union—and to get her unit caught up. She asked for thirty union membership cards and left. The next day, she called Chewing to say she had sixteen membership cards signed, and she'd be getting the rest as the day continued. Done. She turned the unit in a week from a unit with one person who had signed a card, Liz Miller, into the first supermajority on membership cards. This is the science of organizing: invest in identifying the leader, and doing what it takes to help them come to see that their problems can only be solved by uniting with their coworkers in mass collective action. Then they will take care of the rest of their unit more ably than any outsider.

Decisive here was our intensive preparation of the contract unit by unit and article by article, so that we could imagine a way for workers with apparently different issues to see the potentials of united action. Equally important were our precise awareness of where we were weak and a well-developed structure that gave intransigent but highly respected opponents of the union a place to integrate and exercise real influence in shaping the overall effort, on top of a credible plan to win.

Next up was holding meetings to ratify the contract proposals, and using the ratification meetings to plan and role-play the opening session, which was coming up quickly on August 17. We had prepared a draft PowerPoint to review with the nurses, reflecting in charts and diagrams all their top issues ranked and illustrated in dozens of slides. We had slides with the most up-to-date academic literature correlating improved staffing ratios with improved patient care outcomes. We had slides on the skyrocketing cost of housing in once-affordable Philadelphia. We had everything. They were ready. On the first day of negotiations, we rented a fourteen-foot movie screen on which to project their presentation. When management walked into the room, they found over one hundred nurses dressed and ready to once again make Einstein more than medicine.

Ready to Roll and No Ground Rules

The nurses were completely ready with every system in place, all agreed to in the final meetings leading up to negotiations. The chief negotiator for the employer wasn't Buzz Satinsky, but a different lawyer from Fox Rothschild LLP. He walked into the room with my first book, *Raising Expectations*, intentionally displayed, with tabs all over it, and said, "Huge, just like the book said it would be." That was the first test of everyone holding their poker faces, the first rule of the room, and it was a little challenging. I somehow forgot I had written a book detailing every single system we would deploy at Einstein! He opened by saying, "I assume no ground rules and I assume the nurses have a big presentation for us. We are eager to hear from you." The best part was that after the first day, when our side felt very proud of themselves, the nurses' most common refrain became, "Even after reading the manual on it, Jane, he doesn't know what to do with us!" Many of the committee members had studied the book at least as well as the management negotiator, and they understood immediately from here on: the systems worked. We were off and running, with lots of negotiations coming quickly, given the expedited agreement we had negotiated as the deal to get to the table.

Surprising progress was made on a pay issue, unusual for early stages of negotiations. The hospital was in fact desperate to recruit more nurses and came with a proposal for increasing pay for what are called per diem nurses. Per diems are permanent and work odd and flex schedules. They are perfect jobs for some nurses, especially nurses who are married and get benefits from their spouses, because for the flexibility per diems provide, they are rewarded with higher pay, but surrender all benefits. A good per diem system benefits everyone and avoids hospitals bringing in temporary agency nurses. Management was so desperate to increase the pay rates and do so right away, before we got to the rest of the contract, that it gave us leverage to force an even better structure to the program, with more money than they initially wanted to offer. This gave the nurses serious negotiations experience way sooner than usually occurs. We notched a quick and significant win, and it set the tone for the rest of what would come.

Naturally, things slowed down as we attempted to get to the substantive issues of staffing levels and compensation, but we expected that and we knew we had more power to build before we could force a settlement. Our union caucus sessions were filled with article committees meeting in every corner, poring over any counterproposal management gave us on the relevant contract article, strategy discussions, and trainings where nurses would stand in front of the room and practice moving a harder-to-move coworker in role-plays, then leave the negotiations with their freshly minted nurses' bulletin, heading to their units understanding exactly which nurse they needed to get to do whatever structure test we were moving at that stage. But it was time to escalate.

Power Structure Analysis, the Final Phase

On September 16, we convened a citywide half-day retreat to bring all the negotiating committees across the hospitals together for a presentation on our power structure analysis. Phase three was about to begin, which meant getting the nurses to take their campaign to their own community, once they could see who really ran the city, and nurses were set to imagine how their own lives might intersect with the power structure at surprising points. We planned the four-hour meeting to begin with lunch to help nurses build relationships across the city. This was our second time bringing the nurses together across the hospitals, and the timing was good, since all negotiations were slowing as every negotiating team was hitting up against the tough issues.

The unions' senior staff were highly skeptical that a couple hundred nurses would be interested in a detailed, long PowerPoint on the local power structure. Of course, the nurses were riveted by the day, many exclaiming no one had ever explained anything like this to them about who ruled their region, and how their employers' connections were embedded all over the power structure. Midway through the presentation, just after we reviewed the most powerful faith leaders and their ties to the power structure, a hand went up. It was Joyce Rice, from Einstein's Labor and Delivery department. She started her intervention by apologizing that she had just been texting for a few minutes, but after seeing the name of the organization we ranked as the most powerful Black faith organization, the Baptist Pastors and Ministers Coalition, Joyce thought she had seen in her church newsletter that her minister had recently been elected to a new term as the leader of the coalition. That's why she had been texting: she wanted to confirm with him that he was the newly elected leader. I almost passed out. But I had been in rooms just like this before, with workers quickly starting to realize they themselves had power not just at work but in their communities. Not only was Joyce a member of Pastor Brown's church, she was close enough to him that they were casually texting!

After Joyce's rather amazing revelation, we wrapped up the formal presentation, and the nurses began to have facilitated discussions at all their many round tables, answering a series of questions we had prepared to help them think through whether engaging in comprehensive charting—the systematic approach to them unearthing their own connections to the power structure—made sense as a next step in the campaign. Joyce Rice had sealed the deal on that vote, and a decision was made to do two things: begin to group nurses by political precincts across the hospitals to meet literally every elected official from city council to state assembly to state senate, to ask them to write a letter to the CEOs demanding they settle the contracts favorably to the nurses and the patients (also known as their constituents)—and to embark on charting their connections to the faith and other communities they now understood in depth from the power structure presentation.

In the end, nurses from all the hospitals did the political meetings by political precinct, and the mixing of the nurses across hospitals for the meetings solidified their bonds to fight and struggle united and together. It was only at Einstein where we launched a formal effort to engage every nurse about their broader connections. To win a great contract at Einstein, we could leave absolutely no power on the table. There was so much going on at this point, and everyone was exhausted but committed.

This would be the second time I rang up a team of Canadians with whom I had cancelled a training: the British Columbia Federation of Labour. Within days, six worker leaders and staff organizers from six different unions had agreed to fly, on their own union's dime, to Philly for a one-week blitz comprehensively charting workers' connections with the local power structure, and they would take the bulk of the work off our organizing staff's overflowing plates. We rented a house for them, and they showed up eager to learn the method. They were all women, and all terrific!

The Canadian team wanted to see what big and open negotiations looked like, so we were sure to schedule the blitz when they could witness a session. They were highly doubtful that any nurse in Philly would sit down and let them chart some of the most personal aspects of the nurse's lives with total strangers, from another country, across the continent. This was a great week in the campaign. Team Canada was amazed that after their first day they had all had successful conversations with the Einstein nurses. In the evening debriefs we did, we stressed that the reason this work has to come later in the campaign is that high trust must be present among and between the nurses, and nurses have to own and believe in the plan itself. That is why it works, and why we staged the comprehensive charting to be close to the final structure test. Many of the organizers and union members had read about this in *Raising Expectations*; *No Shortcuts*, based on my PhD research, would be published a month later. But like anything, it is one thing to read about something, and quite another to actually do it.

While the negotiations were at the slow and frustrating stage, the community plan was sequenced to keep people busy with meaningful and exciting work. No elected leader refused to meet a group of nurses from their own districts. No faith leader refused a meeting with their own parishioners. And by the time of the strike vote in December, PASNAP produced a gorgeous multicolor sixty-page book for every nurse at Einstein, with all the letters compiled and bound. Workers had done this themselves; they knew their prepared presentations like the backs of their hands at this point, and were scrambling over themselves to reach out directly, as whole workers living in the community rather than paid lobbyists or union executives, to talk about the importance of their fight.

Joyce Rice's meeting with her minister, the leader of the Baptist Pastors and Ministers Coalition (BPMC), generated an incredibly strong letter sent on their letterhead to the CEO, in the name of the one hundred biggest Black congregations in the city. The nurses made sure to take that letter to all their subsequent meetings both with politicians and faith leaders, because everyone in the local power structure knew what the BPMC meant: serious influence.

The stage was set for the end game and strike vote if needed. Harvard was demanding that I return to my postdoc, and I had already gotten several extensions to my leave to get us that far. I did have a book coming out, and a course I was obliged by my fellowship to teach in the winter session that was coming up soon at Harvard. Plus, the nurses were firing on all cylinders. My work was done, though I agreed to continue working with the negotiator we selected to take over for me, the organizing director of the union, Mark Warshaw.

My last official session was a brutal but important one, two days after Trump's election rocked the soul of every progressive and fair-minded person in the country. Certainly, it knocked the radical staff and generally more liberal nurses in a huge way. How could it not? My last day at negotiations was on November 10. The executive director had called to tell me every one of our young staff were curled up in fetal positions on the floor, and it was my job to get people back up, focused, and in fighting mode. I take orders in the class war and walked into the union's pre-negotiations caucus prepped and ready to lay out the bare facts: we needed to quickly settle all these contracts before Trump took over the country and began to dismantle the NLRB. We knew this was coming as part of their larger effort to, in the words of his chief adviser Steve Bannon, "deconstruct the administrative state."[8] I left later that day on the train to New York City, encouraging everyone to remember that we needed to use the power we had built *now* to get it done fast.

From "PASNAP Is the Devil" to "Thank You, Jesus"

Warshaw and I talked often, and he was escalating as fast as he could. The employers all understood that Obama and his people were soon out and a union-busting casino mogul was about to enter the White

House. The pressure was seriously on. At Einstein, the boss was refusing to budge on staffing, the pension, and wages—the key issues needed to settle. Einstein's nurses' many connections to the faith community led to a hastily called evening multifaith prayer vigil in front of the historic synagogue and the oddly huge Greek-looking giant columns outside Einstein's gates. The CEO was getting the message that workers had made their contract an issue for the whole community. But still we saw no movement at the table on the big-ticket items at the new negotiations sessions that the vigil squeezed out of management. Thus, it was time to announce a strike vote. As soon as the message about the strike vote moved in the hospital, management called to offer three back-to-back dates to try to settle, if the union would refrain from taking the vote. This is normal, if the workers have built demonstrable power—and they had. The bosses, after all, were aware of the sixty-plus-page booklet filled with letters to the CEO that the nurses had generated as we had intentionally left them scattered around the hospital. Sides were in their bunkers for the final round.

Though Telemetry was very engaged, it would take Payne, the famously anti-union nurse turned tacitly pro-union leader, until December to start showing up at negotiations in person. Her presence mattered, as she was a unique symbol to management that if she was ready to strike, the entire hospital was ready to walk out. Back in April, Payne's last posting on the anti-union Facebook page the day before the union election read,

> Tomorrow is a big day at Einstein Medical Center. I hope everyone shows up to vote and I hope everyone VOTES NO! Not all unions are bad, but I think PASNAP is the devil. All and all—service above self! VOTE NO!! VOTE HELL NO!!!

She visited several times during the three sessions where management had promised to make real progress, December 13, 14, and 15. Though there had been substantial movement, it wasn't enough to satisfy nurses, who at that point thoroughly understood their power inside and out. At the end of the session on December 15, the nurses decided to call for the strike vote and to refuse any more deals to sit at tables in lieu of a committing to industrial action. Payne played a key role in mobilizing for the vote, a remarkable example of how deep organizing works to harness and redirect worker power toward victory. On December 19, the nurses voted by a margin of 90 percent to authorize a strike. And just like that, management called for negotiations on the next day. Eighteen nonstop hours later, the nurses had won. It was an impressive contract by any standard, and a ridiculously good first contract, especially in light of where they had come from: a protracted legal war with high-powered union busters who stalled them for five months from getting to the negotiations table.

During the last eighteen-hour round-the-clock final day of negotiations, Payne said, "I wouldn't leave. I couldn't leave. I am for fair pay and I was not letting management not give us a fair pay raise."[9] Miller, the night shift activist, who was inseparable at that point from Payne, said,

> I kept saying to people the process is fascinating, a slow chisel away, all the way to the end. I remember when it was finally over, that last day, we got the wages, we got some remaining little stuff, too, but it was big, and the raises were big. And it's all big especially when they [management] don't want to give you anything. I went home thinking, oh my god, I can't believe this shit happened, I was crying.[10]

On that final eighteen-hour day when it was all over, as Payne was walking out, she wrote in chalk on the blackboard, "Thank You, Jesus." And on December 23, the day the workers voted to ratify their first contract, she sent a text message to Pat Kelly. Pat gave it to me, and Payne agreed we could include it in its entirety:

> Hey Patrick. I wanted to personally thank you for all the work and time you sacrificed on this contract. Up until the very end, I still did not believe our contract could be this good the first time around. I know myself that I was not easy to deal with. I have very strong convictions. And so does my floor, telemetry. It was hard for myself and the floor to swallow that the union got in. I did not believe in the process. After last night and waking up this morning I have now realized that we are in fact stronger together. And we can accomplish so much in this profession together. Thank you for being one of the

lead organizers and helping to push this through. We now have a true
voice and damn good contract!!! Enjoy your holidays with your family.
I am sure they miss you!

Payne would go on to be elected to the executive board of the newest
chapter of PASNAP, the Einstein chapter. Kelly and Lawson were elected
cochairs of their new hospital unit. Management decided to test the
strength of the new union to enforce their contract, as they often do
shortly after a first contract is won. They thought they'd punish Telemetry
and decided to contort the interpretation of the holiday vacation language. Within a matter of days, Payne produced a 100 percent petition
with *every single nurse's name* and, in a contractual labor-management
meeting, laid into them until they learned their first lesson and backed
down. The nurses had built a union powerful enough to enforce their
agreement.

Recalling a 2007 study that found that by the end of twelve months
from when a union is certified, 52 percent of workers don't have a contract,[11] the Einstein nurses had a great first contract six months after their
certification, and nine months after they voted to form a union. How
unions negotiate is a strategic choice.

A crafty lead negotiator has good instincts and judgment, disciplined
by years of mentorship and experience, so that they're able to take full advantage when luck opens a window of opportunity, even a crack. But the
real measure of running a campaign is whether that campaign can keep
fighting and win big even after that leader is gone. Using an organizing
approach to negotiations—bringing the workers to the table—means
building real structures that enable workers to take ownership of the
fight themselves. Organizing means persuading workers of the principles of the fight, and ensuring that they are equipped through regularly
scaffolded practice to take this kind of action themselves, winning not
only a powerful contract but also, in the process, a union that is truly
their own.

3

A Punch in the Face (NJEA)

IN A 2015 INTERVIEW WITH CNN, New Jersey governor and Republican presidential candidate Chris Christie told a national audience what educators in New Jersey had known for years—that he believed the teachers' union deserved a punch in the face.[1] Since first running for statewide office in 2009, Christie had made a political brand out of bald-faced contempt for New Jersey's public employees and their unions, targeting particular animosity towards the state's nearly two hundred thousand New Jersey Education Association (NJEA) members. Christie's relentless efforts to dismantle benefits for K–12 employees, slash education funding, and expand charter schools in a largely pro-union blue state had propelled his rapid rise within the Republican Party.

A crucial early salvo in the war between Governor Christie and the NJEA came with the passage of Chapter 78 in 2011. The legislation tied the amount that public employees were required to pay toward their health insurance premiums to a percentage of their salaries and the overall premium amount, phased in steeply over a period of four years.[2] By design, Chapter 78 severely weakened the union's bargaining position on healthcare and imposed the exorbitant costs of coverage that were all too familiar to so many private sector workers onto public sector workers as well. For many contract cycles, NJEA members had prioritized fully employer-paid health insurance premiums over wages and other benefits

Rules to Win By. Jane F. McAlevey and Abby Lawlor, Oxford University Press. © Oxford University Press 2023.
DOI: 10.1093/oso/9780197690468.003.0004

in their contract negotiations. With the stroke of Christie's pen, they were a thing of the past.

Over the next several years, as collective bargaining agreements for local school districts expired, triggering the bill's phase-in, teachers and other school district employees began to see the salary increases they had negotiated wiped out by state-mandated healthcare contributions. Karen Burke, a school nurse who had worked in the Mercer County Special Services School District since 1999, went from paying no monthly premium for her family's health insurance to over $1,000 per month in the span of just a few years. Chapter 78 also required both public employees and the state to contribute more to the pension system. But while Burke and other NJEA members met their pension obligations, Christie quickly reneged on the state's funding commitment.[3] New Jersey's pension system dropped eight credit ratings to become the worst in the nation.[4]

New Jersey teachers refused to let political grandstanding destroy the top-ranked public education system and good jobs they had fought to build. By the time Christie termed out of office in 2018 with the lowest approval rating in state history,[5] NJEA members were headed back to the negotiations table to contend with the financial mess and legacy of bad faith he had left behind.

Bargaining to Build Power

As members across the state began to feel the full financial impact of Chapter 78, NJEA field representatives Jennifer Larsen and Alex DeVicaris knew that the local associations they worked with would need to build power to take on school boards emboldened by Christie's governorship. At the same time, association members, the source of that power, were less engaged than ever. "People were really overworked and isolated and didn't understand why they were being asked to come out. They didn't know what they were fighting for," said DeVicaris. Both former association presidents themselves, Larsen and DeVicaris had been trying to encourage the locals they worked with to do more rank-and-file organizing. After hearing about open negotiations during a session led by this book's coauthor

Jane McAlevey at their union's 2017 Collective Bargaining Summit, they realized that it could provide the catalyst for greater member involvement and enable locals to build the power they would need to overcome the financial and political setbacks of Chapter 78. "[Bargaining] is something that every association does that all members have an idea about. They understand that bargaining happens. They can wrap their heads around it and can see a pretty quick benefit of being more open and transparent in that process," DeVicaris said. Getting directly involved in negotiations would remind members what the fight was about and show them how to win.

Larsen and DeVicaris put together a detailed presentation on what they saw as the core elements of an open negotiations campaign: a member engagement team (a form of contract action team) made up of rank-and-file leaders with relationships covering the entire workplace, one-on-one "targeted conversations" between members leading up to and throughout negotiations, regular communication from the negotiations team about what was happening in negotiations, and negotiation sessions that were open to the entire membership. With sign-off from "two of the most conservative labor attorneys we knew," Larsen and DeVicaris began pitching local presidents on the new approach, focusing on associations with a history of distrust between members and leadership or a particularly contentious relationship with their school board. As staff support coming in from the statewide union, Larsen and DeVicaris weren't dogmatic about how local associations approached the change. The elected leadership of the local associations could "take it to whatever extreme they're ready to go," as long as they were transparent and communicative and prioritized one-on-one organizing. Soon Burke's local, the Mercer County Special Services Educational and Therapeutic Association (MCSSETA), the Watchung Hills Regional Education Association (WHREA), and two other local associations were signed on to try open negotiations for the first time. Another local, the Readington Township Educational Association (RTEA), decided to move forward with transparent negotiations, with leadership agreeing to radically increase communication around negotiations though keeping the sessions themselves closed.

"Let's Do It."

Leah Pray was settling into her first term as president of MCSSETA when DeVicaris broached the idea of opening up the association's negotiations to members. A self-described pessimist, Pray was willing to try something new but worried about her coworkers actually showing up. Turnout from the association's last contract ratification vote—a mere twenty-six people out of a membership of nearly four hundred—still loomed large in her memory. "When you talk to presidents from other districts, the ratification meeting is the largest meeting they have in their district. It's the one meeting you can get people to come to." In Pray's district, members weren't even showing up then.

MCSSETA is made up of certified staff (teachers, therapists, nurses, and child study team members), classroom assistants, and crisis intervention staff. The district is wholly dedicated to children and young adults with disabilities and serves over five hundred students with significant educational access needs, not only from Mercer County but from districts across the state and even nearby Pennsylvania. The school district's three-building campus sits less than ten miles from the governor's office in Trenton.

Pray had been around the association for a long time—her mother had served as president for sixteen years, and Pray had worked in the district for the last thirteen—and she recognized the need for change. "We were coming off a time where everything was very hush-hush. You were not supposed to talk about things, and there was a lot of distrust between my members and the executive board and the negotiations team." Something needed to happen to build trust and get more members involved. Pray also felt strongly that being the elected president of the association didn't make her its sole decision-maker. "I don't want that kind of responsibility," she said, tongue-in-cheek. She liked the idea of having more people be a part of negotiations and brought the idea of opening it up to her nine-member negotiations team.

Keith Whitacre, Pray's cochair for the negotiations and a high school classroom teacher (now happily retired), had been through so many MCSSETA contract campaigns that he'd started to lose track (six or seven?) and served in the cochair role for the last four. Whitacre also recognized the distrust among members but had always thought that closed negotiations was the association's only option. "For as long as I was involved in the negotiations, that was the way that it was," he said. When DeVicaris explained open negotiations, Whitacre was taken aback: "We were always told it had to be private!" But Whitacre, the optimist to Pray's pessimist, thought it was worth a shot. "This was an opportunity to put it all out there and give everyone an opportunity to truly be a part of the process. . . . What if it works?" Whitacre, Pray, and the other members of the team said, "Let's do it."

At WHREA, the negotiations team and the executive committee were similarly ready to make a change. A 250-member local made up of teachers, secretaries, bus drivers, and security and maintenance personnel serving the Watchung Hills Regional High School, the association was also under relatively new leadership. Listening to Larsen present the idea of open negotiations, President Ken Karnas recalled, "I think we all secretly, without wanting to jump the gun, were like, 'We want to do this, we want to do this right now.' " Like Pray, Karnas was headed into his first negotiations as president. He and other district employees had long been frustrated by the lack of transparency and communication from their school's administration, and Karnas didn't want his coworkers to feel the same way about the association. "It was important to us to say [to other members] that we know that you're not getting transparency elsewhere and we're going to be transparent with you."

In Readington, association president Kevin Meyer also saw greater transparency as a way of distinguishing the association from the school board. A middle school special education teacher, Meyer felt strongly about encouraging both teachers and students to advocate for themselves. "Prior to this process, none of what was happening on either side—in our case the board of education and the association—none of what their goals were for what they wanted was discussed with our constituents, our teachers, our members. . . . Their bargaining team shared only with their board, and they only reported out to the public once there was something final. So all these stakeholders want a say in these things and to be represented, but they have no idea what's going on." The 300-member local included teachers, secretaries, paraprofessionals, clerical aides, guidance counselors, nurses, media specialists, child study team members, and maintenance and custodial staff serving K–8 students.

Meyer wanted to make a change, but he and the rest of the association's executive council were also worried that without a history of one-on-one organizing, the association lacked the foundation it needed to effectively transition straight to open negotiations. Instead, he committed to take the first step of having transparent negotiations.

Meetings with the MET

Though NJEA locals had utilized a bargaining survey in the past, Larsen and DeVicaris were adamant that as part of the shift to open negotiations, member input should be solicited through what they called "targeted conversations"—structured in-person one-on-ones—rather than a written questionnaire. "We've had people come back and say, who've been members for twenty years and been through four or five contract cycles and done the paper survey every time, and yet when we go and do [targeted conversations], they come back and say, 'No one ever asked me my opinion before,' " explained Larsen. "They never equated completing a survey about bargaining to being asked their opinion on what was important at the bargaining table." Gathering survey responses, keeping members engaged throughout the negotiations process, and organizing workplace actions would be the work of the rank-and-file leaders who made up the member engagement team (MET).

When Marisa Walsh signed on to be a part of the negotiations team for WHREA's 2018 negotiations and heard the roadmap for member engagement, she thought she knew what she was getting herself into. A high school biology teacher, she had worked for Clean Water Action after graduate school and gone door-to-door doing one-on-one organizing around environmental issues. After seeing prior negotiations play out, she was "familiar with how it feels" to go through a closed process and liked the idea of a "grassroots" approach with greater transparency and member involvement. As part of the MET (in Watchung Hills, a combination of the negotiations team and the executive council), Walsh took responsibility for a dozen of her coworkers—some of whom she knew, others she didn't—and got to work building relationships with her group. By taking assignments to organize coworkers they didn't already know, Walsh and the rest of the MET hoped to grow the universe of people who were receiving regular updates about the contract campaign to include the entire bargaining unit.

Still several months out from the start of negotiations, Walsh and her fellow MET leaders didn't go straight into talking about contract priorities. Initially, they would stop by coworkers' classrooms or work areas with a "fun fact"—something about the union or the existing contract. It was cheesy, but soon coworkers were asking Walsh when she'd have another fact for them. She started getting to know the coworkers she'd been assigned outside of her own hallway—coworkers who weren't classroom teachers. Eventually, she transitioned into more structured conversations to ask directly about what they wanted to get out of negotiations.

Larsen and DeVicaris framed the targeted conversations around three open-ended questions: What do you like about the contract and working here? What would you change about working here, or what would you like to see added to the contract? Who do you like or respect in the building—that is, who do you go to? The team used the third question to continue recruiting other leaders to the MET from outside the existing building representatives and elected officers of the association. "It's a different kind of job than being on the bargaining team or being the building rep where people are in trouble," said Larsen. "It attracts a different kind of person."

School nurse Burke was one such leader in the Mercer County Special Services School District. Burke had been involved socially in the association but had always been reticent to get in the middle of workplace grievances, a central part of the role of a building representative (NJEA's version of a shop steward). After years of being on the periphery, Pray convinced her to chair the association's MET for the 2018 contract negotiations. The member engagement role played to her strengths. With a self-described style that was assertive and funny, Burke wasn't afraid to be direct with her coworkers. Over the years, she had seen her share of staff representatives from the statewide association and felt she could do a better job in getting her coworkers to care about what was happening in negotiations. When she couldn't find someone in person, Burke would use the school's PA system to track them down.

For all of the local associations Larsen and DeVicaris worked with, targeted conversations between leaders on the MET and their group of assigned coworkers in the lead-up to negotiations was the foundation for everything that followed. "When we're doing [conversations] around bargaining, we almost get 100 percent input," said Larsen. "We created a paper to hand to members that asks them what they're comfortable doing and how they'd like to be involved. So we're trying to build a database of how we can get each member involved in some way in the association." The conversations were a means of gathering input but also served the crucial functions of developing relationships between members, laying a groundwork of trust and communication not only for open negotiations but for the ramped-up workplace actions that would accompany it. The conversations also identified new organic leaders to bring into the organizing efforts.

Other People's Worlds

After the targeted conversations with their coworkers, MET members from across departments and buildings gathered to debrief their experiences and tally the issues that came up most often. Then the association held a "World Café," which brought together the MET and the broader membership to talk through contract priorities. Pray had found in the past, that with a paper survey, "There was lots of conflict and misunderstanding about why issues got prioritized." The World Café gave association members the opportunity to come together and set the priorities themselves.

"We sat down and talked about the issues," said RTEA president Meyer. "We started by BSing a little bit and seeing the really outrageous things that we heard from our members and the really consistent things that we heard and the things that none of us had thought about ourselves. And we did it in a social way and then we started looking at it categorically. What things were related to time? What things were related to professional development? Health benefits? Compensation? And then from there we really dwindled it down to a prioritized list which allowed us to make the most effective group of proposals that we wanted to go to the board of education with."

During World Café meetings, members spent time in small groups, each one assigned to a contract issue. The small groups rotated through three prompts: What information or evidence would you share with someone at the local who doesn't understand why this issue is important that explains why it should be a proposal? What evidence or information can you give to the board of education to explain why they should adopt this proposal? Assuming we go to impasse, what evidence or information would you give us to help explain to the public—parents and taxpayers—why we're holding out over this item? At MCSSETA, as small groups discussed bargaining topics, Whitacre and the other members of the negotiations team monitored the conversations "to get information to help us explain to the board about why this was so important."

Pray had started her career as a classroom assistant before becoming a teacher and recognized the value of the World Café in allowing members to understand each other's experiences. "You're meeting with the whole building and people are talking with each other, not at each other . . . and you're explaining why [certain issues] are important," said Pray. "Everyone gets to hear what is happening in other people's worlds." MCSSETA brought certified staff, classroom assistants, and crisis employees together in one association but under three separate salary guides. For classroom assistants, the salary guide topped out at $40,000 per year while the certified staff guide started at $62,000, creating an economic gulf between members. For WHREA, the bargaining unit included secretarial, security, and custodial staff, and bus drivers. "Things happening with the secretaries, the aides, the security people, the nurses, I wasn't really as aware of their day-to-day issues, so that was surprising, knowing what they were dealing with," said biology teacher Walsh.

Members left the World Café with a better understanding of their coworkers' issues. The negotiations team left with a clear sense of members' priorities for the next contract and with butcher paper full of notes on how to best explain proposals. The meeting placed rank-and-file members in the shoes of their coworkers on the negotiations team, preparing them for what actual negotiation sessions were going to look like. "It starts to show the other members that it's really difficult to come up with an explanation that's not just 'it should be that,' " said Larsen. "They start to recognize it's really not easy to be at the table negotiating against their bosses," said DeVicaris. "They've never thought of it that way. The team gets a lot more respect after that."

An Overcapacity Bargaining Council

Closed negotiations had long been the practice in NJEA locals. In order to open up negotiation sessions, field representatives Larsen and DeVicaris decided they didn't need to pick a head-on fight with the school districts over changing ground rules that local associations had agreed to in the past. The rules allowed the association to pick its own bargaining council. There was nothing preventing that bargaining council from being the entire membership.

At MCSSETA, the negotiations team had worked to set clear expectations for members about how to behave while they were in the negotiations room with management. "Everyone had to be quiet, no grunts, no 'Hey, what do you mean?' We had to keep it under control," said negotiations cochair Whitacre. "And everyone was fine with that, they were just excited to be there and to be a part of the whole process, especially because they felt like they had been a part of putting together the contract proposal, that they were really a part of that, so they felt good about being there." Negotiations were scheduled for four o'clock in the afternoon, after the close of the school day, and Pray made sure there would be food. "Educators are always hungry," she explained. After all of the groundwork laid by the MET, eighty-six members filled the school library for the first session, more than three times as many as had participated in the association's last ratification vote. "It surprised the crap out of me," said Pray, though sharing the board's opening proposal in advance—including a wage proposal "TBD"—no doubt helped to drive turnout. "The board's opening proposal showed them that the board has absolutely no respect for what we do as teachers. [Members] were really, really mad, and that helped to get a lot of people involved."

Pray and Whitacre were at the negotiations table along with the rest of the negotiations team and DeVicaris, with rows of members behind them. "The power dynamic felt absolutely different," said Pray. "We were all sitting there and I was astonished at how many people had shown up and I had a big old smile on my face. I was watching as the business administrator walked in, saw all the people, and quickly turned around to walk back out the door. I was like, 'Ooh, she's nervous.' That just kinda glided me through, because I knew they were not happy at all that we were doing this."

As negotiations progressed, the team continued to make adjustments to accommodate the expanded bargaining council. After the first night in the library, later sessions had to be moved to the school gym as attendance grew to as many as 150 members. "One of the things we realized as more people came in, it got harder and harder to hear the discussions," said DeVicaris. "So we started to bring microphones in. And the other side would hate that and they wouldn't speak into the microphone. So we would start repeating what they were saying so that people could hear. And then the members started asking like, 'You're talking about proposal B.4, what is that? I've never heard of that.' So we started developing handouts for them that had all of the proposals on it in plain language and we update that after every meeting and have it for the next meeting and it has all the proposals—which ones have been withdrawn, what the modifications were, when we agreed to things, so that everyone who comes to a session gets the most up-to-date information right there that they can follow along as they're sitting there." The negotiations team also passed out three-by-five-inch index cards to the members in the room so that they could give input to the team at the table in real time. "We would have a runner that would collect them and bring them up to the table. The board a lot of times isn't honest with the rationale behind something they were saying and at any given point a hundred flash cards might come flying up to the table," said Larsen. "We're just picking up the cards and incorporating them into what we're saying and it's very intimidating [to the board] because essentially you know right away you're being called on the card because what you said is just not accurate," said DeVicaris.

During caucuses, "people are running back and forth with microphones so we can hear," said DeVicaris. "When we caucused, the lead team would talk a little bit about what they counterproposed, and then we would turn around and talk to the membership. . . . It was very helpful," said Whitacre. "It was helpful for the membership to give information, it was helpful for us to feel confident about what we were thinking of doing, if they were supporting it. We knew where they stood on a certain issue. Because things may change as you go along, you may not get exactly what you initially asked for but you're adjusting. Having them there gives you information and feedback, and you can ask questions. It made the lead team feel a little more confident about the decisions you were making . . . and it was immediate."

In Watchung Hills, Larsen used a pre–bargaining ground rules session with management to let them know that they would need a bigger room for negotiations. "They didn't like it at all. They couldn't fathom why you would have this many people," said local president Karnas. The board refused to move the bargaining location, so when the first negotiation session came, the WHREA negotiations team filled the school conference room exactly to capacity—twenty-five members—while over fifty members waited outside the room. When the school board president and the district's negotiations team arrived, they refused to enter, claiming it would violate the fire code. "It was clear the board knew that's what was going to happen and they'd looked up the capacity of the room," said Karnas. The association asked just enough members to join the larger group outside so that the district's negotiators would at least enter the room, but the board still wasn't ready to begin negotiating. They aired every possible objection to open negotiations: "that this is going to take forever, that you're not going to be able to caucus effectively, that it's going to be disruptive." They refused to hand over proposals. The district's lead negotiator called the NJEA office and complained about Larsen's representation. But Karnas and the rest of the negotiations team stuck with their plan. With clear expectations for the association's side that had been communicated through the MET, they were confident that their expanded bargaining council would be disciplined and be able to get things done. Eventually, they got the district to hand over its proposals. And they got a bigger room.

"The fact that we had communicated so much with the member engagement team made sure that people were not out of line," said Karnas. "We had plans in place that if someone did step out of line and say something in a meeting, we would escort our own person out." Walsh noted, "Everybody was really eager to be at those meetings. People really didn't know what negotiations looked like and wanted to see what they looked like and show the board we were serious about what we were asking for. . . . Everybody that showed up at the meetings was really happy to be there and definitely they saw the adversarial position of the board and the pettiness of some of the board members. To see that, they understood what we were working with there."

As negotiations progressed in both Mercer County and Watchung Hills, the expanded bargaining councils were faced with crucial strategic decisions. Did MCSSETA members need Chapter 78 relief in the form of reduced healthcare premiums? Or did they want to focus on salary increases that were substantial enough to outpace the increased monthly costs? In Watchung Hills, the board of education had proposed that negotiations focus exclusively on wages and benefits and to leave noneconomic language unchanged from the prior agreement. Then they passed an above-average wage proposal across the table. Were members on board with an economics-only approach? And were they ready to take the board's initial offer?

Pray caucused with the over one hundred MCSSETA members that were in the gym and decided to move off of the association's Chapter 78 proposal. It was a risky move. "In order to do to that, we needed to get a certain percentage [salary increase]. So I really needed people to stick around, because that was the only way we were going to get the salary increase we needed to not make less money," said Pray. "I think people realized that if we were going to do this then they all needed to help us do it. And they did, they were phenomenal." Because members had been in the room since the beginning, they understood they would need to keep the pressure up on the school board in order to win the raises they needed.

At WHREA, Karnas and the negotiations team put the school board's proposal to move forward solely on economics to a vote of the eighty-five members in the room. The members decided that noneconomic issues could wait for the next contract cycle but also that the district's "let's get this over with" wage proposal wasn't enough. They'd continue to fight for more money.

New Faces

As negotiations progressed, the MET continued to meet face to face with their assigned groups to share information from the sessions.

"When there's information coming out from the bargaining team, it goes straight to the [MET] so it can get to the members and they know," said DeVicaris. "Whether it's open bargaining or transparent bargaining, we don't have rumors going on in any of the locals where we bargain because everyone knows the information. And they know if they have a question or concern or they heard something they're not sure about, they know who they can go to to ask that question and they know they will get an answer back quickly."

With many more members in the room, the MET had less work to communicate out the message of what had happened in negotiations. "People can't say they don't trust you because you are literally sitting in the room with them while they are going through this process. And it definitely makes disseminating the information easier. There's no, 'We have to wait until the email server is up and running or the printer has ink.' You don't have to do that because they're right there," said Pray. Instead, the challenge was how to channel the increased interest and involvement of hundreds of members into pressure on the board of education. "Once all those people got involved, we realized we needed to do more." They'd succeeded in getting the board president to show up to negotiations—something that hadn't happened in many contract cycles—but even having her in the room didn't seem to be enough to get things moving.

MCSSETA decided to take their fight to the decision-makers behind their local school board. Because they worked for a special services school district, the board of education and the superintendent were appointed by the county executive rather than directly elected, as was the case for other school districts in the state. Brian Hughes, the county executive and son of a former governor, had been in office since 2004 and had tremendous power over the board. "I have never spoken to him, past presidents have never spoken to him . . . so we needed to voice our frustration to someone. And the people who are supposed to oversee the things he is doing are the county freeholders," said Pray. MCSSETA members decided to go to freeholder meetings every month to update the freeholders and the (absentee) county executive on what was going on in their district. "The first few times, we didn't have that many people, but as we progressed into the second year of negotiations, and we were still not getting anywhere and we were still not getting a response from the board, that's when we really started packing the house," said Pray. Members gave testimony about the administrative disarray in the district and the personal impact of taking home less pay every year. They also met other community members who had no idea that the special services school district existed in Mercer County. Burke and others explained the work they did serving high-needs students and families and their struggle to win a fair contract. Soon, onlookers began signing up to give public testimony in support.

After months of freeholders' meetings and no sign of Brian Hughes, Pray was ready to publicly call him out. It was a packed night, with both NJEA members and members from the correctional workers' union, there on a separate issue, filling every seat and then some. Sitting in overflow, waiting for her turn for public comment, Pray saw an unfamiliar face. "I'm staring at the TV, my VP is sitting next to me, and I'm like, 'Is that him?' And she's like, 'I think it is!' " Hughes had finally made an appearance. "So within seconds I had to change how I worded my speech. Instead of asking the freeholders where [Hughes] had been throughout the years, I got to ask him." Pray's question was not well received. "He did not respond. He did not even look at me. When I said I was the president of the union, he turned his chair and faced the wall. . . . But I asked him where he was. And you could hear the cheers coming from downstairs [in the overflow room] all the way upstairs. Because I think everybody would have liked to know the answer to that question."

Hughes may have been unhappy with being called out, but it was also election time, and New Jersey Democrats couldn't afford to treat the state's teachers the same way Christie had. MCSSETA members had stuck through negotiations and continued demanding real salary increases for nearly two years. Per the state's public sector collective bargaining rules, they had entered into state-mandated fact-finding and were headed toward formal mediation. NJEA president Marie Blistan made a call to Christie's replacement, Democratic governor Phil Murphy, and soon Blistan and Hughes had a meeting set. A week later, MCSSETA members had the deal they needed.

At RTEA, where negotiation sessions were limited to the five-member negotiations team, greater transparency and communication led to increased militancy among the association's membership. Members gathered for meetings after every negotiation session, and the 20-member MET also communicated bargaining updates one on one. The association also reported out to the community, holding joint member-parent meetings an hour before district school board meetings, and the MET encouraged teachers and parents both to stick around and testify before the board itself. For one meeting with 150 members present, school district employees lined the sidewalk and hallway into the board offices wearing matching T-shirts. As school board members arrived, RTEA members clapped to show their collective power. Later in the school year, the association escalated to a work-to-rule action. "We were congregating outside of our entrances, entering school at the same time, leaving school at our contractual hours," said Meyer. Teachers updated their email signatures with their hours of work and set auto-replies to respond to emails received outside of the school day.

For Meyer and the MET, organizing the work-to-rule action was "100 percent easier" because of transparent negotiations. "If we had passed out that directive or instruction association-wide midway through the process with people like, 'Oh yeah, we know we're negotiating,' but having it in the back of [their] minds, had we sprung that on people we wouldn't have gotten nearly the engagement [we did]." Knowing what was going on in negotiations gave members a sense of why they needed to take action.

We Gave Up Nothing

Early on into negotiations, the president of the Mercer County Special Services School Board had requested to meet one on one with MCSSETA president Pray. Pray took the request to her members, who vetoed any closed sessions. But after Blistan's meeting with Hughes, they gave her the go-ahead. Pray and Whitacre sat down with the board president and the board's attorney while the bargaining council, still over one hundred members strong, gathered in the gym. "We said, 'Our members will be here, we'll come in and talk with you but if there's anything we have to discuss with our membership, we'll go back with them and discuss it,'" said Whitacre. Going into the meeting, the board's offer on salary increases had long been stuck at 1.25 percent. Exemplifying the "90/10" rule—that 90 percent of movement in negotiations happens in the last 10 percent of negotiation sessions—the board suddenly came back with an offer of 3 percent. Then, with the board's business administrator on the phone to the superintendent and Whitacre and Pray coming back and forth from the gym, the board came back with a proposal that would get MCSSETA members to a 3.9 percent salary increase by year three of the contract.

"In the past they could hold out as long as they wanted and we would do job actions and go to meetings and stuff but slowly we would lose momentum and it's almost like they knew they could wear you down a bit and go for something that was less than you wanted," said Whitacre. "This time they knew we were still there and the whole membership was there and we were unified and we continued to say, 'This is what we need.' It didn't look like we were losing our momentum." DeVicaris echoed the impact of open negotiations on helping associations stay strong even years into negotiations. "The biggest thing I've found [with open negotiations] is that it really gives the bargaining team the courage and the power to hold out for a better deal. It's not even just that it intimidates the other side or forces the other side to take concessions. It strengthens our own side, our own membership."

Pray and Whitacre walked back to the gym and told their coworkers the latest offer of 3.9 percent. Some couldn't believe it. They'd gotten the district to offer up the kind of raises they needed. "We walked into the gym, told them the amazing deal, and they were all like, 'Yeah!' So then we walked back in and shook hands and walked away," said Pray. The power dynamic with the district had finally shifted. "They're always trying to take things away. We pay a ton for Chapter 78 relief . . . and they want us to take lesser health benefits and get rid of things and get rid of longevity, and they don't want to give you a salary increase." But this time around, "We gave up nothing."

The agreement was quickly ratified. Whitacre wasn't sure if many people would show up for the ratification vote because unlike in past years they already knew exactly what was in the agreement. But over one hundred members turned out. "I felt like they really wanted to see it through, the final product that they had worked for this whole time by

going to these meetings and doing job actions. . . . It was the culmina-
tion of everything and they wanted to see it finished."

For Pray, the ratification came just in time. After nearly two years of
late nights spent in the school gym, she could focus on her upcoming
wedding, just three weeks away.

Expectations Set

Larsen and DeVicaris had approached open negotiations with the theory
that they could revamp how associations functioned to become more
open and member-driven, and that these benefits would outlast the contract campaign. So far, the theory seems to be bearing out.

"Once we started communicating everything with everyone, now
that's the norm so people expect that now," said Pray. "People are automatically more involved, it's just something that happens when you do
this kind of process." But higher expectations for communication and
transparency were also coupled with greater understanding and respect
for members who had taken on union leadership. "There were quite a
few times when people would come up to me and say, 'I can't believe this
is what you guys do. I had no idea this is what you do.' "

At RTEA, the change has also altered how the school board approaches
negotiations. In subsequent negotiations, Meyer took the lead as negotiator rather than NJEA staff. And the board began negotiating without
an attorney present. WHREA member Walsh has seen a similar shift in
the relationships between teachers and the school district. "It's creating
transparency not just in our association but in the school district as a
whole. . . . It's face to face, person to person, there's no separation of
screen or title, or someone that we're paying to be our representation like
a lawyer in a court case," said Walsh. "It's down-and-dirty conversation."

Seeing coworkers take a leadership role in the MET and negotiations
encouraged other WHREA members to become more involved in their
union. Karnas described a teacher in the district who decided to run for
the executive board for the first time because he wanted to play a role in
organizing his coworkers and do the work he'd seen the MET undertake.
For other leaders, the relationships they built through the MET have
continued. "I'm still in contact with [my] member engagement team

list," said Walsh. "Some of the security guards that I wouldn't have otherwise talked to, we see each other and chitchat, 'How's your daughter doing?'—that kind of stuff. It's not the relationship I had before, so that's really nice," she said. "Open bargaining makes the membership who isn't really engaged day to day in the union more engaged and a part of it. It ties you together and knits you together as a community and you all feel invested in the success of the educational community and your contract. So it does a lot for the school too, that you're all together.

"More than anything, it reinvigorated the idea of what it feels like to be in a union," said Walsh.

4

A Flood of First Contracts (NewsGuild-CWA)

JON SCHLEUSS HAS A PROBLEM other union presidents would be happy to have: more first contract negotiations than he can handle. As newly elected president of the NewsGuild–Communications Workers of America (NewsGuild-CWA), Schleuss took office after a hotly contested recount in December 2019 and on a wave of new organizing in the journalism industry that included his own workplace, the *Los Angeles Times*. With the international union adding just shy of 1,500 new members in both 2018 and 2019, and another 1,350 in 2020, Schleuss's "number-one goal" since taking over leadership of the union has been to build capacity for negotiations at new and existing shops. Though Schleuss's ambition to transform the NewsGuild into an organizing union—one shared by a growing number of leaders within the union—is not limited to collective bargaining, the demands of negotiations have created particular urgency around building the capacity of guild members to win great contracts.

It's an uphill battle. The very public influx of new members from prominent media outlets has brought new energy to guild locals and the international union, but dwindling advertising revenue and the near-complete takeover of the industry by vulture capital have led to shrinking and shuttered newsrooms and stark financial realities for many represented shops. The remaining guild members are the ones who have hung on through rounds of layoffs and buyouts. Guild shops are spread thin in small and scattered newsrooms across the country.

Rules to Win By. Jane F. McAlevey and Abby Lawlor, Oxford University Press. © Oxford University Press 2023.
DOI: 10.1093/oso/9780197690468.003.0005

Despite the overall state of the industry, the NewsGuild's newest members have been winning at the bargaining table. Indeed, the union need look no further than some of its own first contract campaigns for examples of highly transparent member-led negotiations producing huge victories. At both the *L.A. Times* and digital media company Law360, bargaining committees of rank-and-file members have used structures built through new organizing to move newsrooms of in-person and remote workers to take increasingly militant workplace actions. Though neither local practiced "big" negotiations, high transparency and largely open negotiation sessions helped to maintain momentum from organizing drives through long campaigns to win life-changing collective bargaining agreements.

Horrible Bosses

In 2016, the *L.A. Times* ownership company revealed its dramatic rebranding: instead of Tribune Company, it would now be known as Tronc, short for Tribune Online Content. "It's about meeting in the middle, having tech startup culture meet a legacy corporate culture and then evolving and changing. And that's really the fun part," said the company's chief digital officer in an introductory video to employees that seemed custom-designed to be mocked on Twitter. The new name wasn't the only shakeup. Tronc brought in new leadership and proposed to dramatically boost revenues through automating the production of video content, the latest and greatest "pivot" for print newsrooms. The technological side of the proposal was vague, but its underlying ambition was clear: to produce more and more easily shareable online content while employing fewer and fewer journalists.

The Tronc rebrand was just the latest in a long slew of upheavals at the company. Since leaving family ownership in 2000, the *L.A. Times* had gone private through a leveraged buyout, declared bankruptcy, emerged under yet another set of owners, spun off as a publishing-only company, and went public once again. Caught between a legacy corporate culture with a storied history of anti-unionism and a tech startup culture that glorified doing more with less, the staff at the *L.A. Times* began to organize. "We had the dictionary definition of horrible bosses," said

Anthony Pesce, a former graphics and data journalist at the *Times*. "Just cartoon-character evil overlords." Galvanized by severe pay disparities, decades of layoffs that had brought the newsroom down to four hundred from a peak of twelve hundred, and deeply unpopular management, workers were ready to fight for greater stability and a voice in their work. Carolina Miranda, an arts writer (now arts columnist) who had been at the *L.A. Times* for three years, had previously taken buyouts at two prior media outlets. "It just became so clear when taking those buyouts how critical union representation is. I looked at my *L.A. Times* contract when I was hired by Tribune and it was at-will employment. There were no guarantees of anything." Miranda, Pesce, Schleuss, and others started secretly talking to their coworkers about organizing. After a majority had signed up in support of the union, they presented Tronc with a demand that the company recognize their union in the fall of 2017.

Tronc refused to agree to voluntary recognition and made it very clear through captive audience meetings and all-staff emails that management vehemently opposed the campaign. But they were too late to slow the organizing efforts already underway. Convinced by that point that they needed new ownership in order to achieve any of their goals in negotiations, the organizing committee focused on getting rid of Tronc. Putting their reportorial skills to work, they wrote and released a report detailing the exorbitant compensation paid to Tronc executives. In the context of the company's financial troubles and cuts to the newsroom, the report was a powerful indictment of the paper's prioritization of short-term profits over real investment in quality journalism. Soon after, the newsroom filed for an NLRB election. In the week before the vote, the paper's top editors wrote to the newsroom in an attempt to third-party the union, framing a vote in favor of union representation as a loss of worker agency: "The question to you is do you want to preserve your independence and the independence of the *L.A. Times* or do you want someone else negotiating on your behalf?"

In early January 2018, *L.A. Times* reporters, data journalists, copy editors, photographers, videographers, web and audio producers, page designers, librarians, and other workers voted 248 to 44 to join the NewsGuild. The unit included not only the main newsroom in downtown Los Angeles but community newspaper offices throughout the region and scattered remote workers. Through negotiations, it would later grow to include the paper's Washington, DC, bureau. A month after the election, and on the heels of revelations that Tronc had been setting up a "shadow newsroom" to replace unionized employees with new non-union hires employed by a separate business entity, the company announced it was selling the paper to a new owner. Management's anti-union email had presented a false choice. By organizing, the newsroom had been able to regain its independence from Tronc. And the newly minted L.A. Times Guild members would be heading to the bargaining table to negotiate for themselves.

If the Tronc era at the *L.A. Times* showed the strains of a 140-year-old print newspaper transitioning to a modern media company, Law360 represents a new model. A subscriber-only newswire founded in 2004 with legal news and analysis for practitioners, the company quickly grew and was acquired by LexisNexis, a subsidiary of RELX, which describes itself on its website as "a global provider of information-based analytics and decision tools for professional and business customers." On the one hand, the newsroom seemed stable and well-funded, buoyed by a much larger business enterprise. On the other, Law360 reporters, editors, and news assistants faced managerial practices unheard of in traditional newsrooms. For Jody Godoy, a general assignment reporter who came to Law360 after several years working in journalism (and who has since moved on to Thomson Reuters), "Just right from the jump the conditions there weren't that great." She had come to expect extreme penny-pinching from media companies. But Law360's corporate approach was next level, with strict productivity requirements and legally questionable overtime restrictions. General assignment reporters faced four-story-a-day quotas, while editors were expected to review fifteen to twenty stories a day. "They had the day divided up into basically two-hour increments, two hours for each story," said Juan Carlos Rodriguez, another general assignment reporter. "And it didn't matter if the story was just a short little press release or a seventy-five-page opinion from an appeals court. You had the same amount of time. You had to crank out five hundred words." While Tronc had envisioned a future in which video production could be automated, the journalists at Law360 were already being treated like robots. Overtime was not only highly discouraged but also financially penalized, with the company adopting a "flexible workweek" approach that meant employees were paid a *lower* rate the more they worked rather than earning time and a half. For Godoy, who had relied on overtime at past journalism jobs to achieve what felt like reasonable take-home pay, the situation at Law360 left her fuming. "The idea that you would do work and not file for overtime was just something that I couldn't stand for, because even though in the past I had been paid less than I thought I was worth, at least I was making overtime so it sort of made up for it."

The problems bubbling under the surface came to a head in 2015 when management bucked industry practice and moved to enforce a noncompete agreement against a former employee who had left to take a job at Thomson Reuters. The reporter, Stephanie Russell-Kraft, was promptly fired from her new job. "That made everybody really mad in the newsroom," said Rodriguez. "A lot of us have worked other places. A noncompete in journalism is just not a thing. Law360 required them. Usually they gave it to you when you started at the company and they told you, 'Oh yeah, don't worry about that, that's just for the tech side,' or whatever. Nobody really thought about it . . . until [Russell-Kraft] got fired." Rodriguez and his coworkers realized the issues they were experiencing in the Law360 newsroom could follow them even if they tried to move on to another news outlet. "It was just a mess," said Godoy. "Once we started talking, we realized we were all suffering because of the practices there."

The Law360 newsroom began to organize and started reaching out to unions. With the help of the NewsGuild, the New York attorney general launched an investigation into the company's noncompete policy. In June 2016, workers scored their first victory as Law360 agreed to discontinue the use of noncompetes. A month later, the organizing drive went public. Despite a concerted anti-union campaign, the newsroom voted overwhelmingly, 109 to 9 in an NLRB election, to join the NewsGuild that August.

Transparent Transitions

It was a new day at the *L.A. Times*. The paper had been sold to a local owner—a billionaire bioscientist named Patrick Soon-Shiong. And the newsroom was finally union for the first time in its long history. But as the now-official L.A. Times Guild geared up for negotiating its first contract with unfamiliar management, they faced an immediate dilemma. "It was simpler in a way to run our campaign against Tronc because it was this big national news chain that wasn't invested in our newsroom and didn't have our best interests at heart," said Matt Pearce, a political reporter and member of the original bargaining committee. As the campaign transitioned from a fight for recognition to a fight for a first contract, they couldn't just beat up on Tronc anymore. "We got this new owner who was signaling that he wanted to invest in the newsroom and had a long-term interest in seeing the paper survive and have people work there. That checked a lot of boxes for us for some of the demands for why we formed a union." The interim executive council, made up of members put forward by the organizing committee and elected by acclamation, were nervous about striking the right tone for their coworkers and their new management. "Tronc was a great bad guy that you could pin all sorts of stuff on because they were just so awful. And this new owner we didn't know as well," said Miranda, the arts writer. "So we couldn't just go attack him. But we also didn't want to roll over. There were certain things we were working towards with our contract, so how do you strike that balance?"

At Law360, the organizing committee faced a similar dilemma. The noncompete policy, an early motivator for unionizing, had been eliminated before the union had even been formally recognized. Nonetheless, support for continuing the union drive stayed strong, with many in the newsroom seeing a collective bargaining agreement as a way of addressing problems endemic to the journalism industry. "I've been in media for a while and I know the precarity of it," said Braden Campbell, a senior reporter covering labor and employment issues who later served on the unit council, the elected leadership group for the Law360 union. "I was at a newspaper before and survived a few rounds of layoffs and then I was at a website before Law360 where I got laid off. Thankfully, Law360 is a very stable and thriving place, but I have a good sense of the importance of having our own say in matters [and] the ability to not be purely at the whims of management." A contract would allow workers to have a say and ensure that the stability they felt would be lasting.

Indeed, at the *L.A. Times*, it didn't take long for the newsroom to be reminded they were still at the whims of their boss. As his first act as owner, Soon-Shiong called a town hall and announced that the company's offices would be moving from downtown Los Angeles to El Segundo, seventeen miles farther south and west on traffic-choked freeways. The *L.A. Times* no longer owned its historic downtown offices—the valuable real estate had been sold off during the bankruptcy—but the company had still leased the building. Soon-Shiong wanted out of the exorbitant rent and for the newsroom to move into a building he already owned. Guild members were caught off guard and they weren't happy. Members tried to negotiate over the change—first over location, then over the open-plan layout of the office—and got nowhere. "For a lot of people that was the moment where we realized, oh, he's going to be really helpful for us, he's going to do a lot of the financial stuff we want him to, but also he's still a billionaire and is going to do billionaire stuff and make decisions that people don't think are desirable," said Pearce. "You still want to have a seat at the bargaining table for exactly this kind of thing."

With new ownership, new management, a new office, and negotiations still on the horizon, the organizing committee saw its role as an important source of openness and information about what exactly was happening. "We had been dealing with a company that was so used to doing things behind closed doors and then at the last minute announcing these faits accomplis to the staff. So for us it was important to operate as transparently as we could as a union," said Miranda. As the Tronc era came to a close, the L.A. Times Guild took an important step in signaling both what it was fighting for and how it would be fighting in negotiations. In anticipation of negotiations, the unit had filed an information request for detailed pay data for bargaining unit members. They had publicized their bosses' compensation as part of the organizing drive. Now they were going to publicize their own. Spearheaded by Pesce and other data reporters, the organizing committee performed an analysis of pay within the newsroom by gender, race, and ethnicity, releasing the results in a detailed report to the entire unit and the public at large. The findings were striking: not only were women, Black, and Latinx reporters underrepresented in the newsroom, they were paid significantly less than their white male counterparts. The median gender gap was $14,000 while the gap between white journalists and journalists of color was $19,000.

The guild's public transparency reaped new rewards when, soon after taking over as owner, Soon-Shiong went on a hiring spree. The bargaining unit grew by around one hundred new workers, many of whom had been following the union campaign and were eager to get involved. "We were concerned that we were going to have to reorganize all these new employees to get on board with the contract campaign but ironically what we found was a lot of our new employees were super excited about the union . . . because our campaign, our organizing campaign had been so public that the public had been educated about our drive. A lot of the other professionals in our field were kind of excited about what we were doing and wanted to be a part of a newsroom that was very active," said Pearce. "We basically organized them before they came in the door."

First Contract Fights: Steering the Process

Danielle Smith had been at Law360 as a news assistant for just over a month when the unionization campaign went public. The news assistant position was her first job out of college, and she wasn't sure what to expect. But when she saw her coworkers organizing, it was clear to her that she should get on board. "It was very much a well-organized movement that I wanted to be a part of," she said. Seeing the company's anti-union campaign only made her more invested in the fight. Just five months later, following their overwhelming vote to join the NewsGuild, she accepted a nomination from her coworkers to join the Law360 union's unit council, a group of 31 leaders from throughout the newsroom of about 140. As the contract campaign progressed, Smith also joined the diversity committee, the environmental committee, and the socials committee, with the union's organizational structure growing to engage more members in more ways. Other coworkers from the unit council, including Juan Carlos Rodriguez, formed a bargaining committee, which also included Godoy. "We had a court reporter, a couple of senior reporters, a couple of general assignment reporters, a copy editor, and a news assistant," said Rodriguez. "And we had four women and four men. . . . Diversity and inclusion was always a huge issue to us from during organizing, and that's reflected in the makeup of our unit council and our bargaining committee." The newsroom also formed a mobilization committee, a form of contract action team, to develop workplace actions as part of the contract campaign.

At the *L.A. Times*, the outgoing organizing committee put together a slate of candidates to form what they called an interim executive committee, like Law360's unit council, to help lead the unit through its upcoming negotiations. "From the beginning I would say it felt like an organizing drive where our newsroom was setting the terms for the union itself, not just the employer," said Pearce. "So when we were organizing the contract campaign, we went through it with a very similar attitude, I think, which is that we always from the beginning assumed that our members were going to be steering the process and were going to be the ones in charge." The interim executive committee was affirmed by acclamation and included Pesce and Miranda as cochairs, along with Pearce, coworker Kristina Bui, and others. The executive council in turn assembled a nine-member bargaining committee that would be in charge of negotiations. "It was really important to us that we have a really diverse bargaining committee," said Pearce. "We wanted to have a very wide array of jobs represented at the bargaining table. We also wanted to have a diverse group by age, race, and gender."

By having the executive council select the bargaining committee, Pearce and others hoped to avoid having a committee "loaded with reporters," far and away the biggest group in the newsroom. In particular, they were anxious to include a photographer as that department had been the "biggest worst"—the most challenging area of the newsroom to organize during the union's initial campaign. Fortunately, Jay Clendenin had emerged as a leader and agreed to be part of the team for negotiations. "It was very important that Jay be on the bargaining committee to send a message to the photo department that their interests were going to be literally represented at the bargaining table," said Pearce. "One of the concerns that we were dealing with was that the reporters are just going to gang up on the photographers and take things away. . . . We felt like if we didn't have a photographer on there we would lose a lot of credibility." In addition to the bargaining committee, other members of the original organizing committee formed a campaign committee, their version of a contract action team, to plan workplace actions.

The first task for the newly formed bargaining committee was to conduct a unit-wide bargaining survey. The committee opted to go deep, with a seven-page online survey containing detailed questions about contract priorities as well as detailed demographic information, including age, race, ethnicity, tenure at the *L.A. Times*, length of journalism career, and job title. The survey also included space at the end for members to flag other issues. Delegates from throughout the newsroom were charged with distributing the survey and having departmental follow-up meetings to go over the responses and identify any issues that weren't captured in the survey results. "We did it pretty methodically," said Bui, a copy editor who served on both the interim executive council and the bargaining committee. "We set up a Google folder where everyone could drop their notes from those department meetings and we set up a spreadsheet where we could track, 'Have you gone to this person and asked them to do the survey? Have they confirmed that they did their survey?' " The multistep process took a few weeks, but all of the follow-up paid off. By the end, a supermajority of the bargaining unit—289 out of 380 people—had completed the seven-page survey. The bargaining committee compiled the results into a report and shared them back with the rest of the membership. "A lot of people's relationship with data collection is you ship it off to some crazy corporation and you never see it again," said Pearce. "Our attitude was if you're going to give us data, we're going to collect it and we're going to give it back to you so that you can see where you stand and you can see what other people's priorities are. Because we had a lot of people with a lot of different jobs and a lot of different life situations, and it was important to us that people understood that their own situation may be dramatically different than others."

At Law360, the bargaining committee and mobilization committee worked together to encourage their coworkers to fill out a similarly extensive bargaining survey. "Just like in organizing, we reached out to every single person in the unit at least once for a one-on-one conversation," said Rodriguez. "Everyone had an ask from someone on the bargaining committee or the mobilization committee to fill out the survey." After the survey was complete, the bargaining committee digested and shared the results in two meetings made accessible to the company's remote workers. Rodriguez as unit chair and the guild's representative, Susan DeCarava, held two Zoom sessions to walk the unit through the results and an outline of contract proposals. Some broad priorities had clearly emerged, including raises, fixing the overtime system, and establishing just-cause protections, which would prevent the company from firing workers without any justification. But some job-specific issues came to the fore with particular intensity as well, including the need to reimagine the role that news assistants played in the newsroom. In an industry that relied heavily on unpaid internships to credential early-career journalists, thus limiting career opportunities to those who could afford to work for free, the news assistant role was an all-too-rare paid entry-level opportunity to get a foot in the door by doing background research for stories. But the way the position was currently structured, it was difficult for news assistants to then move up into other roles. "They were forced into these just mind-numbing jobs of scrolling through court dockets and other news websites looking for stories to pitch for other people to do. They got paid $40,000 per year in New York City, and they were never given an opportunity to write their own stories," said Rodriguez. "There were maybe fifteen of them. . . . But it was important to the bargaining committee to make sure that they were placed at the same level in terms of their priorities as the senior reporters or the senior editors."

Constant Communication

As the L.A. Times Guild got into negotiations, the interim executive committee was determined to keep the level of communication high. Miranda and Pesce had originally planned to divide their co-chair responsibilities so that Miranda would handle day-to-day unit issues while Pesce led negotiations. But Miranda quickly saw that her strengths as a communicator were needed to keep members engaged with negotiations. It was a decided challenge: "How do we take some of these very complicated, very arcane issues we're discussing in the bargaining committee and translate them into something understandable to someone who's not following them blow by blow? And not only translate them, but make them care?" Miranda began attending every negotiation session so that she could better help communicate what was happening.

After each session, the bargaining committee would stay in the room to draft a bargaining bulletin. "We would all be caucusing after the meeting, and someone would start a Google Doc and just start writing," said Alex Wigglesworth, another committee member who began at the *Times* as a digital editor before becoming a reporter. The bulletins were detailed, including proposal language, excerpts of table talk, and context from other guild agreements. "I think we constantly went back and forth with 'Are we bombarding them with too much information. Are we boring them to tears with the minutiae of this article? Are we being transparent?'" said Miranda. "It took us a little bit to figure out that when we sent our updates, we would send a few brief bullet points up top. That way if all the person read was those bullet points, they'd at least have a sense of where we were. Then we would do a more detailed update below. There were people that never read past the bullet points, then there would be people who read every word and send us questions about what we were doing about x and y. But even if people didn't access the information, they knew that it was there and I think that was important." Because not everyone in the bargaining unit worked out of the same El Segundo office, the emails were an important backstop for people who didn't have stewards checking in on them in person. Drafting immediately after negotiations made for some late nights, but it was worth it. "Even when we were there until like two o'clock in the morning, we were still trying to do a memo because we felt it was really important to bring people along with us and let them know what was going on," said Wigglesworth.

The bargaining bulletins weren't the only emails members were getting straight from the negotiations room. Though members could generally attend negotiations on request and there was broader turnout for some sessions, members the bargaining committee were often the only ones in negotiations. When the bargaining committee needed to consult with the broader membership, they would send a "quick check" out over email to the newsroom. "Quick checks were typically an email poll. Sometimes we would send out an email poll and then the stewards would go around and nudge people to say go check your email," said Bui. "We generally had a good sense of where people were, but sometimes issues would move quickly enough that we thought we had to do another check-in."

At Law360, the bargaining committee fell into a similar pattern of drafting a shop paper, called *The Amicus*, after every session. "We went into great detail about what we had done, what we had accomplished, what we still had to do, the positions that we were being met with from the company," said Godoy. "We spent a lot of time on that after each bargaining session. . . . It was a bit of a running joke because we had gone through such a hard day of bargaining and then we had to sit down and write a shop paper." The work of reporting was never ending, but for Godoy it was also a personal point of pride. "It was really important for us and for me in particular to strike the right balance between motivational language and making sure people understood the stakes and making sure that things were fact-based and that [members] were getting the information they needed." The bargaining committee encouraged members to contact them with any questions and feedback and would bring concerns to the next negotiation session. Later on in negotiations, the committee also began recording Facebook Live updates during caucuses or after negotiations to post to the newsroom's private Facebook group, another way of making sure that the unit's remote workers were still being engaged.

Maintaining Momentum

The Law360 union had already done away with noncompetes before ever sitting down with management. And for a while, negotiations seemed off to a smooth start, with members scoring an early victory when the company agreed to eliminate the quota system. "We felt like we were making progress, and then all of a sudden we realized we were being slow rolled by management," said Rodriguez. "We were starting to quibble over words in proposals or having philosophical arguments about whether it was appropriate to include a particular provision in the first contract, things like that." The process really ground to a halt when it came time to discuss jurisdiction—the scope of work that would be covered by the union contract. Strong contract language defining the union's jurisdiction was important to ensure that supervisors or subcontractors didn't start to carve away at what was "union work," reducing the size of the union over time or preventing the union from growing alongside the company. After months of back-and-forth to get the company to move off its initial position—no jurisdictional language whatsoever—the mobilization committee stepped into action.

What started with union T-shirts, signs, and buttons soon escalated to using bargaining updates as a workplace action. For fifteen minutes, everyone in the newsroom would come to the front of the office or the kitchen to hear an update from the bargaining committee. Eventually the update moved to the sidewalk in front of the office. Union members had embarked on their first walkout. The next time they left for half an hour. The gatherings served a dual purpose: "It's an action showing everyone standing together but at the same time everyone is being informed and then it's also a public forum where they can ask questions and have things answered," said Smith.

Looking for a way to include remote workers in the escalations, the mobilization committee decided on a work-to-rule action that would be kicked off by a sign-off email at the end of the scheduled workday. "It was a reply-all to the entire company, including managers," remembered Rodriguez. Even though the committee had worked up to the action through escalating structure tests and felt like their coworkers were ready, it was still a scary moment. "That was a risky move because we didn't know how many people were going to do it. That was one of those moments where you had to roll the die. . . . You needed people who were working remotely by themselves in Michigan or in a group in DC or LA to also do it. Everyone in New York had to do it." But the bargaining unit proved ready, and managers' inboxes were flooded with emails from over one hundred workers, a strong majority of the bargaining unit, signaling their refusal to take on voluntary overtime.

As workplace actions intensified, the bargaining committee quickly realized that these actions were the only real way to get the company to move at the bargaining table. "I had to be convinced to go along with some of the more militant stuff as we built up," said Stewart Bishop, a senior reporter who served on the bargaining committee. "Seeing how the company reacted to some of the smaller actions we took helped persuade me that the bigger stuff was good." The newsroom was in motion, but things in negotiations were still dragging on, with wages and other economic issues still outstanding. As the contract campaign approached the two-year mark, they realized they needed to escalate further. The unit council decided to call for a strike authorization vote.

At the *L.A. Times*, the bargaining committee also grappled with the slow pace of negotiations. After carrying momentum through a yearlong organizing drive, the L.A. Times Guild had managed to keep their campaign going even after the advantageous ownership change. Another double-edged victory came when that new owner immediately put significant wage increases on the table. "We were in this weird position where upfront they were being a little more forthcoming with money than I would guess most employers would be, and that created a strategic problem for us because that meant that we had to be much better at communicating with people," said Pearce. The bargaining committee leaned heavily on their communications plan but also turned to the campaign committee to keep the newsroom engaged in the fight.

The campaign committee developed a timeline of escalating actions to accompany negotiations—a mix of internal and public-facing, fun and more confrontational. "Sometimes we would use caucus time to bring [the campaign committee] in and explain where we were in bargaining and where we thought the pressure points were and then they would come up with an idea for how we could press those points," said Bui. "Towards the end the committee started coming up with job actions on their own to keep the pressure up and they would come in to let us know what they were thinking, and [ask] did this [action] make sense in parallel with what we were working on at the table." Members wore guild T-shirts. They changed their company Slack avatars to the L.A. Times Guild logo (nicknamed the banana eagle). They tweeted coordinated messages about issues on the bargaining table.

As time progressed, the bargaining committee recognized a disconnect between the company representatives negotiating, including lawyers who had negotiated Soon-Shiong's healthcare contracts, and the editors and other managers who better understood newsroom issues and were more directly being confronted by workplace actions. "I think they were trying to play an 'out-of-mind, out-of-sight' attitude towards it, and we needed to make it their problem to help us get this contract wrapped up—to make it clear that, 'If you're not going to help us get this thing done, so we can go about our lives, we're gonna make you miserable until then, so please come in the room with us and look us in the eyes,'" said Pearce. "We really wanted our managers, who understood our work and a lot of the reasoning behind our proposals because they're also journalists—we wanted them in the room," said Bui. The campaign committee strategized on how to get their managers to engage with negotiations. "When managers would have a meeting every day—it was like a budget planning meeting that they would have in an open area on the fifth floor—we would have members come out in T-shirts and sit and kind of have a stare-down because there are booths all around it. And it would escalate so that one week we would just sit there and stare at them and then one week everyone's phone alarms would go off at the same time and then we had one where we all got up at the same time and marched around and then went outside the building," said Wigglesworth. "Having that messaging, letting people know that that's how things were and then having those actions, it let them feel like they were helping to put pressure on management to hurry up and get furious about their proposals. I think it was helpful because we had the messaging and then we had an outlet."

The stare-downs worked. Editors started to attend negotiations—and members turned out en masse to fill the other side of the room. According to Pearce, "We would have these very impressive bargaining sessions where we would have the entire masthead of the newspaper sitting on one side of the room and this huge mass of reporters and other visual journalists on the other side of the room as the bargaining teams are sitting at the table talking to each other." Once everyone was in the bargaining room together, the guild finally began making new progress. "For us it was important to drag the managers into the room too, because I'm sure they would have loved to be insulated from the process and have lawyers deal with their problems for them. We had this long contract campaign, and things really didn't get moving until we started demanding that our editors get directly involved."

Going Public . . . Again

The fight for union recognition at the *L.A. Times* had been very public: "One of our strategies was to turn our company and our newsroom into a fishbowl, and tweet about it, and use our unique visibility as journalists to have our independent means of expression on social media to outline all the crappy stuff the company was doing," said Pearce. But with a more sympathetic owner in place and general reservations among many members about relying on outside support, the first contract campaign had largely remained internal to the newsroom itself. "There are a lot of guardrails around the idea that if you're a journalist you're objective and you don't make yourself part of the story," said Bui. "We knew that there would be a lot of resistance from the newsroom to trying to engage with the labor movement around collective bargaining, just because a lot of journalists have very conservative attitudes about maintaining our independence," said Pearce. When the unit did do public-facing actions in the lead-up to negotiations, they had taken pains to deliberately frame them in positive and supportive terms. They held a bake sale for members of the newsroom impacted by the move to El Segundo. Later, they held a drive to urge new readers to subscribe to the *Times* in support of the guild. "Every time we went to the public with some kind of ask, it took a lot of conversation with the shop," said Bui. "When we did anything like that, it was talking to membership and letting them know that we felt like this was something that we needed to do in order to build pressure, and [asked] how could we do it in a way that wouldn't make their jobs harder. But as the campaign went on and people saw what those public-facing actions could look like, they warmed up to them just by participating in them a little more."

It took a slow build throughout the negotiations process and an unexpected skirmish at the bargaining table for the unit to decide to go public once again in a big and confrontational way. The guild had made what they thought was a straightforward initial proposal on intellectual property that addressed the rights of union members to individually profit from their work, including through book publishing and film rights. "The company came back with this completely retrograde thing basically saying we guarantee nothing and saying we not only own the rights to your work, we also own your name and the right to your image," said Miranda. "They basically wanted a blanket release for everything so that if some company approached them about making a podcast or movie, they would already have sign-off from us."

For members of the bargaining committee, the issue was far from abstract. Pearce had spent years on the ground reporting on Black Lives Matter protests in Ferguson, Missouri. What if he also wanted to publish a book based on the reporting he had done? Without strong IP protection, the *L.A. Times* could claim total ownership over his later work. The issue was also strategically important because it resonated with more senior reporters in the newsroom who made more money and had generally been less invested in the campaign. The guild drafted an open letter to *L.A. Times* management signed by over 75 percent of the bargaining unit. Then members of the newsroom began tweeting publicly about the company's proposal. Like the issue of noncompetes at Law360, the issue soon gained broader attention. The guild's escalation was strategically timed to coincide with the *L.A. Times* Festival of Books, a flagship event for the paper, and generated its own media coverage and significant social media attention. The L.A. Times Guild was back in the public eye, and the open letter and the Festival of Books action worked. The bargaining committee was able to reach a tentative agreement on contract language that would protect book rights for *L.A. Times* journalists. And renewed public attention to the ongoing union fight at the newsroom would continue to be helpful as negotiations moved on to the topic of job security.

The Best Thing

As the two-year anniversary of their successful NLRB election came and went, and under the banner "Two Years Too Long," the Law360 union voted overwhelmingly in October 2018 to authorize a strike. The next day, thirty members in red T-shirts turned out to negotiations at the

NewsGuild of New York offices to present their wage proposal to the company. Smith, the news intern who by that point had been able to move into a reporter role and who had sat in on many sessions, found the moment particularly moving. "All of us being there and them seeing that and how much we cared about this . . . I think it really did have an impact." Following the strike vote, the mobilization committee kept the pressure up, delegating the offices of the LexisNexis CEO, erecting an inflatable Scabby the Rat outside of the Law360 newsroom, and holding an hourlong picket in the middle of the day. The company quickly caved on wages, and with a strike looming, the contract as a whole was settled in six weeks. After negotiating late into the night, the bargaining committee sent an early morning *Amicus* announcing the settlement.

After collecting and responding to questions through a Google form and spreadsheet and holding two newsroom meetings to review the tentative agreements, the bargaining committee held an email ratification vote. On December 18, the contract was ratified unanimously, with virtually the entire newsroom participating. "It's hard to even sum it up," said Godoy. "The immediate and tangible quality-of-life increase for the entire unit in the form of an average of 20 percent raises—it's the best thing I've done in my life. That's not hyperbole, it's the best thing I've done for anyone, anywhere, anytime, to be involved and help that come to pass." The contract also memorialized the end of noncompetes and the quota system. And it included successorship in case the outlet was sold as well as strong protection from subcontracting, provisions that are particularly challenging to win in a first contract. News assistants were bumped up to a starting salary of $50,000 and were granted the right to receive reporter training and to begin writing stories after being at the company for six months.

At the *L.A. Times*, with the number of contract proposals still under discussion dwindling and contract negotiations approaching fifteen months, the guild took stock. "We made a list of the remaining issues and the bargaining committee took a full-day caucus. We went into a room and sat down and did a grid of where we stood on the six outstanding issues," said Miranda. "We held membership meetings and sent out more email blasts and talked about it in our Facebook group and said, 'These are the things that are remaining, here's how we view our priorities.' As things wound down, it came to the point of, 'Here's what the membership is telling us, here's where we think they're willing to give in order to get a victory elsewhere.' It was a lot of listening to people and having these meetings and being available for calls and sending the delegates out to do some of the survey work," said Bui. Finally, in October, the bargaining committee felt like they'd gotten where they needed to—with "bulletproof" jurisdictional language to prevent the shadow newsroom that had loomed under Tronc.

"We sent out the full contract but we knew that people would probably not read all those pages. So we also put together a summary, kind of breaking the contract up into the highlights," said Bui. The election committee held an online vote. Out of 480 members, the unit voted 388 to 3 to ratify the contract, which included average raises of over $11,000, detailed wage scales addressing pay inequity, and just-cause protection. The contract also enshrined the *L.A. Times* Metpro training program, which offered fellowships to early-career journalists from diverse backgrounds and provided fully paid positions within the bargaining unit. As with the improvements to the news assistant position at Law360, the L.A. Times Guild had been able to win contract language impacting not only the workplace conditions for journalists, but also the conditions under which aspiring journalists could gain entry to the industry.

Building beyond Bargaining

In the aftermath of winning their first contract, the members of the L.A. Times Guild bargaining committee stayed busy. Schleuss ran for and was eventually elected president of the NewsGuild-CWA. Pesce ran for and was elected president of the newly formed guild local, the Media Guild of the West. After Pesce left the *L.A. Times* for a job at the *Washington Post*, Pearce took over as head of the new local, which has grown to include members at the *Arizona Republic*, *Pop Up Magazine*, and *Voice Media*. Wigglesworth joined Pearce as vice president of the local. Bui took a buyout from the *L.A. Times* to join the NewsGuild organizing staff.

In New York, Juan Carlos Rodriguez continued to serve as unit chair for the Law360 union. A year after winning their first contract, Rodriguez, Smith, and Godoy joined their guild representative, Susan DeCarava, in running to take over leadership of the NewsGuild New York on an organizing-focused platform. At the end of 2019, DeCarava was elected president and Rodriguez, Smith, and Godoy joined the local's executive committee, supporting workers in first contract negotiations at the *New Yorker*, *Pitchfork*, *BuzzFeed*, *New York* magazine, and several other newly organized publications.

5

Radical Roots (MNA)

GREENFIELD, MASSACHUSETTS, IS A SMALL rural town with a proud union history. Once the "tap and die capital of the world," workers in Greenfield played a central role in the growth of American manufacturing during the early twentieth century, making tools that were essential to the precise, standardized production of the literal nuts and bolts used in everything from household appliances to military munitions. During World War II, Greenfield Tap and Die (GTD) was so essential to the wartime supply chain that the federal government installed an antiaircraft gun outside the company's Sanderson Street campus near the center of town.[1]

GTD's plants were strategically important for American manufacturing and the wartime economy, and no less so for industrial organizing efforts. Beginning in the 1920s, Greenfield became a stronghold for the famously rank-and-file–led United Electrical, Radio and Machine Workers of America (UE), which organized the town's tap and die plants wall to wall. Following World War II, during the peak of red-scare attacks on more radical unions within and outside of the Congress of Industrial Organizations (CIO), GTD and other UE shops fended off numerous raids from the rival International Union of Electrical Workers.[2] By the late 1950s, however, overseas competition and a series of mergers and acquisitions shrank the size of GTD's workforce from its peak of four thousand employees to fewer than one hundred, still represented by UE Local 274.[3]

Rules to Win By. Jane F. McAlevey and Abby Lawlor, Oxford University Press. © Oxford University Press 2023. DOI: 10.1093/oso/9780197690468.003.0006

The legacy of rank-and-file–led industrial unionism exemplified by the UE has, at least in Greenfield, outlasted the industrial economy itself. Today, the healthcare sector dominates the region.[4] Baystate Franklin Medical Center, just on the other side of Sanderson Street from GTD's main campus, is now the largest employer in Franklin County, and is owned by Baystate Health, one of the largest health systems in New England.[5] The old GTD headquarters now houses Baystate's administrative offices, with "Greenfield Tap and Die Corp." still engraved above the door. But while healthcare has replaced manufacturing as the main driver of the region's economy, Baystate Franklin has become its own epicenter of militant union organizing. Nurses represented by the Massachusetts Nurses Association (MNA) have used collective bargaining open not only to nurses but to the broader community as a tool to strengthen rank-and-file leadership within their union and to keep Greenfield's strong labor tradition alive.

Consolidating Care

By way of personal introduction, Donna Stern, a psychiatric nurse at Baystate Franklin, readily declared, "My philosophy is really like the old CIO model. I believe in wall-to-wall unionization." Stern, a former social worker and longtime member and leader in the MNA, a nurses-only union, was clear: "I don't like craft unions." For her, both hospital- and sector-wide organizing were a necessity and an inevitability. "All healthcare workers should be under the same umbrella, but we're not there yet."

While community hospitals throughout western Massachusetts have been brought under shared control over the course of more than three decades of acquisition and consolidation by Baystate Health, the system's workers remain largely fragmented. MNA isn't the only union at Baystate Franklin—nurses are represented alongside small bargaining units of security guards and operating engineers. But the majority of the hospital's 1,150 employees,[6] and the vast majority of Baystate Health's 12,000-person staff, including nurses at the much larger Baystate Medical Center in Springfield, are still without a union.

What was then called Franklin County Public Hospital first organized in 1970, following passage of a state law that authorized collective bargaining for nurses (and during a period in which the Taft-Hartley Act's exclusion of nonprofit healthcare workers from coverage under federal labor law was still in effect). In the 1980s, Baystate took over the hospital, inheriting the nurses' unit. Though it took two decades before Baystate Health became actively involved in the day-to-day operations in Greenfield, corporate cost-cutting began to surface in the early 2000s for both Baystate Franklin nurses and patients. "They realized they could make a ton of money," said Stern, "no different than any other area in the capitalist system." The fact that Baystate Health was, on paper, a nonprofit hospital didn't seem to influence the company's behavior.

A small craft union faced with the corporatization of healthcare, MNA used open negotiations at Baystate Franklin to build broad support among nurses and the community to win common-good contract demands and improve their quality of work and the quality of care for Baystate Franklin patients. After a bitter contract fight lasting over two years, including two twenty-four-hour strikes followed by two employer lockouts, Baystate Franklin nurses were able to maintain the union difference within Baystate Health and win detailed contract language addressing the hospital's profound staffing crisis.

Drawing a Line

When asked about the most recent contract campaign at Baystate Franklin, which began in 2017, Stern and her coworker Suzanne Love both insisted on first talking about 2012. For Stern, a bedside nurse for fifteen years, the 2012 contract campaign was when she really came into her own as a leader in the union. "I was not born a union leader. I became a union leader because of circumstances and because of the nature of what is happening and what has been happening in healthcare and the corporatization of healthcare, and how that impacts not only our working conditions but how it impacts patients' safety," she said. Stern was "thrown right into the fire" as union cochair for the 2012 negotiations, a role she would reprise in 2017.

MNA members were a small minority of Baystate Health's overall nursing staff, and the lack of density showed. Baystate Franklin nurses had lost their traditional pension plan and accepted a two-tiered leave system. Going into 2012, the hospital appeared hopeful that it could eliminate altogether the union difference between the wages and benefits at Franklin and what Stern and others referred to as "the mothership"— Baystate Health's non-union flagship hospital in Springfield. "You could see the writing on the wall that Baystate was inching its way towards making it so [that you'd ask] what's the point of even having a contract? If you have what everyone else has, why do you even need a union?" said Stern. Stern and her coworkers realized, "They're just going to keep taking and taking and taking and taking and taking, unless we draw a line in the sand." Rather than accept concessions as inevitable under the circumstances, they decided to fight back. "It was the first time we'd ever taken a strike vote. It was the first time we'd ever gone on strike. It was forty-four negotiation sessions. It was almost two years of a bruising battle." It was also nurses' first time deliberately framing their contract campaign in terms of issues impacting patients and the broader community, highlighting Baystate's growing practice of sending Greenfield patients to Springfield for treatment, by demanding the company "keep care local."

For Love, an emergency room nurse for eleven years, 2012 marked the beginning of her serious involvement with the union. As membership chair, Stern had been the one to present Love's union orientation when Love first started at Baystate Franklin, fresh from a student nurse apprenticeship program. These orientations were important for new nurses to learn about their rights under the union contract, but also because MNA did not rely on employers to collect union dues through payroll deduction. Instead, the union signed up new members to pay dues directly, taking away any power an employer might have to strategically terminate dues collection during a contract dispute. Love found Stern's orientation rap appealing. "I thought it was interesting—I like being involved in processes and organizations and volunteering," she said. But she was also consumed with schoolwork, still attending classes on her way to earning her associate degree and later a bachelor's degree in nursing. Love resisted urging from a coworker that she become the ER shop steward. But the coworker saw Love's natural leadership and never gave up. After three years, Love was out of excuses. "She came back to me and said, 'Oh, okay, I see you graduated now.' " Soon, Love was regularly attending negotiation sessions for the 2012 contract and getting more involved.

Nurses had long practiced open negotiations at Baystate Franklin, the legacy of former MNA organizer Mike Fadel, who shared Stern's CIO predilections. The openness allowed members like Love to see right away what the union was all about. "I got pulled in that way, by being at the sessions and seeing what it was like," Love said. "We could really stand up for ourselves as a group with a collective voice." Not only that, but she genuinely enjoyed being in the negotiations room with her coworkers. During caucuses, the mood was casual and social, and there was always food. "It struck me as a good way to get to know people who I work with who are outside my department, because it can become very isolated," said Love. Working in the ER, Love and her coworkers often suffered the downstream consequences of problems elsewhere in the hospital. With the hospital constantly running short staffed, the medical-surgical unit and other departments would often refuse to accept patient transfers from the ER, leaving them stranded. In the past, Love would get frustrated with the "med-surg" nurses when patients began to "back up," overwhelming the ER nurses. But talking with them during the downtime in negotiations, Love realized, "Maybe there's other stuff going on behind the scenes that we in the ER don't know about."

The 2012 contract campaign gave Stern and Love a first taste of what it meant to fight back against Baystate—and to win. After two years of negotiations, a strike, and an impasse declaration from Baystate, nurses won wage increases, improved healthcare benefits, and a new overtime system they hoped would force the hospital to increase staffing. Later that year, Baystate Health broke ground on a new surgical center in Greenfield, signaling that the company had reversed course and was investing in providing more services locally.

Up until 2012, "Many of the nurses hadn't worked anywhere else . . . and they still thought their employer gave a crap about them," said Stern. After that contract fight, they realized, "You work in the same building that you've always worked in, but you don't work for Franklin Medical Center anymore, you work for Baystate." The 2012 contract had been radicalizing. Open negotiations brought in new leaders like Love and showed them what it took to win a nonconcessionary contract. Still, nurses hoped that after such a long and drawn-out campaign, their next negotiations would be more straightforward. "I think everybody was hoping and praying that this contract would not be like the last contract, and we couldn't have been more wrong," said Stern. "It was brutal." When the new overtime language failed to fix Baystate's chronic understaffing problem, nurses geared up to place safe staffing levels at the front and center of their next negotiations campaign.

Putting Together a Platform

In early 2016, nine months before the expiration of their hard-won contract from 2012, the MNA bargaining committee gathered at outgoing cochair Linda Judd's farmhouse outside of Greenfield. The fifteen-member group had been formally elected at the unit's annual business meeting and consisted of one shop steward from each department along with the unit cochairs, a treasurer, and a secretary. Stern was returning as senior cochair and was joined by a new junior cochair, Jillian Sicard, who would be taking over for Judd. Love had also joined the bargaining committee for the first time after officially becoming the shop steward for her coworkers in the ER. The gathering was MNA negotiator Dana Simon's first time meeting the committee. Like his predecessor, he was committed to open negotiations and wanted to get a sense of key issues from the leaders on the bargaining committee before drafting a bargaining survey.

The backyard meeting that night lasted three hours and was just the first of several the committee would hold to focus and tailor the survey before it went live to the whole membership. Finally comfortable that they were asking the right questions—both to solicit meaningful input from their coworkers and to draw them into the negotiations process—the bargaining committee took responsibility for distributing it to everyone in their "turf" and collecting responses from a majority of the bargaining unit. But the survey wasn't simply one-and-done. After collecting majority input, the committee distributed the survey a second time, this time with a narrowed list of priorities for members to rank from 1 to 10. "Everyone could see what everyone else wanted to focus on," said Love, "and then the top points are what we then bargain over."

The committee also pulled together membership meetings to discuss the survey results and give other members space to bring forward any issues that had not been adequately captured through two rounds of surveys, followed by open meetings to review concrete proposal language, during which draft proposals underwent further on-the-spot edits.

The lengthy, iterative process for developing contract proposals produced clear consensus around high-priority issues like understaffing and healthcare benefits that impacted nurses hospital-wide. But it also allowed more nuanced departmental issues to rise to the surface, including downsides of the union's seniority system. Under past contracts, requests for summer vacation were granted based on seniority. While the system worked well in most departments, in one department the two nurses who had been at the hospital the longest each regularly requested five full weeks of summer vacation. With only one nurse granted vacation at a time, this meant that none of the other twelve nurses in the department—many of whom had school-age children—could take time off during those ten weeks. They brought the issue to the bargaining committee and came up with a proposal to cap summer vacation requests to a maximum of two weeks. The new system would still give priority to the nurses who had been there the longest but would also give other nurses the opportunity to take some time off while their kids were on summer break. It was a fair solution that didn't fundamentally undermine the bargaining unit's longstanding seniority structure. But it was also unavoidably disadvantageous to the two most senior nurses. Knowing that the proposal had the potential to cause conflict in the department that might boil over into negotiations, Stern went to them and explained why they had drafted the proposal. "Because we did the background work and paid them the respect of talking to them directly first about why we're making this proposal, I think they accepted it more readily than if we had just done it without involving them in the process," said Love.

The existing collective bargaining agreement showed clear evidence of past proposals stemming directly from nurses' on-the-ground experiences, many of which further strengthened the value of seniority. MNA had negotiated that nurses who had been at the hospital for twelve years or more would no longer be required to take on-call shifts, which required that they be able to arrive at the hospital within forty-five minutes, rotate to the night shift, or have their days off moved. "It's those tiny details that really show something's been bargained over," said Love. "It's special circumstances, it's special considerations that can get written into a contract that really can make bargaining worthwhile. It can make your work situation a little more easy and gracious." And according to Love, "It's that room for input that allows for details to come out of what individual departments would benefit from."

With a suite of proposals hashed out through meetings, surveys, and more meetings, the bargaining committee was ready to start negotiations. They had a clear set of big-picture priorities as well as a sense of the more tailored departmental issues that nurses wanted to address in negotiations. "We went into bargaining with a platform," said Simon, the negotiator. "We could go out to our membership with, 'Here's the platform we're running on.'" With that platform came an open invitation, and express encouragement, for members to come to negotiations and be a part of making the platform a reality.

Making the Case

The 2017 contract campaign wasn't the first attempt at open negotiations for the committee or for Simon. In his experience, members came to negotiations with one of three motivations: super-militant members who were eager to speak in favor of the union platform, a "great middle" who wanted to see the negotiations firsthand but would much rather observe than participate, and the fence-sitters who "aren't quite sure they think the union's particularly smart." One of the virtues of open bargaining was that the third group couldn't stay on the fence for very long. "If you have a room full of everybody and management's as bad as Baystate, that last category, boy that takes one meeting for them to say, 'Oh my god. . . . I'm so glad I'm on the right side.'"

Indeed, it didn't take long for the Baystate management to begin organizing nurses against them. At the table, the company proposed to reclassify nurses who worked thirty-two hours or fewer as part-time employees, a change that would increase the rates they paid for health insurance and reduce their paid time off. Nurses had long had the choice of working three twelve-hour shifts, a total of thirty-six hours per week, or four eight-hour shifts, a total of thirty-two hours per week. But the year before negotiations, the hospital had started encouraging nurses to take the thirty-two-hour schedule, claiming shorter shifts would promote patient safety. Many nurses had agreed to make the change, including Love, though she soon switched back. The part-time proposal made it instantly clear what had actually been motivating management to push nurses toward shorter shifts. "I think it was a setup that they were trying to get most of us to move," said Love. When nurses realized exactly what the company was trying to do, "The room just exploded. . . . I had to tell everyone, 'Just wait 'til they're all out of the room before you say something,' because people were so mad."

As a general rule, the bargaining committee told other nurses in the room to keep a blank face and not show any reaction to the company's proposals. But there were exceptions, and this was one of them. When the company left to caucus in another room, the union formulated its response. "People were really mad, and Dana [Simon] is a believer in, 'Well, let them see that you're really mad and that they've gone too far with the proposal,'" said Love. "As we're doing this heated discussion amongst ourselves, he said, 'This is great, capture that.'" When management walked back into the room, nurses were ready. "Instead of just one or two people talking, we went down the length of the table and everyone in the bargaining committee told the chief nursing officer what they thought of the proposal." The strategy worked. "They took it off the table right away," said Love. "I've never seen it happen so quickly. Within an hour, they had taken away that proposal."

With as many as seventy-five members in the room at a given time, caucuses provided an important space to plan for the presentation of the union's proposals as well as for how to respond to management's proposals. Indeed, the bargaining committee often turned to other coworkers in the room to provide further explanation or rationales for particular items. For the significant number of nurses who wanted to watch but were reluctant to speak in front of management, caucuses gave them the chance to build their confidence by planning who would speak in what order and going through practice role-plays with Simon. "I like to have people give their rap of what they're going to say and then I play the boss and I just cut them to ribbons," said Simon. "And sometimes it's funny because it's just so disingenuous the bullshit that comes out of me. And sometimes it's very helpful, too, because you realize, 'Did you see what you walked into? I saw you coming a mile away. Don't do that. That second argument you made? That one's the money.'" By taking the time to think through arguments and make a plan for the bargaining table, members felt more confident and prepared to speak directly to management.

As safe staffing continued to be the central demand in negotiations, nurses spent significant caucus time brainstorming all of the ways they could demonstrate to management how the issue impacted both nurses and patients. In one caucus, conversation shifted to the frequency with which nurses were called at home to come back into work: during days off, vacations, and even the middle of the night. They realized that working for Baystate, even their time off was never truly theirs. But how to convey that feeling to management? Bargaining cochair Sicard remembered that most of the call-in requests she'd received from the hospital had been via text message. She pulled up the texts on her phone. "Things like, 'We desperately need help. Can you come in right away? We're dying here. We're drowning,'" said Simon.

Sicard spent an evening at home transferring all of her text messages into a Word document. The bargaining committee printed it out—twelve single-spaced pages. At the next negotiation session, Simon nonchalantly passed the document across the table and then read sample texts from each page. "Management was horrified," said Stern. "They couldn't hide anymore. . . . You could say, 'Oh, maybe nurses are exaggerating,' or 'Maybe it's not as bad.' And managers are trying to protect themselves so they're minimizing the problem. But then when the evidence is in front of them, you can't minimize it." Later, the human resources director told Simon it was the worst moment of her professional career. Sicard's idea had had a huge impact at the table. "The process of talking and talking and talking about these issues and having large groups of people, it becomes a competition for who can be more productive and come up with the next best idea," said Simon. "It creates a culture that if I come up with this idea and I come up with the goods, it will immediately be used and be really gratifying."

A Community Contract

Sicard's text messages were a perfect encapsulation of the impact that understaffing was having on nurses at Baystate Franklin. But from the beginning nurses realized it would be important to also demonstrate what understaffing meant for patients. As they had for past contract campaigns, the bargaining committee decided to open up negotiation sessions to the broader Greenfield community.

Dave Cohen and Judy Atkins, longtime residents of the Greenfield area and retirees from the UE, had been involved in supporting MNA members for the last three contract cycles, beginning when Baystate Franklin negotiations had coincided with Occupy Wall Street protests on the Greenfield Common. Cohen and Atkins were dedicated leftists and fixtures in the Greenfield labor movement. They were also Baystate Franklin patients. Cohen had recently undergone treatment for prostate cancer but had been unable to get the care he needed locally. "I had to get radiation treatment, but they wouldn't do it here in Franklin County and so I had to drive every day to Springfield for eight weeks during the winter. That wore pretty thin, having to drive forty-five minutes for ten minutes of treatment and then drive forty-five minutes back home," Cohen said. "And when I'd get there, there'd be a room full of people from Franklin County." According to Atkins, Baystate offered bus service to and from its hospitals in Greenfield and Springfield, but the bus only made one round trip per day, leaving patients who needed transportation waiting for hours before they could return home. When MNA campaigned to "keep care local" in 2012, the demand resonated beyond the union's membership. "There was a real fear that Baystate's real intentions were to shut down Franklin Medical Center or just make it into an emergency room over time," said Cohen. After the 2012 contract victory and Baystate's subsequent groundbreaking on a new surgical center in Greenfield, it was clear that the combined pressure from nurses, patients, and other community members had kept the company from pulling up stakes.

Though not all open negotiations campaigns necessarily bring in community members from outside the bargaining unit, MNA had seen that it was a strategy that could work for them. Cohen remembered that when he and Atkins first met with nurses about getting community members more involved during the Occupy days, they were apprehensive about asking for help. Good jobs were few and far between in the hill towns surrounding Greenfield, and nurses at Baystate Franklin were better off than a lot of their neighbors. "They thought they made too much money and people would hate them because they made too much money," said Cohen. But Cohen and Atkins knew from their experiences in UE that good jobs could be a source of community pride rather than resentment. "We spent a lot of time talking to them, saying, 'No, this is a good union area, if you put out the issues, people will understand and won't hate you because you're earning a decent living.'" It didn't take long for nurses to see that their fears were unfounded. "Of course the community loves nurses, and they realized that quickly," said Atkins.

Over the last two contract cycles, nurses had continued to develop relationships with community members and organizations and to build public awareness about the impact of healthcare consolidation on nurses and patients. In 2017, with help from Cohen, Atkins, and a committee of other local community leaders, nurses hoped to focus public pressure around the issue of safe staffing, another common-good demand, by once again bringing community members into the negotiations. Baystate tried to block the move, proposing conventional ground rules that would limit negotiation sessions to Baystate Franklin workers. But Simon and the bargaining committee said no. Ground rules may have been conventional, but they weren't required. "These rules are so old," said Love. "It was like they were [printed] on an old mimeograph machine. One of the rules is no smoking at the bargaining table. That's a pretty old set of rules." Because the existence and content of ground rules are a permissive and not mandatory subject of bargaining, the union wasn't obligated to negotiate over them. Moreover, with management refusing to pay nurses on the bargaining committee for lost time spent in negotiations, a common incentive for unions to consider ground rules, there was no reason to. "We just held the line and refused to agree."

Love had been shut out of negotiations when she tried to attend MNA negotiations for nurses at another hospital. Because of restrictive ground rules, she and other union and community members who didn't work at the hospital were only allowed in the room during caucuses. "There was someone sitting outside with her seven-year-old and they would not let the child in the room for bargaining because she's not a nurse at the hospital." Love wanted her own family and other members of the community to be involved in the negotiations process. "My husband is interested in this stuff. He might want to come and be a part of it. We have many supporters that would want to be a part of it. Not only because of the strong labor history in Greenfield, but also the community has a vested interest in the community having enough nurses." The exclusion of outside nurses and family members from negotiation sessions underscored the artificiality of distinguishing between "union members" and "community members." Nurses were workers. And they were also community residents who, along with their families, neighbors, and friends, relied on the hospital as a healthcare provider.

The lack of ground rules at Baystate Franklin negotiations facilitated participation by Cohen, Atkins, and others, as did their location: two churches in the heart of downtown Greenfield, including Saints James and Andrew Episcopal Church. "It's a church that is known as an activist church . . . and it was right next to our office, which is also right next to places that people hang out," said Rudy Renaud, a city council member who left her day job at another union to join the MNA staff and be a part of the Baystate Franklin fight midway through the 2017 contract campaign. The church also happened to be her church. The bargaining committee tried hard to advertise that their negotiations were open to everyone through copious food and welcoming signage. "People would feel like it was a place to stop in and even just grab a cookie and a coffee," Renaud said. Many were familiar faces. "We were sort of like a mini drop-in center for some of the patients who were really high risk who needed food or a snack or whatever," said Stern. "Sometimes they would stay and listen to negotiations, too. But it's building trust with the community. It's not just about the contract."

Having patients and other community members in the room gave nurses the confidence and credibility to talk about the broader impacts of staffing shortages on patient care. Love remembered one particular session devoted to discussing safe staffing where the church was packed. "It was great to see these nurses who were there feeling the safety of numbers," she said. One nurse told management about a patient who had stuck with her: a seventy-eight-year-old man who had gone four days in the hospital without getting his face shaved because none of the nurses could take the time away from other patients to help him. "That's all about patient dignity," said Love. The presence of patients in negotiations, particularly patients who relied on the hospital's mental health care and emergency services, underscored that nurses were fighting not only for themselves but for the people they cared for. "You have one co-chair in the emergency room who literally sees everybody who comes in off the street and then you have the other co-chair who's a psych nurse," said Stern. "There were a lot of our patients that were also involved in supporting because they were saying, 'This is not okay. I've been taken care of by these nurses and I can't believe you're making them work how many hours in a week?' "

In Stern's eyes, by advocating for nurses, patients were also advocating for themselves. They too were coming to see the impact of Baystate's profit-driven decision-making on the quality and availability of health-care. "They only care about certain patients, and I think that really came out," said Stern. "They care about certain patients, patients with the right health insurance . . . the ones that go into the surgical building or the ICU or go in for colonoscopies and other outpatient procedures, because those are the moneymakers." In a rural community with high rates of drug addiction and mental illness, the patients most dependent on access to community healthcare were being left behind.

For Stern, negotiating a contract was about improving her working conditions but also ensuring that she and her fellow nurses would be able to provide for their patients' needs. "I always look at the contract as two parts. There's the nuts and bolts, what's the health insurance, the raises, those things are important. . . . But then there's this whole other, I call it the soul contract with the patients," she said. "So you have a soul contract and then you have the contract with management, and it's like, how do you negotiate both of those contracts? And they're not mutually exclusive. In fact, they're intimately connected."

Having supporters like Cohen and Atkins from the Greenfield labor community in the room for negotiation sessions didn't just provide sup-port for the common-good demand for safe staffing. It also allowed the bargaining committee to draw on outside experiences and perspectives when thinking through strategies and tactics for the campaign. During long caucuses, when conversation turned from contract proposals to

how to increase pressure on the hospital through workplace and outside actions, community members were there to help to plan pickets,
strikes, and other escalations. Even with sixty people in the room, the
conversations managed to be productive. When the group started to run
short of ideas, someone would pull up the Greenfield community calendar to scope out upcoming events for possible leafleting or turn to a
power structure map of the hospital system and think about stakeholders
they hadn't engaged with yet. As with providing evidence for contract
proposals, having more people in the room generated more ideas. It also
helped ensure that there was buy-in from members and community and
that people were on board to participate. "When you get everybody together, it doesn't mean you're boiling it down to the lowest common de-
nominator of boring," said Simon. Coming up with an action as a group
resulted in actions that were both more strategic and more fun for the
members participating in them.

"You always start off slow, right?" said Stern. "You know, you start off
with pickets, local pickets, and then you start to crank it up and then you
start talking about, 'You know, these pickets aren't seeming to do it.' So
now we're heading towards strikes. And in addition to strikes, we're going
to start taking the show on the road and we're going to start targeting the
mothership. And also we're going to start targeting the board members
of the Big Baystate," the larger hospital system. One day in negotiations,
Renaud had the idea to purchase a twelve-foot-tall inflatable fat cat. Soon
the fat cat was popping up outside of the hospital's executive building
and outside the offices of board members. After another brainstorming
session, a "Support Baystate Nurses" sign appeared at the top of the Poet
Seat Tower landmark overlooking downtown Greenfield. "In the middle
of the night, I don't know who did it, but some crazy kids went up there,"
joked Renaud. Nurses went to the Veterans' Day Parade. The Franklin
County Fair. The hospital's annual "Wheeling for Healing" event. They
put ads on local radio. "Just everything we could do to just constantly hit
at them and give them PR everywhere we went," said Renaud.

Though many voices participated in brainstorming new ideas, it was
ultimately up to the bargaining committee to decide if a given tactic
would help or hurt their position in negotiations. "We are deciding what
we're to be arguing for in bargaining and how far we want to take outside

actions," said Love. But buy-in from nurses and community members gave the committee the backup they needed to stand tall against any blowback from the boss. After deciding in a caucus to distribute flyers about the hospital's "dealing and stealing" at the Wheeling for Healing fundraiser, it was Stern as cochair who took the heat. "The doctor who oversees the event, basically lost his, excuse my French, but he lost his shit in the cafeteria with me. And I turned into Daenerys from *Game of Thrones*. He basically ended up having to apologize to me because he was so out of control," said Stern. It hurt not being able to get along with everyone in the hospital. But Stern also saw the attack for what it was—a sign that management felt their power being threatened. "There's still this thing between nurses and doctors, there's still this old-school belief that, 'You nurses should know your place, and how dare you challenge.' "

One-to-One; One through Five

Stern had learned a lot about how to organize from Fadel, the former MNA organizer, in the 2012 contract fight: "the old-school model of one-to-one communication," as she described it. But direct communication came easily to her. "It kind of goes along with the philosophy of nursing, which is you include your patient in the process," she said. Why should organizing her coworkers be any different? Throughout negotiations, Stern and the other members of the bargaining committee communicated with their coworkers through as many methods as possible, but in-person communication remained paramount. "Facebook is helpful. Email is helpful. Texting is helpful. But there's still nothing that beats that one-to-one communication and your coworkers seeing you showing up at like two o'clock in the morning to have a conversation with them," she said.

The bargaining committee worked to continue to engage members even after they had completed the bargaining survey process and announced their platform for negotiations. They made sure the date and location of each negotiation session was posted on Facebook and on the MNA bulletin boards in each department's break room. At the end of every negotiation session, members would stay in the room and draft a detailed bargaining leaflet to distribute in the shop the next day. The text of the leaflet would then get posted on the Baystate Franklin MNA private Facebook group page. Sometimes Simon or the MNA communications staff would make adjustments to the final leaflet overnight based on questions or comments that came through the Facebook group. Though MNA had been hesitant to make use of Facebook in the past, Stern, Love, and the other bargaining committee members helped to set the tone to keep the group productive. "We had discipline of message," said Stern. "Discipline, discipline, discipline. Because I had already gone through a bruising contract before, I knew the key was discipline of message. I also reinforced over and over and over again, you don't get into power struggles and fights on Facebook. . . . If someone has questions, it's always face to face."

After a dry run online, the final leaflet would be printed the next morning and distributed by the committee to their coworkers via rounds through the hospital. The leaflets helped fill in the gaps for members who weren't able to attend negotiations, but also gave members who had been in the room a jumping-off point for talking to their coworkers. "When you get over the course of months a majority of the bargaining unit having at least borne witness to a few bargaining sessions, when you put out a leaflet, they'll really read it because they've decided they can also tell their coworkers, 'This leaflet that you just read, it's not telling the half of it. I was there. They're being diplomatic,'" said Simon. The bargaining committee also continued to hold regular membership meetings to discuss negotiations as a group.

Though the committee provided detailed leaflets, the best communication came from open negotiations themselves. Toward the end of the campaign, management released its own flyer claiming that the union had turned down a 23 percent wage increase. "We had a small minority, but a very worried minority overnight that was saying, 'What the hell? Really, we turned down 23 percent? What the hell?'" said Simon. The bargaining committee was quickly able to put out its own leaflet that laid out the facts of what had happened—but more importantly could be backed up by the supermajority of workers who'd seen the negotiation session firsthand. The worried minority quickly turned sheepish that they had fallen for the boss's messaging. "If you try to do that and they haven't been there and you tell them that management's lying, you're in a he-said, she-said, 'I just feel as a union member, I feel caught in the middle.' We didn't have any of those people because it was open bargaining," said Simon.

A year into negotiations, with little progress at the table, the bargaining committee decided to move forward with a strike authorization vote and communication among the membership began to intensify. "We realized we were just at a standoff, we're not getting anywhere," said Love. "And so we spent a lot of time going to the hospital, going around to departments, talking to members. We had open meetings. We also would reserve a room in the hospital, the conference rooms. And we members of the bargaining committee took turns being there for like a fifteen-hour, eighteen-hour time period so that everybody at every shift time frame would have a chance to come in and talk to us about why we think we need to go on strike." The bargaining committee had recommended a twenty-four-hour strike, but the hospital had made it clear that they would be locking out nurses for an additional three days. So Love and Stern prepared their coworkers for being out of work for a total of four days. "It takes going from unit to unit, unit to unit, one to one, one to one," said Stern. "It takes asking the hard question: 'Are you going to vote yes? Are you going to vote no?' Because the thing that I learned about the first time is you never want to go into a strike vote not having a pretty good sense of what your numbers are going to be." The committee went through a list of coworkers and ranked everyone on a scale of 1 through 5 based on their support for the strike. When the time came to vote to authorize the strike, they knew they had the votes. "We held it over two different dates and times so that there was as much opportunity for people to vote," said Stern. In the end, over 80 percent of the unit turned out, many of them driving over thirty miles on their day off to participate. The strike was officially authorized.

All on the Line

Nurses at Baystate Franklin had struck for the first time in 2012. But they had never been locked out before—in fact, the Baystate lockout was the first in the history of the MNA. Management thought they could lure the union into a misstep by instituting the lockout twelve hours before the strike was scheduled to begin. By law, the union had to give ten days' notice of the start of their strike and picket. In starting the lockout early, management hoped to trick nurses into picketing before the time they had officially announced, triggering an unfair labor practice charge. The plan backfired. Instead of nurses walking off the job, they were being shut out of the hospital, an even worse optic for Baystate.

At precisely their announced hour, Baystate Franklin nurses began to picket. Being locked out "just pissed nurses off," said Stern. "The lockout just enraged them." The lockout had also galvanized the broader community. "The turnout from the community and organizations was ginormous," said Simon. "We had students coming in from UMass Amherst, like forty-five minutes away, and from all over the place. All sorts of community people were populating the picket line." Atkins and Cohen were there with other UE members and retirees, as well as members of Franklin County Continuing the Political Revolution, an organization they had founded to carry forward organizing that had started under the auspices of the Bernie Sanders campaign. Renaud's city council colleagues and her old union, the SEIU, had also turned out along with local firefighters and several other local unions. And many nurses had brought their family members. Love's husband struck up a picket line conversation with Atkins and Cohen about their experiences in the Greenfield labor movement. Two years later, he would publish an article on the history of the UE at GTD.

After four days, nurses went back to work. But progress at the bargaining table was still slow. A second strike and lockout followed six months later, further solidifying community support for the nurses and distrust of Baystate Health. When Stern tried to go into the hospital shortly before the second lockout was scheduled, four Greenfield police officers blocked her from entering and physically pulled her away from the entrance. The incident was caught on video and reposted by the *Greenfield Recorder*. "That did not play well," said Stern. "Police officers putting their hands on a nurse who literally was just trying to get into a building legally before lockout began." The incident was especially galvanizing for nurses themselves. "There were a couple of baby nurses and it was really funny, they said, 'We had no idea you were so badass.' And I never thought of myself as badass or that anyone was paying attention. But I realized that it actually motivated them to show up for the action. You know, those moments of bravery that you don't really think of yourself as brave. You just think this is the right thing to do. They do make a difference."

After the second strike and lockout, the hospital finally began to make movement toward settlement. Another run-in between Stern, cochair Sicard, and the police as nurses tried to reenter the hospital only further lowered management's stock with community members. MNA had also filed twenty-three unfair labor practice charges against Baystate, many stemming from management's response to the strikes. Baystate decided to clean house, getting rid of the president, the director of nursing operations, and the head of human resources—and they hired a new advertising agency. "It's all these little cumulative things that are not so little," said Stern. "It's accumulation of action, action, action." According to Love, a month after the second strike, nurses went into negotiations and management just caved. "They said, 'Well, we think that we can settle something today. . . . We'll meet all of your concerns and we can get this thing settled today.' We were so shocked. I don't know what changed other than they got sick of it." Nurses won back a health plan that the company had previously eliminated, a 7.4 percent wage increase, and a ratification bonus. But finally addressing the hospital's short staffing through staffing grids was far and away the biggest victory.

Safer Staffing Secured

In 2012, nurses had won contract language that incentivized hiring more staff, but the 2017 contract in effect required it, specifying the minimum staffing levels for each department and each shift. It was an amazing victory, forcing the company to hire and immediately expanding the bargaining unit by nearly 10 percent. "I think the thing that made me happiest is not seeing my coworkers have to work thousands of hours of overtime in any one calendar year," said Stern. "And not seeing my patients be put at such high risk." After some hesitation, the bargaining committee scheduled the ratification vote and the victory party back-to-back. They didn't want to seem presumptuous, but they also knew their coworkers were similarly thrilled about everything that had been accomplished in the contract. Both the turnout and the yes vote were overwhelming, as was the celebration that followed.

Though Baystate Franklin nurses had won huge staffing improvements at their hospital, the issue remained a priority for MNA statewide. Almost immediately, Stern, also a member of the union's board of directors, pivoted into campaigning for a ballot question that would fix nurse-to-patient staffing ratios in state law. Legislating staffing ratios would ensure safer conditions for nurses and patients regardless of whether a hospital was unionized. It would also eliminate a key incentive for companies like Baystate Health to fight nurse unionization. In November 2018, six months after the contract victory at Baystate Franklin, the initiative was defeated, with MNA being outspent two-to-one statewide by the Massachusetts Health and Hospital Association, an industry association led in part by Baystate Health's CEO. But Franklin County was a bright spot on the electoral map, posting some of the only positive margins in the state. Years of relationship-building between nurses and their community, against the backdrop of Greenfield's long labor history, showed plainly at the ballot box.

6

The New Boss in Town (UNITE HERE)

RICHIE ALIFERIS HAS STAFFED THE front door of the Omni Parker House Hotel in Boston for forty-four years. His tenure as a door attendant has spanned most of his life and a full quarter of the Parker House's history as the longest continually operated hotel in the United States. Since he began working at the Parker House while a student at nearby Suffolk College, Aliferis has seen the hotel industry change from small, local, and regional family-owned businesses to global, publicly traded hospitality behemoths. "When I first started in the hotel, individuals and families owned the hotels. They weren't these big corporations. When I started it was the Dunfey Hotel and it was an Irish Catholic family from New Hampshire." That Irish Catholic family from New Hampshire, a pillar of Democratic politics in New England, would eventually become the owners of Omni International Hotels, before selling the company to a Texas-based billionaire who'd made his money in oil and gas.

The growth of Omni from a New England company with a family face to part of an international conglomerate with an inscrutable name, TRT Holdings, paled in comparison to the trajectory of another hotel company founded by a family. Unlike the Dunfeys, this family was two thousand miles away, but like the Dunfeys, this family had religious roots too. A Mormon family from a town in Utah that bears their name, the Marriotts opened their first hotel in Arlington, Virginia, in 1957. The company grew rapidly over the course of just two generations to become the dominant

Rules to Win By. Jane F. McAlevey and Abby Lawlor, Oxford University Press. © Oxford University Press 2023.
DOI: 10.1093/oso/9780197690468.003.0007

global hotel operator and brand. By 2016, Marriott International achieved the status of largest hotel company ever in existence with its acquisition of Starwood Hotels and Resorts. Marriott's merger with Starwood brought together thirty of the most publicly recognized hotel brands in the world, including Westin, Sheraton, Ritz-Carlton, St. Regis, W, Renaissance, Courtyard, Aloft, Moxy, and many more, under the Marriott umbrella. Though the Omni Parker House remains the oldest hotel in Boston, Marriott is now far and away the biggest game in town, operating three of the city's largest eight hundred–plus room hotels and continuing to develop properties under its newest brands.

Aliferis had closely watched the changes to the hotel industry in Boston not only as a career hotel worker but as a member of the executive board of his union, UNITE HERE Local 26. The local had consistently organized to keep up with the booming hotel industry, going from nine unionized hotels at the start of Aliferis's career to thirty-four by the time the Marriott-Starwood merger came about. In 2008, Local 26 successfully locked in a citywide contract just before the market crash sent hotel revenues south. Despite the Great Recession's impact on the hotel industry, the union continued to grow rapidly, and the 2012 hotel contract, negotiated citywide with the city's hotel association, established the union's pension plan and its strike fund for the first time.

In the past, UNITE HERE had often focused on pressuring a particular company to set the citywide standard. Aliferis was used to that company not being his employer. "They only have fifty-five hotels, so they're not a real big player." One contract cycle had focused on Starwood; another on Hilton. Though Marriott was already the second-largest hotel company before the 2016 merger, decades of successful union avoidance meant the company had far fewer union properties than its closest rivals, and it had stayed out of the negotiations hot seat by virtue of its low union density. But that was about to change.

Marriott's acquisition of heavily unionized Starwood not only made it the largest hotel company in the world but also meant that the company was suddenly operating a significant number of union hotels for the first time. In Boston, Marriott now employed nearly 40 percent of Local 26's hotel worker members, far more than Omni or any other single company. And unlike Starwood, Marriott couldn't be expected to agree to a contract negotiated with another company or with the city-wide hotel association. "Marriott doesn't play nice in the sandbox. They like to do their own thing," said Ian Seale, a banquet server at the Boston Park Plaza, owned by Highgate Hotels, another smaller player. Seale had started his career working in hotels in Barbados, but like Aliferis had now spent four decades in the industry in Boston. Though neither worked for Marriott, they knew that negotiations with the company would have major implications for what workers would ultimately be able to win at the other unionized Boston hotels. Because a key feature of Marriott's union avoidance strategy had been to match the union wage in major hotel markets, a strong contract would likely also mean improved standards for the many Marriott workers in Boston still without a union.

History Made at Harvard

The Marriott-Starwood merger raised important strategic questions for hotel workers looking ahead to their next contract negotiations, but first the local had to get through negotiations for 750 members who worked in dining services at Harvard University. Local 26 members at Harvard had been fighting for many years to get the university to address the financial impact of long summer layoffs. In 2016, after intense delibera-tion over contract demands, the bargaining committee decided on a new approach. They reframed the issue as one of annual earnings, rather than year-round work, and demanded $35,000 per year for all dining services workers. When the university, a $40 billion institution, refused to agree to the union's eminently reasonable demand, the workers embarked on the first open-ended strike in Local 26 history. After three weeks, in the middle of the fall 2016 semester, they won.

"The Harvard campaign was proof positive that [Local 26] can pull off a big action and strike and assert the power of the union," said John Flannery, a door attendant at the Fairmont Copley Plaza. Flannery had once been skeptical of the union's elected officials, at one point running for union office against its eventual president, Brian Lang. But he'd seen the local's steady growth under Lang's leadership and stayed involved as a shop steward. "We were more thinking in the present before. Since 2011,

2012, we started thinking more about the future as far as our union and what it could be and what it should be," said Flannery. The union established a strike fund and a pension plan, set ambitious new organizing goals, and started to do more community-oriented organizing. The victory at Harvard showed Flannery and others that the new approach was working, with dining services workers pulling off a successful strike and winning broad public support.

Sticking with What Works

Like Flannery, Aliferis and other members of the executive board took a number of lessons away from the Harvard contract victory. After decades of being a local that threatened to strike, Local 26 had become a union that had indeed struck one of the wealthiest and most powerful institutions in Boston and won. But building the internal organizing structure to support an open-ended strike hadn't been easy. Moreover, the formulation of an easily communicated, common-sense demand—$35,000 per year for all dining hall workers—had taken months of discussion and deliberation among dining services members. Looking ahead to citywide hotel negotiations, union leadership hoped to replicate what had worked so well at Harvard. In order to fuel the kind of mass participation they would need for a successful strike, the union planned to have a large negotiations committee with leaders from hotels across the city and negotiations open to all hotel members. To pull it off, they would need to start planning right away.

Citywide Conversations

In early 2017, just a few months after the Harvard settlement, Boston hotel workers came together to start identifying key issues for their own negotiations. The Local 26 leadership wanted to leave plenty of time for hotel workers to deliberate over demands and develop a strategy for dealing with Marriott's new dominance. Organizers convened a series of meetings for all union hotel workers in the city—thirty-four properties in all—to begin discussing goals for the contract. The meetings, held over the span of two weeks, drew two thousand of the local's five thousand hotel worker members.

Maryann Silva had worked as a banquet server at the Ritz-Carlton Boston for seventeen years. While Ritz-Carlton had once been a standalone hotel company, it too had been acquired by Marriott. Silva had always been a union supporter: "I didn't shy away when my brothers and sisters might need me to stand behind them or with them." But, she said, "I did shy away from getting involved because I didn't really know what the contract was all about." Silva went to one of the citywide contract meetings in 2017 and started talking with workers from hotels throughout Boston. "Those types of meetings helped to bring people like myself out and [encourage us to] be more vocal," Silva said.

As Silva and other Local 26 members discussed their work, retirement was front of mind for many. The local's pension fund was newly established, and the accrued benefits even for the most senior workers were modest. The reality of what it meant not to have retirement savings soon began to register for younger workers as well. Ye Qing Wei, a room attendant at the Sheraton Boston, a Starwood-turned-Marriott hotel and the largest in the city, hadn't fully understood why her own mother, also a room attendant, was still cleaning rooms. "I'm fifty-two, so I don't realize why people who are seventy are still working." Then she and her mom did the math together. "My mom, she worked over twenty-five years in the hotel. She has $1,100 right now for retirement. So she said, 'I pay $400 for rent and I pay $300 for my insurance. How am I going to survive with only, like, $400 left?'" At a minimum, workers wanted to be able to afford the monthly premium for Medicare supplements to maintain the level of coverage they had under the union's health and welfare plan.

Another issue that rose to the top was Marriott's "green choice" program, which gave hotel guests a financial incentive to decline daily housekeeping services. Though the company led with the environmental benefits of washing fewer sheets each day, the program was also an excuse to schedule fewer room attendants and save significantly on labor costs. The program reduced the number of room attendant shifts overall, but also meant management could no longer predict in advance what the demand for housekeeping would be. As a result, many more low-seniority room attendants were moved to de facto on-call status, without regular schedules or any guarantee that they would be able to work enough hours in a given month to qualify for health insurance benefits. When her kids were younger, Wei remembered feeling like she couldn't ever say no to a call-in shift, even when it was on one of their birthdays. "I needed the hours. I didn't know the next day if I would be scheduled or not," she said. "It really affected my life, my schedule. It was out of control."

Starwood had pioneered green choice as a cost-saving measure, and now Marriott was eager to implement the program company-wide. Despite the reduced number of shifts for room attendants, the green choice program didn't reduce the amount of work that needed to be done—the guests still produced the same amount of mess and trash over the course of multi-night stays. Because of green choice, however, room attendants were forced to deal with the mess all at once, during one room cleaning, rather than spread out over several shifts. It also meant dealing with ad hoc guest requests—fresh towels, an additional trash pickup—that weren't factored into their workload. The move away from daily housekeeping services and the larger loads of dirty towels and trash compounded the physical toll of the work. "It was killing my back, my coworkers' backs," said Alganesh Gebrelibanos, a room attendant at the Westin Copley, another Starwood-turned-Marriott hotel, for twenty-five years. "At the same time, it was killing my benefits." There was nothing fundamentally incompatible with the hotel reducing its environmental impact and providing room attendants with fixed schedules and sufficient time to do their jobs. But Marriott's cost-cutting had pitted the two against each other. Gebrelibanos and other room attendants hoped that, through negotiations, they could get the company to finally address how the company's bottom-line-driven approach to environmentalism was impacting them.

Retirement and the green choice program were both high-priority issues for room attendants, the largest department in each hotel and the bulk of Local 26's hotel membership. But smaller departments also took advantage of the citywide meetings to voice their key issues. Door and bell attendants were particularly adamant that their earnings had begun to fall behind workers in other departments and that the wage scale needed to be adjusted to bolster their take-home pay. After talking with his coworkers about the upcoming contract negotiations, Juan Eusebio, a "door ambassador" at the W Hotel, another Starwood-Marriott property, became focused on winning a significant wage increase for his department. "The door ambassador position was a good position. You made good money in tips." But, Eusebio explained, "Not many people carry cash these days, and the industry has changed." The impact of a cultural shift around cash tips was further compounded by the growth of Uber, Lyft, and other ride-hailing apps. Hotel guests no longer relied on doormen to flag down taxis for them, and the associated tips had dried up. "You have the reputation being a doorman or bellman, you make a lot of money, quote unquote a lot of money," said Flannery, the door attendant at the Fairmont Copley Plaza. But once the door and bell attendants started talking to workers in other departments, they found ready support. "A restaurant server or bartender could have a gratuity line put on their bill. . . . Well, we don't have a gratuity line," he said. "Once you start to explain it to people, the lightbulb goes on." The door department found common ground with the room service department, which was also feeling the financial impact of new technology. Instead of calling for room service, guests now used app-based delivery services when they wanted to order food.

The meetings in early 2017 kicked off conversations among hotel workers across the city about what they wanted their next contract to look like. Toward the end of the year, they would reconvene to concretize their demands and start making a plan to win.

Getting Organized

Eusebio had started talking with his coworkers about contract issues at the hotel but had yet to attend a citywide union meeting. In late 2017, Local 26 hotel members gathered at the Teachers Union Hall in Boston for an all-day citywide bargaining convention to officially kick off their contract campaign. Many of the same members were in the room from earlier meetings, including the local's established network of shop stewards. But the stewards and the local's organizing staff had also been working hard to identify and recruit new leaders to help build out leadership committees within each hotel as well as what would become the bargaining committee for the contract. It was important to represent not only the various departments in each hotel but also the local's "extreme diversity," with members from China, East and West Africa, Haiti and the Caribbean, Central and South America, and elsewhere around the world, such that one group rarely constituted a majority.

Eusebio was one such leader who'd been recruited in the lead-up to the citywide convention. He had become involved with the union right away after starting at the W in 2010 as a bellman, helping to organize the hotel under a card check agreement the union had negotiated with Starwood. The W was his first job ever—he was newly in the workforce after studying hospitality at Fisher College—but he was already frustrated with the low pay and myriad responsibilities that seemed to go far beyond his job title. "I was doing not only the bellmen's job, I was also the runner, and there was no houseman after six o'clock, so any call for houseman duty was me too. So I was doing all of that and getting paid six dollars per hour" before tips. After talking with another door attendant from an already unionized hotel, the decision to support the union was an easy one. In the intervening years, however, Eusebio had more or less checked out. "We had shop stewards and everything, so I distanced myself for a bit," he said. Still, he was the one whom coworkers went to when they had issues, and now the local's staff organizers had gone to him as well. Eusebio agreed to attend the citywide convention.

The agenda of the convention was equal parts political education and planning, recapping the local's ongoing transformation under its last three presidents to focus on both raising contract standards and growing the power of the union through organizing, and looking ahead to how the hotel contract fight would continue that work. For many longtime members, it was a history they had helped to make: a history that included dramatic improvements to the union's health plan, the creation of a first-of-its-kind homeownership assistance fund, and of course the recent establishment of the union pension and strike fund. When Aliferis first started at the Parker House in the early 1980s, he paid $500 every three months for health insurance. Forty years later, union members paid just $12 per week, or just over $150 every three months for family coverage, even as the overall (and therefore employer-borne) cost of coverage had increased dramatically.

For Saihua Deng, the union's progress could also be seen in steady improvements to room attendant workloads—measured in terms of the number of rooms or "credits" that attendants were assigned to clean per shift—from contract to contract. Given the physically exhausting and often debilitating work of rushing to make dozens of beds and scrub over a dozen bathrooms in the course of eight hours, a reduction of even one credit made a huge difference. Deng had worked as a room attendant at the Newbury Boston, a Highgate Hotel, for thirteen years and served as shop steward for her coworkers. When she first started, the citywide standard was sixteen credits per shift. In the next contract, room attendants were able to win a citywide "room drop" to fifteen. But Deng thought that fifteen wasn't good enough, especially given the time it took to travel between the hotel's two buildings and because management had long assigned just thirteen credits to room attendants working in one of the buildings while matching the citywide standard for the other. The system was unfair, and she had organized her coworkers to fight back. It took eight years and two turnovers in management, but Deng and the rest of the Newbury room attendants had eventually won an additional room drop for their hotel, above and beyond the citywide contract. "My whole department was really united, and we worked together because it was affecting our job," she said. "We really wanted to fight for it and we never gave up, even eight years, every year I would fight. Every time the manager changed we would fight." Deng knew that getting a hotel to agree to fewer than fifteen credits was possible, but she also knew better than anyone the work that it would take to win.

By that point, members' contract priorities were beginning to coalesce around key issues: equality and respect, healthcare for all, full employment, and real retirement. Members at the convention broke off into small groups, once by department and once mixed with other departments, to discuss the priorities and continue to bring forward issues that had surfaced at each hotel. They also began to talk about what it would take to actually win their demands from the various hotel employers. "I went to the convention meeting and I saw everybody together. . . . I was like, *Wow, this is different. I didn't know it was like this.* We were getting organized," remembered Eusebio.

Workers came away from the citywide convention with assignments to start holding weekly committee meetings within their hotels as a way of continuing to build toward negotiations. For newly identified leaders like Eusebio, the convention had lit a spark. "I wanted to get more involved. I wanted to have a voice. I wanted to make decisions. I wanted to have control," he said. A leadership group within the W formed and started meeting regularly. "I was leading the organization in the hotel without even being the shop steward."

With thirty-four hotels gearing up for contract negotiations, each was in a different place in terms of existing level of organization. At the Westin Boston Waterfront, another Marriott property that had first organized under Starwood management in 2000, there were a few union stalwarts, but most people were no longer involved. "You have a few diehards who people listen to, but it was never enough. . . . We didn't have a team there that was enough to move people," said Courtney Leonard, a server in the lobby bar. She'd worked non-union and union hotel jobs before being hired at the Westin Waterfront, a hotel her mother had helped to open. When a Local 26 staff organizer asked her if she would consider coming out on union leave to help build a team that could really move people, she said no, twice. But after dropping in on the citywide convention and volunteering with the union for a few weeks, she finally said yes. In February 2018 she left her server job to organize full-time, an opportunity created by language in the existing contract that allowed members to take time off from the hotel to temporarily join the union staff. "Literally I'd just sit in the cafeteria all day, eight hours a day, ten hours a day, just talking to people that I've worked with for so long." For Leonard, it was important that voices from the food and beverage department were heard, particularly on issues like sexual harassment and pay disparities. But she also wanted to make sure that people across departments were hearing and understanding each other's issues.

As the leadership committee in each hotel organized its coworkers around the key contract priorities and continued to add new items under the primary themes identified in citywide conversations, the local also began to focus on negotiations strategy. Hotel workers had generated a transformational set of demands to bring to the bargaining table. How were they going to win them?

All In on Marriott

It seemed clear from the beginning that Marriott would be the limiting factor on what Boston hotel workers would be able to achieve in
their next contract citywide. As the largest company and the most historically anti-union, they were the "biggest worst" in terms of Boston
hotel employers. In early 2018, following up on the citywide convention, over four hundred workers from the various union hotels came together once again to determine what that would mean for their strategy.
They decided to go all in on Marriott, negotiating from start to finish
with the company before beginning negotiations with Omni, Highgate,
Fairmont, or any of the smaller players. Workers would demand that
other hotel companies agree up front to "Me Too" agreements—binding
the companies to the outcome of the Marriott negotiations. Those hotels
that agreed could shield themselves from a strike. Hotels that refused to
sign had no such guarantee. In either case, however, their negotiations
would have to wait.

Aliferis, Seale, Deng, Flannery, and other leaders at non-Marriott
hotels concentrated on pressuring their employers to sign Me Toos and
talking with their coworkers about just how significant the Marriott
negotiations would be for them. At hotels across Boston, workers
marched on their human resources offices to delegate management with
the Me Too demand. Roughly half of the hotels signed. "They believed
that Marriott was going to take Local 26 on. So whatever comes up with
Marriott, they couldn't hope for anything better," said Seale. "Or, they
just didn't want to be bothered with it [so] they would sign on to the
Me Too. And there's some places that held out that wanted to have their
own thing."

At the same time, a formal bargaining committee had come together,
made up of both established shop stewards and new leaders like Eusebio
and Leonard. Crucially, the committee included both Marriott and non-
Marriott workers. If the Marriott contract would ultimately be extended
to hotels citywide, non-Marriott workers needed a seat at the table in determining what the contract would say. The committee numbered thirty-
four; there were fourteen Marriott workers and twenty non-Marriott
workers, plus President Brian Lang, and the financial secretary-treasurer,
Carlos Aramayo. The union also planned to have open negotiations for

the first time, encouraging any hotel member from across the city to attend.

After a year of preparations—for members like Leonard and Wei, who had also come out on union leave, countless hours spent in the hotel cafeteria—and with the contract expiration looming, the union had built an organizing structure citywide. After months of developing and distilling contract demands through conversations within and across hotels, and increasingly through communication with unionized Marriott workers in other cities also headed into negotiations, one over-riding theme had emerged: One Job Should Be Enough.

Big Bargaining

Deng had been a union member for fourteen years, but she had never been to negotiations. "Before, when there were negotiations, they were never open like that, where everybody can come and watch. . . . The union always had the committee to go to the negotiations and sit down with the hotel managers, but this time they were open," she said. "Everybody can go to the meetings, can go to sit there and listen to the whole conversation. The whole meeting, the whole time, you can go and watch." Negotiations began in a too-small conference room in the Boston Convention Center. "They put us in a room that was about the size of a closet," said Leonard. "I remember being out in the hallway and we were all chanting 'cause there's probably three or four hundred of us." Marriott eventually paid for a bigger room.

As negotiations bounced between banquet halls and union halls, things started slow and stayed slow. But with hundreds of their coworkers watching, the bargaining committee hammered the company on the core themes of the campaign, while connecting them to workers' lives. Leonard remembered a banquet server sharing her story of losing two children to overdoses and being unable to qualify for health insurance because she worked on-call at several hotels. "I'm standing there beside her because I just don't know how else to be helpful," said Leonard. "And the company's faces are just blank. . . . I don't know how you listen to stuff like that." Leonard herself stood up to share her own story about being sexually harassed on the job. "I think making them listen to us was one of the most powerful things I got out of bargaining. . . . Everybody was so willing to be so raw and so open in those meetings." For Leonard, those moments were as much about the other members in the room as the company. "It helped build everybody as a stronger team, opened everybody's eyes."

Union members would meet for an hour before the company arrived for negotiations, with bargaining committee members gathering even earlier. "We would all talk before we met with the company," said Eusebio. "We already knew what was the plan, what was the goal." Lang took the lead as negotiator, but according to Eusebio, "We already knew what he was going to say. He was just on that message. And we stayed on message. . . . Very disciplined, that's how we did it." During caucuses, members would go around the room sharing input on next steps. Their discipline was tested when the company first put raises on the table—proposing to pay for them out of healthcare savings, money that workers had already negotiated in the previous contract. "It was so hard to believe because of who they are and what they're supposed to stand for," said Silva, the Ritz-Carlton banquet server. "It's just unbelievable how little they wanted to give us." But everyone stayed on the program. "To me it was a strong showing of the committee structure that we had. Both the bargaining committee and the organizing committee were that strong because how do you get that many people in a room who don't want to explode?" said Leonard.

For Marriott workers and non-Marriott workers alike, the company's wage proposal made it clear where things were headed. "Starwood—negotiations, anything you ask, they don't want any problems, they are peaceful," said Gebrelibanos, the room attendant from the Westin Copley. Marriott, on the other hand, wouldn't agree to anything. "That set the standard that it was going to be a tough fight and they weren't going to give an inch and we had to be more together than ever," said Seale. For Gebrelibanos, the explanation for the company's strategy was obvious: "Marriott was taught that no one will come out for a strike." Local 26 had taken strike votes as part of its last three hotel contract campaigns, but hotel workers in Boston had still never been out on strike. The company seemed happy to wait the union out at the bargaining table on the assumption that this time around would be no different.

Marriott on Strike!

Local 26 members had anticipated that winning their key contract priorities from Marriott might require escalating to an open-ended strike. As negotiations dragged on, leadership committees within each Marriott hotel continued to build and test their level of organization to gauge if they were ready, not only to win a strike vote but engage in an actual strike. Between negotiation sessions, Leonard led her first delegation to her general manager: "I was like, 'Oh my God, I'm going to faint, I'm going to faint, I'm going to faint,'" she said. But when she saw the crowd of coworkers behind her, she knew she had to go through with it. Other days, workers at the Westin Waterfront "buttoned up" by wearing union buttons to work, staged a march in front of the human resources office, and did a silent action in the hotel lobby. "All of that was so necessary. . . . Through all those things, you could slowly see people building confidence in each other, confidence in me," she said. On Labor Day, Leonard, Wei, and other hotel workers staged a civil disobedience action near Copley Square, risking arrest. Two weeks later, the bargaining committee called for a strike authorization vote.

Marriott's surrender-nothing approach had allowed the leadership committees within each hotel time to build toward a strike through structure tests. Several months of negotiations had also allowed Marriott contracts in other major hotel markets—including San Francisco, Honolulu, Kauai, Detroit, Oakland, San Diego, and San Jose—to expire, and hotel workers around the country were now uniting under the banner of "One Job Should Be Enough." In San Francisco, UNITE HERE Local 2 had adopted a similar citywide "big bargaining" strategy, with a bargaining committee of over 120 rank-and-file leaders from Marriott and non-Marriott hotels. Lead negotiators from various UNITE HERE locals had also been in close communication with one another, even bringing some global demands to the company to try to resolve them uniformly across hotels. If Boston Marriott workers were to go on strike, it looked increasingly likely that they wouldn't be alone.

Strike preparations were well underway, but Eusebio, the bargaining committee member from the W, still didn't feel ready to give up on negotiations. "I was really, really, really scared," he said. "I'm young in the labor force, and the first couple of years, I was not great with my money. . . . In my mind, I was like, if I'm thirty, I should be in a better financial situation." Other members of the committee were also grappling with what it would mean to go on strike, even as they urged their coworkers to pledge to vote yes. "I had just recently been divorced, and my mom lives with me," said Silva, the banquet server from the Ritz-Carlton. "She's ninety-eight, and it was just hard to go out there and not know, not having a paycheck every week. It was a very hard decision to make." Wei, the room attendant from the Sheraton, had two kids in college. "I was very scared because my household gets more income from me. My husband works in a factory. They never have benefits, they never have increased their wages since he's worked there over fifteen years. So in my family, my income is important." The potential sacrifices of going on strike were daunting. But after witnessing firsthand that months at the negotiating table had yielded little, the bargaining committee saw a strike as the only way to achieve the ambitious goals they'd set for the contract.

On September 12, Marriott workers voted 96 percent in support of strike authorization, with 77 percent participating. The strike was going to happen, whether Eusebio felt ready for it or not. "I got on board and I knew it was the right thing," he said. He talked with his girlfriend and his mom and started planning out a strike budget for himself. At the next negotiation session, workers busied themselves assembling picket signs. When the company had nothing to present, they were chanted out of the room for the second time. On October 3, Boston Marriott workers were officially on strike. Over the course of the next week, Marriott workers in seven other cities would join them.

For workers on strike, walking the picket line and staffing strike support became a full-time job, with members signing up for a set picket shift and collecting strike pay. Members at non-Marriott hotels continued to go to work, but also rallied to support the strikers. Deng's hotel, the Newbury, had once been a part of the Ritz-Carlton, and she and the other room attendants still knew many of the workers there. "After work every day, we walked to the Ritz-Carlton to support the people," she said. "We are kind of like brother, sister, before, helping each other. We know each other. So when they go on strike, we go there to support them." Though Seale wished that the union's strategy had included taking all of the union hotels in the city out on strike together, he was committed to doing what he could to make the Marriott-only strike successful. "We would try to figure out times before work, after work, in my case in between work, where we could go to different hotels and be on the picket line with Marriott workers. Because they essentially were fighting for us." Seale's hotel had signed a Me Too agreement, so whatever contract resulted from the strike would become the new contract for his hotel. Members who were still working at non-Marriott hotels also signed up to authorize a $10-per-week additional payroll deduction to bolster the union's strike fund in recognition that the striking workers were taking home significantly less in strike pay from their hotels than they would otherwise.

With the vast majority of Marriott workers across seven Boston hotels out on strike, negotiations continued. But it soon became clear that the company was taking advantage of the sessions to draw energy and attention away from the picket lines. It was a boss strategy to wear down the workers. The bargaining committee made the decision to shrink down to a smaller group of ten leaders from the Marriott properties and focus their energy on keeping the strike going strong. The negotiating committee continued to report out to the picket lines through daily picket updates, phone calls, texts, and flyers. But the power of a supermajority strike was what was going to make the company agree to the workers' core demands. "It was almost winter time, we were outside from 7 a.m. to 7 p.m. at each door in Marriott, marching and yelling," said Gebrelibanos, who moved to Boston from Ethiopia in 1994. "I come from a very different country, and for me with Marriott it was a war. . . . We had to stand up there and fight."

After forty-six days on strike, and one failed settlement attempt, the negotiating committee reached a tentative agreement with Marriott on November 17, on the heels of agreements reached by striking Marriott workers in Detroit, Oakland, San Jose, and San Diego. By that time, the smaller committee was meeting with the company in the office of then-mayor Marty Walsh. Eusebio, who'd remained on the committee throughout, remembered crying with happiness when it was all over. He called his girlfriend, then his coworkers. The bell and door departments, his group, had won a five-dollar per hour raise. "You know, I said it and everything in the meeting, but inside me I was like, we won't get five dollars. Maybe two dollars." Not only that, but they had secured a higher vacation wage to make up for lost tips. After years of never taking a vacation, his coworkers could finally use their vacation days. They'd gotten everything they'd asked for.

Winning for Everyone

As Marriott workers convened at the Hynes Convention Center the next day to ratify the contract, the news kept getting better. The new agreement included increased funding for retirement, a cap on the use of the green choice program, new protections from sexual harassment, language addressing the implementation of new technology in the hotel, and wage increases across all departments. The union had also won the right to strike again—mid-agreement—if the company tried to subcontract out or eliminate food and beverage jobs. Wei, the Sheraton room attendant, also remembered tearing up as she spoke to the crowd of nearly a thousand Local 26 members who'd gathered to celebrate and cast their votes: "I said, 'We got it. We stayed together.' " She was especially proud of the older women in her department. "With the rain, with the snow, with the cold, people who are seventy years old stayed with us for the whole time. . . . In the history of our local, we never go on strike. So I feel very proud with my coworkers." Marriott workers voted 98 percent to ratify the agreement. By early December, Marriott settled with hotel workers in Hawaii and San Francisco as well, bringing strikes around the country to an end.

The Boston contract settlement was a victory not just for Marriott workers but for the many others at Omni, Highgate, and other smaller hotel companies who would see the same benefits under Me Too agreements. For some with property-specific issues to hash out, negotiations weren't over. Deng and her coworkers at the Newbury were quickly back at the bargaining table, this time with their own boss to address the impacts of an upcoming hotel renovation. But the Marriott strike had given them a massive boost, and they were able to win guaranteed income and six-figure buyout packages for food and beverage workers impacted by changes to the hotel restaurant. For other hotels without signed Me Toos, achieving the citywide standard set by the Marriott strike would take organizing toward a credible strike threat of their own. At the end of 2019, workers at the Battery Wharf Hotel, the final holdout in the city, went on strike. After seventy-nine days, they reached a tentative agreement under the terms of the Marriott contract, just over a year after it was initially settled.

7

━━◦◦((◦))◦◦━━

Hollow Applause (ver.di)

IN LATE 2020, DURING THE second peak of COVID-19 infections in Germany, wages for nurses and other healthcare workers at Berlin's public hospitals were up for renegotiation. The Tarifvertrag für den öffentlichen Dienst (TVöD), a national sectoral bargaining agreement negotiated by trade union Vereinte Dienstleistungsgewerkschaft—known as ver.di—covered not only public hospital employees but a total of 2.3 million workers employed by the German federal government and municipalities.

Berlin's two major public hospital systems, Vivantes and Charité, had been chronically understaffed before the pandemic struck. Under Germany's healthcare finance system, known as G-DRG (German Diagnosis-Related Group), flat fees for individual patient procedures created a strong incentive for hospital management to eliminate positions and save on staffing costs. With Berlin's public hospitals on the front lines of the city's COVID response, the problem became even worse. "It was just really bad," said Stella Merendino, an emergency room nurse at Vivantes Humboldt-Klinikum, one of the system's nine Berlin hospitals. "And the pandemic just came on top." As case counts spiked periodically throughout 2020 and into 2021, insufficient staffing left nurses and other healthcare workers questioning whether they could keep going. From the balconies of Berlin, healthcare workers received nightly applause. But inside the city's hospitals, they were on the brink. "We don't know how we survived," said Merendino. "We had colleagues sit downstairs

Rules to Win By. Jane F. McAlevey and Abby Lawlor, Oxford University Press. © Oxford University Press 2023.
DOI: 10.1093/oso/9780197690468.003.0008

in the changing room crying after their shifts and being completely alone." Merendino loved being an ER nurse. "You're the one thing that is standing between a patient and potential death. You make a difference right in the moment. . . . You're right there and are the person who is helping them right now and is there for them in basically their worst days." But seeing hospital management's indifference to how nurses were struggling "was the kind of thing that made you doubt your whole job."

For some public healthcare workers experiencing peak frustration and despair, the 2020 negotiations offered an outlet—a way to build power with other essential workers in Berlin. When COVID began, "Everybody basically went into hiding," said Silvia Habekost, an anesthesia nurse at Vivantes Klinikum im Friedrichshain since 1988, and a longtime activist in ver.di and various political groups. "But we didn't." Habekost and other union activists from Vivantes joined with members from Charité to demand a "Corona Hospital Treaty" from the state of Berlin. The energy and collaboration carried forward into the TVöD negotiations that fall, with healthcare workers building support for a set of hospital-specific demands. After four days of warning strikes called by the national union, the TVöD settled in late October, with some nursing classifications securing raises well above the contract average.

Habekost, who had been organizing for decades to fight changes to the German healthcare system, saw the 2020 TVöD negotiations as a sign of progress. Against the backdrop of COVID-19, healthcare workers had been far more active than other workers in the public sector, and it showed in the final agreement. She and other organizers had been successful in signing up "quite a few" new ver.di members. And after years of conversation about the prospect of nurses from Vivantes and Charité taking action together, they had finally done it.

But for other public hospital workers in Berlin, the TVöD negotiations seemed like business as usual. Anja Voigt, an intensive care nurse at Vivantes Neukölln Hospital in Berlin and another longtime member of ver.di, felt detached from the process and from her union. "You have a working fight every two years, it's every time the same. The union says, 'So that's your demand. The demand this year is 2 percent more in wages.' " As Voigt described it, "It's like a film. . . . It was every time, okay, I get a little bit more wages this year and they're sending two workers in front of my hospital with a trade union flag for one day or two days, as just like a symbol. No real action or fighting."

When it came to the TVöD, Voigt saw her union as a distant third party, negotiating on her behalf: "These white men sitting in the closed room, and the press gets informed of the results before the union members get the results." But for Merendino and her coworkers in the ER, the 2020 negotiations hadn't even registered, though the need for collective action was very much on their minds. "We were all very dissatisfied and very sad about everything. And in the summer of 2020 we thought for the first time about striking. Like, we had colleagues say, 'You know what, if we're so important right now, why don't we strike now that it hurts them the most?' But it was always just a thought. We didn't know that people were actually planning something like that." Like a majority of workers across both hospital systems at the time, Merendino wasn't a member of her union. Working in the Humboldt-Klinikum ER, she didn't know anyone who was involved in the organizing efforts. But all of that would soon change.

Sectoral Shortcomings

The TVöD had successfully secured wage increases for healthcare workers and a modest COVID bonus to acknowledge their service during the pandemic. But it left untouched *the* pressing issue for nurses and other healthcare workers: the staffing crisis in German hospitals. In Germany, staffing levels had traditionally been treated as within the purview of management, and beyond the scope of ver.di's national sectoral negotiations. But in other countries, staffing levels were not only routinely (though contentiously) negotiated, but staffing demands were core drivers of organizing among nurses and other healthcare workers. Staffing impacted all aspects of workers' experience on the job—first and foremost their capacity to provide quality care to their patients.

German public hospitals had also exploited another aspect of the German sectoral system and low levels of worker organization by outsourcing large portions of their workforces. The hospital systems no longer directly employed therapists working in clinical settings, laboratory assistants, cleaners, transportation, kitchen workers, and other support staff. These workers were instead hired through subsidiaries. This in turn meant they could be paid below the wage standard set by the TVöD. Because these subsidiaries weren't signatories to the sectoral agreement, they didn't have to abide by its terms. All in all, seven different Vivantes subsidiaries employed more than twenty-five hundred workers outside the bounds of the TVöD. Despite working through the same pandemic, the outsourced staff received neither the raises nor the COVID bonuses paid out to their coworkers covered by the sectoral agreement. The low wages also created their own staffing pressures, with the public clinics unable to compete with private facilities for therapists and other staff.

Lynn Stephainski had worked at one of Vivantes's rehabilitation centers for four years as a physiotherapist. Stephainski was hired at the outset by a Vivantes subsidiary, but a small handful of her more senior coworkers had been direct employees at Vivantes's main hospital before transferring to the clinic upon its opening. As a result, they were still paid the higher wages set by the TVöD. But Stephainski and all newer hires at the clinic were paid far lower. "It's completely stupid. They do the same exact work as I do," said Stephainski, "but I get a thousand euros less." Unbound by the national public sector agreement, the wages and working conditions of the subsidiary employees became a convenient place for employers to cut corners and costs. This two-tier outcome was a close cousin to union-busting contract proposals in the United States, which maintained higher wages and benefits such as pensions for an existing workforce but eliminated them for new hires. In both cases, two-tiering set the stage for the union standard to decay over time and created new divisions within the workforce that employers could continue to exploit to their advantage.

The ability for German employers to exit sectoral agreements— whether through the backdoor of outsourcing, or by directly renouncing their participation in signatory associations—has led to a steady decline in coverage. Though the German sectoral bargaining system still produced collective agreements that covered many more workers, ver. di faced many problems familiar to US labor unions: low membership, even lower levels of worker participation, and a sense among workers that the union was engaged in negotiations on their behalf rather than an organization of and for the workers themselves. Without sustained worker organizing and a credible threat of mass strikes, sectoral negotiations were artificially constrained to a set of heavily moderated demands unlikely to drive additional employer exits from the sectoral negotiations. Though workers could negotiate at the company level on topics not addressed sector-wide, doing so risked the issue being eventually elevated to the sectoral table and potentially watered down as a result.

Such employer gamesmanship flourished in the absence of worker organizing. Despite the risk that employers would continue to exploit the dual tracks of the sectoral system to their advantage, the open issues of staffing and outsourcing gave Berlin healthcare workers a direct strategic opportunity to continue organizing and fighting back. With a strong investment from the national union, the progress Habekost had been a part of in late 2020 exploded in 2021, with the existing core of activists working to identify hundreds of new organic leaders and sign up thousands of new members in teams and departments like Merendino's emergency room. This time, the company-level negotiations seemed unequivocally to match the moment, with healthcare workers standing together across three negotiating tables to demand safe staffing and basic equality. Against the backdrop of Germany's first post-Merkel federal elections, and state and local races in Berlin, hospital workers across the city took to the streets and ultimately struck together under the banner of "Berliner Krankenhausbewegung" (the Berlin hospital movement) to jointly demand "Mehr Personal & TVöD für alle" (more staffing and the TVöD standards for all workers). Voigt herself was at the negotiations table along with Habekost and twenty-three other coworkers representing teams and departments across the hospital system. An extensive network of newly elected delegates stood by to make any decisions as a larger body. At the same time, Charité healthcare workers and Stephainski and other staff employed by Vivantes subsidiaries were also at the table. All in all, a total of 75 tariff commission members and 750 delegates participated directly in contract negotiations across the three units. The delegate system and the accompanying organizing structure not only produced a successful monthlong strike but made healthcare workers a political force in the Berlin parliamentary elections.

Staffing Up

Like Silvia Habekost, Dana Lützkendorf was one of several key leaders in the 2021 Berlin hospital movement who had seen privatization and the profit motive seep into the German healthcare system over the course of twenty years. An intensive care nurse at one of Charité's three Berlin hospitals, she had just started her nursing career when Germany transitioned to a financing system called DRG in the early 2000s. Under DRG, hospitals received a flat fee for patient procedures, which in practice translated to the DRG payments underwriting the staff portion of the budget. As public funding for hospital infrastructure, maintenance, and repairs lagged, hospital management dramatically reduced staff to make up the difference. The advent of DRG not only caused public hospitals to act more like private companies but also spurred the growth of the actual private healthcare sector in Germany, which skimmed profitable procedures and left costly cases to the public system. As nurse-to-patient ratios plummeted, Lützkendorf became an active ver.di member and began educating herself about the state of nursing globally.

When Lützkendorf first became involved in negotiations in 2011, "the bargaining was all about wages. But we expected the hospitals would try to cut personnel. We knew that our situation would not improve if we didn't fight for more personnel. So that really became the core question for us." Lützkendorf started talking with other activists about the issue of staffing and realized that the TVöD's silence created an opportunity: under German labor law, they could negotiate a separate company-level agreement to fill in any issues not addressed under the sectoral agreement. Though theoretically possible, they also knew it wouldn't be easy. "It's quite a high barrier in Germany because usually it's the authority of management to deal with these issues. We were quite aware that in order to have a collective bargaining arrangement around staffing, we'd need a lot of support and to be quite strong," said Lützkendorf.

In 2015, healthcare workers at Charité took an important first step by striking for ten days to demand a company-level agreement addressing staffing. Though the language they negotiated proved difficult to meaningfully enforce, they had successfully established that Charité workers could have a voice in their employer's staffing decisions. Staffing was no longer merely a management prerogative. The strike made an impression on Berlin's political left and helped to inspire other German nurses, who soon improved upon the standard set at Charité through their own company-level agreements.

Following the 2015 campaign at Charité, healthcare workers in the German cities of Mainz and Jena launched campaigns to win staffing standards through company-level agreements, each effort building on the last. These campaigns were bolstered by staff support from a group of organizers hired by ver.di known as "Organizi.ng," who had come to specialize in expanding the ranks of union membership through issue-focused campaigns and the development of new rank-and-file leaders, and from mentoring and coaching by this book's coauthor Jane McAlevey. After the successes in Mainz and Jena, both were looking for the opportunity to support Lützkendorf and other ver.di members at Charité and bring the staffing fight back to Berlin. A 2017 attempt to reach a new staffing agreement through another strike had largely fizzled, and Lützkendorf and the core group of union activists needed new strategies to move forward.

David Wetzel joined the nursing staff at Charité's Benjamin Franklin medical center shortly before the 2017 strike. He had attended demonstrations in support of Charité nurses in 2015 while still in training at a small Catholic hospital in Berlin and had become more and more involved in politics as he learned firsthand about the German healthcare system. He was eager to get involved in organizing, but talking with his coworkers, it seemed like many felt disillusioned in the staffing agreement aftermath. "They had great expectations with the strike, but they got disappointed," he said.

Though the 2015 strike had garnered significant participation from workers, the contract negotiations themselves were led by a group of just five union members and two union officials. In 2017, the campaign was similarly closed off. "It was a group of I think around twenty people, maybe only fifteen people. And of course they were highly politically motivated. They knew each other for a long time because they were fighting for better payment way back in 2011 . . . and then between 2015 and 2017, this group more or less stayed the same." Meanwhile, other nurses seemed frustrated that the 2015 negotiations hadn't yielded more and lacked an understanding of why. After five days of striking, workers voted to go back to work without reaching a new agreement. Lützkendorf knew that something had to change in their organizing. But, she said, "not everybody wanted or was able to take that step. Some of the old activists dropped out. But others found it a very good development."

In early 2019, McAlevey's organizing primer *No Shortcuts* was released in German, and by the end of the year, Lützkendorf, Wetzel, and a small group of other politically active Berlin healthcare workers from both Charité and Vivantes had joined McAlevey's Organizing for Power trainings through the Rosa Luxemburg Institute alongside staff from Organizi.ng. The book, and the accompanying trainings, gave workers a shared vocabulary and set of tools for talking about the kind of union and movement they were trying to build. They realized that to be successful, they would have to go beyond existing union strongholds like Lützkendorf's ICU and find new organic leaders in new departments. McAlevey's emphasis on power structure analysis also prompted them to strategize about what it meant for their hospital systems to operate as extension of the Berlin state, and the political opportunities it might create.

By 2020, the issue of outsourcing at Charité and Vivantes had also begun to take on momentum. That year, therapists employed at Vivantes's main hospital struck and won their demand to be hired back as direct Vivantes employees. But therapists at the systems' rehabilitation clinics and hospital support staff were left behind. "Patients came to us and friends came up to us and said, 'Ah, congratulations! You're back in the big hospital and getting paid better!'" said physiotherapist Stephainski. "And we said, 'No, no, no, it was the other therapists.' We started to think about what is now wrong." Subsidiary workers at Charité were already fighting their own company-level agreement on wages. Stephainski and other rehabilitation workers started to meet together and to reach out to workers from the other Vivantes subsidiaries. They also got in touch with officials at ver.di about commencing company-level negotiations. In November 2020, they began negotiations. But with COVID cases spiking, the sessions didn't last long.

Three Units, Two Demands, One Deadline

By late 2020, in the wake of the TVöD settlement and with the threat of COVID-19 still looming, a growing cross-hospital coordinating committee, along with organizers from Organizi.ng, had the loose contours of a plan to win meaningful staffing standards in Berlin's public hospitals and significant raises and benefits for the subsidiary workers. Lützkendorf had by this time gained a national leadership position within ver.di, heading the department of health, social services, welfare, and churches, and had successfully secured support for the campaign, which would once again unite workers from Berlin's two major public systems: Charité and Vivantes. The lack of progress in negotiations for Vivantes's subsidiary workers created the opportunity for them to join as well. Together, the three units had two simple overarching demands: more staffing and the sectoral wage standards for all workers. Because Charité's outsourced workers had recently settled a company-level agreement addressing wages, they would not directly participate, nor would workers employed by a joint Charité-Vivantes subsidiary. The campaign would also deliberately aim to create a crisis not only for the management of the two hospital systems, but for the Berlin politicians who oversaw them.

The plan matched the scope of workers' ambition and was strategically timed. Together, Charité and Vivantes accounted for over 40 percent of the hospital beds in the state of Berlin. Against the backdrop of the pandemic, public awareness of and appreciation for healthcare workers was appropriately high. And Berlin was headed into elections at the city, state, and federal levels, with Chancellor Angela Merkel and the governing mayor of Berlin both announcing they would not run for reelection. Lützkendorf, Wetzel, Habekost, and others who had gone through the Organizing for Power trainings began to recruit their coworkers to the cause. Unlike in 2015 and 2017, where worker involvement at Charité largely consisted of activist nurses in the intensive care unit and a few other departments, this time the initial group of organizers planned to cast a much wider net. They needed to identify leaders in each station in the hospital—oncology, anesthesiology, emergency, intensive care—and talk to their coworkers who weren't nurses. This included midwives, X-ray technicians, and other nondoctor healthcare workers covered under the terms of the TVöD, as well as the subsidiary workers, many of whom worked in different facilities or shifts.

To begin building and strengthening democratic structures within each unit, workers held initial elections to establish a skeleton tariff commission, or negotiations committee, to make an initial bargaining demand to each employer and to get the campaign off the ground. But because a central goal was to identify new organic leaders, workers planned to hold a second election later in the campaign to fill out the tariff commission and to elect a second, much larger delegate body. Under ver.di rules for the healthcare sector, tariff commission membership was limited to twenty-five workers and twenty-five alternates. Though the commission was required to reflect gender parity, it was otherwise elected at large. In contrast, the coordinating committee planned that the delegate body would be elected team by team, with one delegate for every ten workers, up to a maximum of four per team.

On March 1, the Berlin hospital movement was officially launched. By the end of the month, after numerous phone banks calling existing union members, 665 healthcare workers gathered together via Zoom to embark on the first majority structure test of the campaign: a joint petition across the nursing stations throughout both hospital systems directed not at management but at the Berlin government. The petition plainly set forth the campaign's dual demands: more staffing and the TVöD for all. The coordinating committee set a goal of majority participation, and after an additional training session, workers began circulating the petition among their coworkers along with an ask to become members of the union.

"We did it by the book," said Habekost, the anesthesia nurse who was among the original coordinating committee. "It was not like the few of us going through the hospitals and collecting signatures. We wanted to find organic leaders in the teams, and they would then sign up their coworkers." ER nurse Merendino was one such leader who quickly emerged during the signature-gathering process. After hearing about the campaign from an organizer from Organizi.ng, Merendino had one question: "When can we start?" She immediately signed up to become a ver.di member for the first time and went to work. "I think it took me with two colleagues two or three weeks to get 85 to 90 percent of the employees organized in the union," she said of the emergency department at her hospital. Soon she moved on to talking with workers in other stations. "We would do our shifts and then afterwards we would go through the wards," said Merendino. "I talked to people and they would listen to us because they would see someone like them. We were still in scrubs and we were talking to them about how we finally want to change something." Merendino described nurses as "just very pessimistic, I guess." But, she said, "if you have a few members that are really active, well, they drop basically like dominos."

The petition set the tone for the negotiations to come, signaling mass participation, unity, and solidarity across the two hospital systems, and a new focus on Berlin's politicians as the people with the power to improve conditions in the state's public hospitals. In April, the campaign's community organizing kicked off with a Berlin city assembly, which drew over four hundred participants, including members of Berlin's activist left, members of various political parties, and other trade unionists. On May 12, the dual organizing focus was again on display when five hundred workers and five hundred community members jointly delivered the final petition—two banners containing 8,397 signatures—to Berlin's city hall. They had reached their goal: well over a majority of the nurses across Vivantes and Charité. With the petition came a hundred-day ultimatum. If workers' demands weren't met by August 20, just over a month before the Berlin elections, healthcare workers across the city would go on strike. Underscoring the threat, Vivantes rehabilitation workers chose the same day for a one-day warning strike.

Delegate Democracy

With the first majority actions behind them—a highly public petition to Berlin politicians and the announcement of their hundred-day ultimatum—it was time to hold the next round of leadership elections for the campaign. The coordinating committee had a vision for the delegate body to play a direct and important role in the negotiations process, helping to ensure transparency, high participation, and democratic decision-making. Though ver.di's tariff commission structure, with its limited composition, posed challenges for big and open negotiations, workers hoped that having a full tariff commission and a large and representative delegate body would still enable them to deepen their coworkers' involvement, understanding, and control over the negotiations process. But in order for both bodies to be effective, they would have to be representative of all workers who would be covered by the three agreements.

Denise Klein-Allerman became a union member when she first started working as a midwife at Vivantes Klinikum im Friedrichshain in 2013—her father told her she had to—but had never been actively involved. She didn't see other midwives organizing with the union, just nurses. But that changed after a meeting in early 2021 with a midwife who had been a part of the staffing fight in Mainz. Klein-Allerman recalled the midwife describing how "the conditions got so bad that she had the feeling that she had to do something" and could immediately relate. She also took the midwife's campaign advice to heart. "She said, 'There has to be a midwife on the tariff commission. Otherwise your voice is not heard.'" From that point on, said Klein-Allerman, "it was just an impulse that if there is no midwife that wants to do it, I would do it. . . . You know this feeling that you have to do it, otherwise it is a lost chance? If there's no midwife, we won't have a chance." In April, Klein-Allerman and one of her coworkers, midwife Kim Lenzen from Vivantes Humboldt-Klinikum, were elected to the tariff commission to represent midwives. "It never happened before that two midwives were in the tariff commission," said Klein-Allerman. Both midwives took the "once-in-a-lifetime chance" of representing their colleagues seriously, visiting the delivery stations at other Vivantes hospitals and helping to recruit and support the midwife elected to the Charité tariff commission as well.

In order to bring forward new leaders who had never been involved in the past, the campaign's coordinating committee made two important structural choices. First, rather than select delegates from a list of workers who had self-nominated for the role, workers were presented with a blank ballot to vote for whichever coworker on their team they respected and trusted the most. Lenzen described the criteria she used for deciding which coworker to vote for: "When she says, 'We need to go on strike to get our terms right,' we must trust her and do as she says. Or when there's a demonstration and she gives the time and place, you come." For Klein-Allerman, "In my department, it was already clear who would be the team delegates. . . . My team already saw, okay, these three midwives are very motivated, they are very into the campaign already. So of course it was clear that they became the elected team delegation."

Second, each team was only able to select their representatives after a majority of workers within the team had completed a survey to weigh in on that team's demands. By ensuring that the elections took place in the context of majority engagement with and consideration of the team's specific negotiations proposals, this structure encouraged workers to select the coworker they felt would best carry their demands forward. Departments that lacked majority participation risked being left behind: their representation plainly depended on their level of organization. Though the campaign's basic goals had already been established, it was up to each team to determine what "more staff" meant to them. Ratifying each team's negotiations demand was no easy task but required surveying a majority of workers on each team, followed by lengthy deliberations on what staffing levels made sense on each shift in each station. "The first sentence was everywhere, 'We want more staff,' " said intensive care nurse Voigt. "It's easy to say. But then we were asking, 'Okay, what do you mean more staff? . . . How many patients can you care for in one shift?' " Only when a team had hashed out these questions and reached majority consensus could they select their representatives. "In the end, we had a lot of demands," said Voigt, laughing. "But for me it was the best way to do the thing."

Throughout this same period, the campaign's political and community organizing efforts were also highly targeted, with rolling petition deliveries to politicians in districts with Vivantes or Charité hospitals, followed by public rallies outside the hospitals themselves. "We were their district hospitals," said Merendino, "so it was their business to deal with it. It wasn't just only a big Berlin thing. It was district per district per district per district. So every politician knew what was going on and they had to do something, because we would be on their doorstep nearly every day. We would call them, we would email them, we would make appointments with them—with all the different parties."

By early July, a majority of teams had ratified their contract demands and selected their team delegates. After intensive work in small groups, it was time for them to come back together as a larger movement. Over two days in July, delegates from across all three units held a "delegate strike" and came together to plan for the dwindling days before their ultimatum expired. On July 9, after a day of training, delegates old and new were finally able to see the sheer scale of the organizing structure they had built when a thousand workers gathered at the Alte Försterei Football Stadium, home to the aptly named Union Berlin FC. Indeed, the event was a visual representation not only of the number of leaders who had emerged to lead the Berlin hospital movement, but the social power they carried with them: use of the stadium (and the support of the team) had been secured through workers' community organizing efforts in Neukölln, one of many significant social connections that had emerged as workers engaged in power structure analysis and comprehensive charting—identifying friends, family, and faith connections who could lend support.

The delegates convention at Alte Försterei allowed each bargaining unit to present their demands to the body as a whole. But the tariff commissions had also decided to vote on two other procedural matters before the delegate bodies that would buck established ver.di practice and set the stage for the negotiations ahead. First, the tariff commissions voted to signal that they would carry out negotiations as a full group and not shrink down to a smaller "negotiations team" as was commonly the practice. Second, the tariff commission took a formal vote to elevate the delegate body's role in negotiations, committing that they would not make any decisions at the negotiations table without consulting the delegates first. Though the language of "consultation" had been massaged to not impermissibly delegate the authority assigned to the tariff commission under the ver.di constitution, the commission members themselves were clear on what it meant: the delegate body, not the tariff commission, would be driving the decision-making in negotiations. In front of the thousand workers and several ver.di officials, the three tariff commissions confirmed, with official votes, that they would stick together and that the delegates were in control.

After the formal deliberations had come to an end, workers invited the top leaders of Berlin's three main political parties in for a presentation of their demands. Later, press and supporters were also invited. "We were kind of scared that if there are only a few people coming, it would just look really bad, that huge stadium," said Merendino, who spoke before the crowd that day. "But the seats were all taken. It was all full." The stadium's concession stands opened up on the football club's dime, and a party broke out to conclude the convention. "The football club actually made a banner on the other side of the stadium so that we could read it. It said something like, 'We stand behind you,' " remembered Merendino. "It was really, really cool. It was just a really amazing feeling."

No Emergency Contract, No Problem

With the September election looming on the horizon, and their ultimatum deadline quickly approaching, all three units began to look to escalate. The Vivantes subsidiary workers had held occasional negotiation sessions throughout 2021, but progress was slow despite multiple one-day warning strikes. Meanwhile, Charité management had finally signaled a willingness to start negotiations. On August 3, Vivantes subsidiaries held another one-day strike, and workers at both Vivantes and Charité decided to move forward with preparations for their own warning strikes. The first day of negotiations with Charité followed three days later, with each team presenting their demands: "We're saying, 'I'm from the radiology department. Our problems are one, two, three, and we as the radiology department of Charité are demanding . . . ,' " said Wetzel. "We had a PowerPoint presentation that went on for an hour, maybe an hour and a half." Charité management took a break, came back, and had nothing substantive to say in response. After the tariff commission and the delegates debriefed with workers at Vivantes, they decided to move forward with the first warning strike.

In the United States, healthcare workers are required to give notice prior to striking to allow their employers time to hire replacement workers to continue emergency services. Under the German system, which prohibits replacing striking workers, healthcare unions are required to maintain minimum staffing levels, effectively prohibiting a mass-participation strike. While the German prohibition on replacing striking workers gave strikes real power, in the healthcare industry, it had some complications. Before workers could protest the hospitals' refusal to negotiate, workers would have to negotiate an emergency contract with the very same hospitals.

They got nowhere. Still chastened by the 2015 strike, Charité management refused to reach an agreement. Vivantes management, which had shown itself to be particularly hostile throughout the campaign, took the same tack. So workers set out to decide for themselves what staffing levels were needed. They looked to previous emergency staffing agreements and how the hospital was currently staffed on its worst days. "We said we'll take the night-shift level," said Habekost, "which was still higher than the average of the last three months. I mean, that shows how really low the staffing levels are. And that's what we put into the agreement, and in the end the union signed it but management did not." Staffing levels had become so bad that management's status quo wasn't sufficient to care for emergency patients during the strike.

Though the German system of emergency strike staffing put workers at a disadvantage—unlike US healthcare workers, they couldn't use their strike to force the hospitals to take on an entirely new set of staff and the payroll that accompanied it—workers' solidarity across hospitals and units provided some strategic strength. Nurses and other care workers at the main hospitals would still be required to maintain emergency operations, but subcontracted workers who provided noncritical services and those working in nonemergency clinic settings could strike without qualification, shutting down whole facilities and operational segments. Indeed, as part of an earlier power structure analysis, workers had identified the stations that performed the biggest high-dollar nonemergency procedures, targeting their strike efforts where it would cost the hospitals the most.

But the hospitals' efforts to thwart the warning strike didn't stop at their refusal to negotiate. At 2 p.m. on the first day of the planned three-day warning strike in August, Vivantes management secured a legal injunction to block the strike. The idea that a public sector employer would seek to enjoin a labor action by German public sector employees was virtually unheard of. Charité management had expressly told workers they respected their right to strike. But the Vivantes human resources director, a transplant from the private healthcare sector, was clearly advising the hospital to adopt hardline anti-union tactics. Indeed, they had already successfully used the court to block two smaller actions: a one-day strike by Vivantes subsidiaries and the July delegate strike.

Vivantes's boss tactics were one thing—ultimately, to be expected. But the court going along with it was another. Upon news of the injunction, Vivantes workers crashed a meeting of the Social Democratic Party (SPD), Berlin's governing party, and refused to leave. The next day, the court lifted the injunction. On August 25, workers across all three units were on strike together for the first time in the campaign. Five days later, they began casting ballots to vote to embark on an open-ended strike.

Delegates Next Door

With the threat of an open-ended strike across Berlin's public hospitals and the election just weeks away, all three units began to negotiate in earnest. Workers had succeeded in organizing well over a hundred Berlin politicians, including forty sitting officials, to attend rallies, walkthroughs, and other events at their hospitals. The Berlin hospital movement was regularly in the news, with Merendino appearing in the newspaper and on TV and even publishing her own guest column on the staffing crisis. The pressure on both hospital systems was steadily mounting. On August 31, Vivantes management met with the tariff commission for the first time. Management immediately protested the presence of the full tariff commission, arguing that the room would only fit a group of ten. "It was really new for our employer, this big, strong tariff commission," said ICU nurse Voigt. "But we said, 'No, everybody or nobody.'" The tariff commission's insistence on attending negotiations as a full body also got some pushback from ver.di's negotiator, who declared it "not standard." But the tariff commission had taken the vote at Alte Försterei (the football stadium strike delegate conference) in anticipation of any resistance and stayed united. "So, okay," said Voigt, "we'll make new standards." In addition to a full tariff commission, the hundreds-member delegate body was also meeting simultaneously in another room, ready to weigh in if needed.

As at Charité, negotiations began with workers' presentation of a PowerPoint of the staffing demands from every team in the hospital. "Our employer was a little bit speechless," said Voigt. When the hospital's negotiators tried to bring up other issues to distract from the question of staffing, "We were straight on every time," said Voigt. "'Hey, come on, that's not what we want.' We didn't want to talk about new notebooks for our trainees. That's not important for us." Before they returned to the negotiations table a week later, the results of the strike vote had been announced, with union members voting over 97 percent yes across all three units to strike indefinitely.

After three more days of negotiations, the team delegates met at Berlin's Zion Church to discuss their progress and plan next steps. They decided to move forward with the open-ended strike. On September 9, the strike launched with one thousand healthcare workers gathering for a centralized demonstration. Though strike participation was limited by the emergency staffing requirements and the fact that only ver.di members could collect ongoing strike pay, workers nonetheless successfully shut down twenty-eight stations across both hospital systems.

For workers at Vivantes, the strike had not only provided the necessary pressure to get management to the negotiations table but had logistical upsides as well. Because cafeteria operations in the hospitals had closed as a result of the subsidiaries' strike, the space was available for delegates to gather during the negotiations. It was just down the hall from where the tariff commission would be sitting. The strike also freed up many of the delegates, who, unlike members of the tariff commission, did not receive paid release time for negotiations, to spend significant time in the cafeteria to consult and deliberate in person.

As negotiations progressed, the delegate body provided needed expertise and moral support to the tariff commission. "If you have any technical medical question, you can immediately get the answer," said Voigt, who served on the Vivantes tariff commission. "You can go next door and ask them and you not only have one, you have a hundred or sometimes three hundred people there, three hundred colleagues. So if I have a question about the ICU, I have ten colleagues from different ICUs. And so you have a really good answer in the end." When negotiations entered into marathon sessions, delegates provided an energy boost. "Sometimes we negotiated thirty-six hours into the night, and all the times they were there. You can go and talk with them, drink a coffee with them." Even when there was nothing new to report, the tariff commission would take breaks to check in with the delegate body to make sure they knew what was happening. "In the middle of the night, three o'clock, four o'clock, I'd go into the cafeteria and they were there. . . . They were waiting and supporting us," said Voigt. After starting out in a building ten minutes from the actual negotiations, Charité delegates were also eventually able to secure a space next to the negotiating room, remaining on call for any decisions that needed to be made during the negotiations process.

Tariff commission members routinely communicated with the delegates from the negotiations room using a Telegram group chat. When it came time to caucus or make a decision, the tariff commission would join the full delegate body for discussions and votes, the procedure they had chosen to adopt at Alte Försterei. Each delegate also had their own Telegram groups for coworkers on their teams that they would use to communicate live updates and get quick feedback. Direct communication from the negotiations room to the delegate body made for more efficient and productive caucuses. "We would inform delegates even before there was a pause in negotiations about what was going on and asked them to prepare and discuss some questions," said Lützkendorf, who served on the tariff commission at Charité. "So that when the negotiators came out of the room and came back to the delegates, they had already formed opinions and discussed the issue." Though early on in the campaign, workers had created and distributed more traditional bargaining updates via flyers, as more people became connected to the campaign through Telegram and social media, the delegates came to rely on rapid digital communication.

Voigt remembered a particularly heavy discussion when workers had to decide how the penalties for understaffing would function. They had already decided that, in order to enforce whatever staffing ratios were established, employees who worked when their team was short-staffed would earn points toward paid time off. Now they had to settle on the total number of points that would equal one paid day. Voigt's instinct was that three points made sense, but to her surprise, the team delegates were willing to take a more moderate position. "The team delegates in the end decided five points for one day off," she said. "I didn't understand this, but I had to accept this." Recognizing that negotiations involved compromise, Voigt found that compromises "are better understood when everyone is involved in the process." That was the value of the delegates. "We don't have to decide things with twenty-four people. We decided it with three hundred people." Though the tariff commission didn't immediately return to the negotiations room and reduce their demand, they knew the range within which to negotiate.

For Klein-Allerman, Lenzen, and the other Vivantes midwives, the key ratio under negotiations was how many births per year would be assigned to each midwife. Management, citing a German Hospital Association average of 127 births per midwife per year, offered to set the ratio at 110 births. Midwives had initially proposed 65 births per year. They explained to management everything that wasn't reflected in the proposed ratio, including births where the baby had died and unexpected emergencies. They stuck with their proposal. And management began to move. "Then it was a hundred births per year per midwife," said Lenzen. "Then they started to go down to 95 and we stayed with our 65 births the whole time. We wouldn't change anything about that. And Denise was like, 'Oh my God, we can't do this, we can't be like that. We need to get them something too.' And we said, 'No, we stay there. We stay low. They can come to us.'" After thirty hours of negotiations, management claimed impossibility. "Management sat there and said, 'I can't get any lower, I really can't do this.'" The proposed ratio would require hiring thirty-five new midwives. "How can I get these midwives?" the negotiator asked.

Over the course of the campaign, Klein-Allerman, Lenzen, and their coworkers had developed relationships with the midwives' "faculty association," a professional organization for German midwives, even bringing representatives into meetings with management. At the midwives' request, the faculty association quickly sent out an email to their membership asking if they would go to work at Vivantes if the staffing ratios improved. "After three days, 287 midwives from Berlin said, 'Yes, of course we would come back if the working terms would change.' And this was the point where I told the high management, 'You have enough midwives. I can give you the email addresses when we get this contract,'" said Lenzen.

Outside of negotiations, the strike remained strong. With just a few days before the Berlin elections, Berlin politicians and the leading political parties were being put to the test with repeated demands directly from healthcare workers to support the strike. On September 20, just a week shy of the elections, strikers held a huge meeting in Zion Church, with politicians from the major parties who were candidates in the elections. Though healthcare workers had successfully garnered media attention throughout the campaign, this meeting was purposefully closed to the press. In that setting, looking politicians from all major parties in the eyes, the healthcare workers shared their personal horror stories of trying to care for patients amid extreme staffing shortages—stories of deaths and serious damage to patient health that didn't have to happen. "I think this was the moment where the politicians really understood what happens in our hospitals," said Voigt. "This was the moment for me when they made some decisions that they didn't dare before." Healthcare workers' personal experiences, and the fear that their stories would become more public, had finally moved them.

Though the election one week later came and went without the planned settlement of the strike, less than twenty-four hours after the polls closed, Franziska Giffey, the victorious SPD candidate for mayor, showed up again to meet the striking workers at Zion Church, but now acting in her capacity as head of the state, not merely a candidate making promises. She signaled her immediate interest in settling the strike as she worked to secure a coalition government and appointed former SPD leader Matthias Patzeck to serve as mediator for the subsidiary negotiations. Negotiations at Charité began to pick up in intensity, and after twenty-five days on strike and twenty-one straight hours of negotiations, workers reached a tentative agreement on enforceable staffing ratios just before seven in the morning. They had shown that agreement was possible.

The strike at Charité was off, but workers continued to stand together, with a roving demonstration on October 9 drawing five thousand people, including workers from all three units. "We walked through the city from one point to another. And the atmosphere was really good because many people from Charité supported us," said Klein-Allerman. "They already had their contract, but we still knew that it's one big campaign, Charité and Vivantes. They have to work together. The Vivantes employees will profit from the contract between Charité people and the Charité management."

Three days later, Vivantes workers had a contract of their own. The hospital system's negotiator, said midwife Lenzen, "got this pressure from the side of her colleagues and the side of the politicians, and then Charité got their contract. And she started to negotiate with us." After that, things moved quickly, and soon the tariff commission had a proposed agreement to put before the delegates. "It was their voting, not the tariff commission, that decided to take this contract," said Voigt. "They voted for this. There were 250 people or a little bit more. So it was laid on a lot of shoulders. There were some compromises, and some were really hard for almost everybody." But at the end of the day, Vivantes workers had won their very first staffing agreement with ratios for every department. "A lot of us were very, very tired," said Voigt. "I imagined I was going home. But they're standing there, three hundred team delegates with champagne and confetti. It was such a great moment. So we made a little party."

With mediation ongoing and the other two units settling their strikes, the Vivantes subsidiaries stayed on strike an additional ten days before suspending the action. Over the course of the next week, they reached agreement on a schedule of wage increases that would take subsidiary workers over time from 85 percent of the TVöD to between 91 and 96 percent. Stephainski and other therapists, who struck in particularly high numbers, would reach 96 percent of the TVöD by 2025. For the first time ever, all subsidiary workers would also receive career steps—raises tied to their years of service. And crucially, the six subsidiaries, who had each previously had their own company-level agreement, or no agreement at all, were now united under a single collective agreement with Vivantes. The ultimate agreement was not without compromises: the fact that the smallest unit with the easiest-to-replace workers was the last unit on strike forced the delegates to make some difficult final decisions. But the power of the strike was enough to win significant improvements.

Mehr Personal und TVöD für alle

After the tentative agreements, the full text of the collective agreements were hashed out over the course of November. In early December, the agreements were finally ratified by union members, whose numbers had grown by a staggering twenty-three hundred over the course of the campaign. The campaign's two demands had been largely achieved. Healthcare workers had defined staffing ratios for every station and shift in the hospital, with a system of earned paid days off for any violations. They had also secured a "free charge nurse," a standing position without direct patient assignments who could provide floating support to nurses who needed a break or some extra help. In Wetzel's Charité oncology ward, the staffing ratios for the day shift dropped from one worker to every ten patients to one to seven. Midwives had secured an overall ratio of one midwife per every 90 births, down from the industry average of 127. And the therapists, medical workers, and other support staff employed through Vivantes subsidiaries received huge raises, their first in a series to significantly close the gap with the TVöD.

Looking back to the beginning of the campaign, midwife Klein-Allerman remembered seeing a photo at a training session with Jane McAlevey. "I can remember that she showed us a picture of striking hospital workers in California where thirty-five hundred people struck to reverse the privatization of a community hospital system. And they were able to. And then I was thinking, *Wow, that's really cool.* And now it's the other way around," she said. "Maybe you can show some pictures of the Berlin Krankenhausbewegung?" she suggested.

Conclusion: Participation in Negotiations Helps Build Governing Power

There's an old saying. You don't wanna watch sausage be made, and you don't want to watch a bill be made. Sometimes it's not a pretty sight, but the end result—I mean, unless you're a vegan, of course [laughter]—the end result is usually pretty good.

—US vice president Kamala Harris, on the Build Back Better Act[1]

HOW UNIONS NEGOTIATE IS A strategic choice: how you do it structures what you can win and what kind of union you build. The temptation to fall into stale, default approaches—top-down, backroom, low-participation— risks, at best, stale results, a low-turnout ratification vote, and a workforce that struggles to enforce even the few contract provisions it can remember. At worst, the very reason for the negotiations, the union itself, can end up on the chopping block. Winning tough negotiations requires bringing people into the process, to learn and debate how the "sausage" should be made and what should be in it, and to become a central part of crafting and executing a strategy to win it. Transparent, big, and open negotiations, bolstered by a high-participation organizing strategy throughout contract preparations, trusts not only that workers *can* use their intelligence and power to participate in negotiations, but that also, by doing so, they will be better positioned to make sure the end result, the contract structuring half of their waking lives, is more than "pretty good." After all, the heroic workers at the Smithfield "foods pork factory" built a high-participation union and won a life-changing contract against impossible odds, all while making actual sausages every day.

The twenty elements of high-participation negotiations function like key ingredients in a successful recipe: the amounts required might, in a

Rules to Win By. Jane F. McAlevey and Abby Lawlor, Oxford University Press. © Oxford University Press 2023.
DOI: 10.1093/oso/9780197690468.003.0009

pinch, vary or be substituted for something very similar, but the basic items and the steps do matter. The twenty elements are a set of principles about how to approach contract negotiations if the goal is a life-changing victory by and for the workers, such as 100 percent employer-paid family healthcare, a real retirement plan, wages sufficient enough to enable good housing, and more. Workers don't just win better contracts with this approach: they emerge with newfound solidarities and relationships at work and in their communities, and are better equipped to pull the lever for a candidate and party who will, like a good contract campaign negotiator and good union, involve them in the process of building a fairer and more just society.

To sum up, this approach is designed for winning a transformative contract—one that will cost the employer a lot of money and control—through maximum participation of all workers covered by the contract directly in the formulation of demands and the strategy to win them. Winning concessions this size requires building to a supermajority of 90 percent unity and participation among the workers, the level of demonstrable solidarity required to confidently call and sustain a strike as workers' ultimate point of leverage. Serious demands require maximal power.

A three-phase power structure analysis is required:

1. Who holds power in the labor market, and where does the employer's quantifiable power fit into that picture?
2. How does the workers' power structure in workplace relationships operate, and who among the workers can strengthen the union to achieve a supermajority structure?
3. What points of pressure on that local power structure do the growing corps of high-trust worker leaders have, and how can they, as whole workers living full lives in the community, move actors who can push the boss toward meeting workers' demands?

The workers' own power structure will be built and changed through structure tests, which aim to turn routine activity into opportunities for organizing: for example, one-on-one issue survey conversations until a majority of workers have participated, mass involvement in information requests from the employer, direct elections of volunteer negotiations representatives of every position and work shift to a massive committee, article-by-article contract proposal construction, and unit-by-unit ratification of demands. This builds a set of proposals that has been demonstrably endorsed—for the union and the employer—in the blood, sweat, and tears that workers put into crafting them together, and the motivated and informed organization ready to fight for them.

As negotiations begin, with this massive and directly representative committee, all workers are not only invited but actively encouraged to attend and see for themselves what the boss makes of the demands they have created together. Refusing any ground rules penalizing or gagging necessary communication about negotiations, the workers nonetheless will enforce pokerfaced discipline by following rules enabling their collective intelligence to achieve its maximum deliberate effect, calling caucuses as necessary to privately share information or debate counterproposals. The committee will take special care to ensure that scheduling and location are conducive to mass participation, and, should the employer delay negotiations with their own caucuses, to have productive organizing work ready for workers: for example, updating materials like article checklists to help members dropping in get up to speed on arrival, or writing quick negotiations bulletins to keep members who could not attend informed of what happened. It is widely understood as a basis of hard-built trust that the lead negotiator's mandate comes from the workers, and at no point will they accept off-the-record meetings without approval from the committee.

With demonstrable power established inside and outside of the negotiations room, and deep levels of ownership of the struggle among an expanding circle of workers, the workers use the trust built throughout this process to involve their whole community in their struggle for fairness. Should the employer continue to refuse key demands, escalation of higher-risk structure tests will eventually make clear that, should a strike be necessary and a vote called, 90 percent of the workers will participate in the strike vote and likely overwhelmingly approve. Whatever is necessary to arrive at a tentative agreement that the massive committee seeks to put to the membership, this highly engaged body will nevertheless take the time to consider it before putting it up for a true all-member ratification vote. Through the entire process, accurate, fast, and endless communication is crucial to offset and inoculate against the many fictions the employer creates to deny a fairer distribution of the profits. Fights are contested locally, and only if many locals understand the fight can a global army be constructed with the power to create a crisis for the global elite.

Building that army methodically, unit by unit, shift by shift, means realizing the direct continuity, not simple similarity, between democratized unions, the protection of democracy, and a role for working people in politics writ large. As this book argues, overcoming apathy and helping people sort fact from fiction in a union campaign starts with engaging people more meaningfully in thinking through the process itself. We lay out a clear and comprehensive approach to how unions can engage workers in large numbers before and during contract negotiations, which themselves, like civic elections, officially happen only every few years. The problem with most unions *and* political parties is that they believe, wrongly, that when it is time to vote to ratify a contract or elect a government, these organizations can merely flip a switch and activate an otherwise passive base. What this book demonstrates, in part, is that what we do *between* contract expirations dictates whether the next contract will be better, the same, or worse. As we are learning every day of the 2020s, the same goes for politics.

Public Policy and Collective Bargaining: Getting Their Future Right

Collective bargaining is a powerful policy tool, and key policies won by unions in negotiations have historically set the floor for subsequent local, state, and federal legislation on a wide range of issues, including antidiscrimination policies, sick leave, safety and health provisions, and wages. This is why understanding how and when collective bargaining has won, at every level, is so important. As labor laws have been badly skewed in favor of employers since passage of the Taft-Hartley Act of 1947, which amended the 1935 National Labor Relations Act in ways outrageously favorable to the corporate class and against workers, winning strategies against a rigged system have all the more to teach us.

To return to Vice President Harris's comments in the epigraph for this chapter, before the disastrous failure of the Build Back Better plan—which promised unprecedented public spending toward long-overdue priorities for working people—how presidents, political leaders at all levels of government, and civil society groups negotiate is also a strategic choice. The 2021 conclusion of the never-ending behind-the-scenes negotiations of the signature policy for the Biden-Harris administration was far from pretty good. The end result fell miserably below what the working class needs. Because so many campaign promises on issues important to voters failed to materialize in the first full year of the administration, Biden's poll numbers were at historic lows at the one-year mark, and continued to sink.[2] Whether it is union negotiations or public policymaking, shielding working people from messy sausage making, so that all they get is the surprise of a deeply disappointing Best Alternative to Negotiated Agreement (BATNA), has had even messier results.

Along with collapse of Build Back Better, other bold policy initiatives the Biden-Harris team entered office with were buried in the same grave, including the Freedom to Vote Act, the John Lewis Act, climate legislation, and something called the Protecting the Right to Organize (PRO) Act. The PRO Act was a raft of legislation that would have transformed the terrain of labor struggles across the country: banning several favorite union-busting tactics, eliminating right-to-work laws, undermining union avoidance by false-freelancer operations like Uber, expanding the array of solidarity actions that workers can legally take, limiting employers' ability to stonewall by surface bargaining, and beefing up NLRB penalties against unfair labor practices. Naturally, the all-out opposition from nearly every corner of business was baked into the proposal. It stood about as much chance as every other attempt at pro-worker labor reform since Jimmy Carter won the White House with a filibuster-proof Senate. Clinton and Obama also had the White House and a more reliable Senate majority, and yet nothing good to improve labor law has happened in fifty years. With Biden's razor-thin nominal legislative majority, building structures to overpower the kind of legislative boss fight it was bound to face was a tall order indeed. Whatever happened in those backroom negotiations, it clearly was not enough to move the bill through both houses of Congress.

With the collapse of the PRO Act, the national discussion about collective bargaining—to the degree there still is one—has overwhelmingly narrowed to the seemingly novel idea of sectoral bargaining. In this model, unions are legally enabled to sit down with employers across an economic sector—such as hotels, hospitals, fast food, or retail—and create overall minimum standards for wages and benefits. Although it can be highly useful and likely could be an improvement on the narrowly enterprise-based US system, sectoral bargaining is still a form of negotiations. Like any negotiations, workers' success at the table depends directly on strong worker organization. The proponents of this reform as a silver bullet for labor point to sectoral bargaining in Germany and Sweden, implying that this single-policy formula is why these countries' workers have a relatively high standard of living: universal health care, robust paid sick leave, amazing paid parental leave, and most recently, salary maintenance at full or close to full pay while sheltering in place during the pandemic.

Comparisons like this get the facts backward, however. Workers in Germany and Sweden didn't achieve their decent living standards because of sectoral bargaining. They achieved the sectoral bargaining system in the shape they did *because* they had built organizational power by fighting like mad, up to and including attempted revolutions in the earlier half of the twentieth century. The sectoral bargaining system that emerged was a reflection of that newfound power. The owners of capital had to accommodate workers' demands if they wanted to keep their system running smoothly—that is, if they wanted to keep making money.

But as in any series of negotiations, when a system like sectoral bargaining—which was won through struggle—becomes an empty, formalistic process that involves fewer and fewer workers as active participants in the struggle, then all the predictable inertia in the power structure of a capitalist society inevitably shifts power in favor of capital, given their obvious structural advantages. To the extent that workers with sectoral agreements do not have the independent organizational capacity to fight back, the robust social safety nets of many European countries will soon look like the nearly nonexistent one in the United States. Like all institutions of democracy, collective bargaining depends on active, mass participation, whether it happens at a national, sectoral, or enterprise level. Democratic institutions that see a decline in active participation inevitably weaken, like an atrophied muscle.

On the flip side, back when unions represented one in three workers overall in the United States, even more highly unionized workers in the auto and steel industries achieved sectoral bargaining in practice without any legal changes, enforced purely by the workers' coordinated power. This model, known as *pattern bargaining*, meant that workers built enough power to line up their contract expiration dates across all employers simultaneously, and forced their employers to the negotiations table together. Facing these employers as one massive workforce, workers were capable of waging supermajority strikes across this decisive, nationwide sector, if the employers failed to meet their significant demands. Workers built the power to force employers to share a far greater portion of their profits with the people who produced them—the workers. While legal support for sectoral bargaining may have made this process easier, any good outcome for workers with or without that framework depends, as it does today, on the level of high-participation organization.

In chapter 6, we saw how Boston's hotel workers exercised this same kind of brilliant strategy, along with Marriott workers across the country. In chapter 7, a similar approach led to hospital workers in Germany winning demands well beyond the purview of their officially mandated sectoral-bargaining agreement. Whether the future of collective bargaining in the United States is sectoral or not, it could be a dead letter or even a vehicle in a race to the bottom if the labor movement doesn't build the power to shape the process of legislative change and enforcement. That kind of power, and not a smart technocratic fix, is the closest thing we have to a silver bullet.

Building the Power to Set the Rules

This same exact dynamic was at play the only time the NLRA was amended to benefit workers after Taft-Hartley's passage turned back the clock. Hospital workers, carved out of the NLRA collective bargaining rights by Taft-Hartley, fought for and won reinclusion in the act in 1974. In the intervening years, a few states, such as New York and Massachusetts, had granted hospital workers collective bargaining rights because of effective organizing and the use of the strike weapon. But the NLRA amendment happened because hospital workers were organizing and waging strikes and they created a massive crisis for hospital employers in enough key labor markets that Congress decided to restore those rights to all hospital workers. Though some of the details of the final amendment were less than satisfactory to some organizing unions, such as 1199, restoring the right to collective bargaining nationwide was a win for hospital workers in the majority of states where they had been previously denied.

A more recent example of this kind of power was on display when thirty-four thousand teachers, with the overwhelming support of parents and students, collectively shut down nine hundred public schools in Los Angeles in 2019. The original contract demands presented to management by United Teachers Los Angeles (UTLA) were formulated by teachers, students, and parents as part of the teachers' union's goal of ensuring that all three stakeholders had a share in dreaming of, and thus being invested in winning, the schools they deserved. These demands included issues that went beyond the bare bones of an employment contract, but nonetheless deeply affected the places where teachers worked, students learned, and parents entrusted their children. One of the parents' contract demands that the union took up was to prohibit Immigrations and Customs Enforcement (ICE) officers from stalking parents through student attendance lists and arresting them as they picked up their children from school.

Over the course of the fight, the superintendent of schools filed a legal objection to many contract proposals, claiming they were not so-called mandatory subjects of bargaining and thus had to be kept off the table. This concept comes from a 1958 Supreme Court case called *Borg-Warner*, which defined specific issues as mandatory (must-bargain), permissive (can bargain, if both agree), and prohibited (off the table).[3] The employer refused to permit negotiations over the parent-driven demands, and would get a legal injunction prohibiting an otherwise legal strike if the union insisted it stay on the table. The teachers' union had built enough trust with the parents to explain to them that they would tactically withdraw the demand in order to continue building the strike,

CHART 5. Mandatory, Permissive, and Prohibited Subjects of Bargaining

MANDATORY	POWER SHIFT	PERMISSIVE	PROHIBITED
Rates of Pay		Indemnity Bonds	Featherbedding
Wages		Management rights as to union issues	Whistleblowing
Hours of Employment			Discrimination based on race, creed, color, religion, or national origin
Overtime Pay		Preferential Hiring	
Shift Differentials		Retiree pension benefits	
Holidays		Scope of Bargaining Unit	Interfering with union affairs or officials
Severance Pay			
Pensions	Items shift from	Including Supervisors in Contract	Closed Shop
Profit Sharing Plans	"permissive" to "mandatory"		Hot cargo clauses
Holiday bonuses	column based	Additional parties to the contract	Discriminatory treatment
Company-provided housing, meals, and discounts	on the amount of power the workers, and	Use of a union label	
Employee Security	their allies,	Settlement of Unfair Labor Practice charges	
Job Performance	can build.		
Union Security		Continuation of past contract	
Management-union relationship		Membership of Bargaining Teams	
Drug testing of employees		Employment of Strike Breakers	
Subcontracting or relocating members work		Plant closings	
		Employer provided childcare	

SOURCE: Adapted from Patrick Hardin, John E. Higgins, Christopher T. Hexter, and John T. Neighbors, *The Developing Labor Law*, 4th ed. (Washington, DC: Bureau of National Affairs, 2001).

but then reintroduce it once the execution of the strike gave them the power required to corner the employer into shifting items, in practice, from the permissive to the mandatory column. After an exhaustive and methodical series of twelve full structure tests, UTLA was able to create and sustain a crisis for their employer big enough to not just win much-needed raises and traditional rule-making improvements, but to change the legal terrain: to make the permissive become mandatory. They won the contract demand banning ICE agents from schools, among many others that had been deemed, from the get-go, as well off the table.[4]

Supermajority union power changed not just what was in the contract but the terms over which they could fight.

To win something like the PRO Act, let alone anything more, labor needs to be prepared to use the strike weapon to create a national-scale crisis—nothing less will do it, and that will take a whole movement of people experienced in and taking ownership of the process, the demands, and the plan to win. This is how we need to understand the relationship between negotiations in unions and fights over public policy. This is not just a hypothetical comparison—they are two components of the same process. Deciding how the work of keeping everyone alive will be organized, even in small but important shop-floor details, is making policy. Setting a pattern of benefits that comes to be locked in place as a right for the entire population is making policy. Giving people the resources, preparation, and opportunity to govern in their workplaces is not fundamentally different than how social movements, anchored by strong unions, should approach governing in society.

Pedagogy Matters

At their best, unions can and should be both schools for and actors in democracy. Some of the supposed chief negotiators for the working class in the political realm could stand to learn a lot from the best unions in this country—most particularly that their leverage against money and entrenched power is almost nothing without an informed, engaged base at the table with them, strategizing and pushing, in targeted ways in the strategic labor markets and Congressional districts on which key votes hinge, and making these wins their own.

Most people who have never experienced union busters at work have a hard time believing how absurd and vicious their misinformation attempts, intimidation, rule-breaking, sore losing, and procedural warfare can be—and even less that people fall for it, or at least disengage from the relationship-destroying tension they pour over the entire union effort. After the shock to many of the 2016 election, and the all-out "Big Lie" offensive trying to overturn the 2020 results, the intensity and effectiveness of these tactics might seem more familiar. Polarization is a strategy, and it works—tactically driving scared people into active far-right distrust or confused and frustrated disengagement, all while working to change the rules of the game altogether. Sophisticated union busters have peddled the same kinds of "big lies" for decades, and they can be beaten.

In unions as in civic life, shutting people out of strategy and negotiations—and thinking elected leaders can get a better deal in a backroom without using workers' power—likewise closes everyday people out of seeing a credible path to a better life for all of us. Even worse, it primes the pump for the generic union busters of the world, the "Trumpist"-style, minority-rule types, to do their worst with the people left behind. In Germany, the rising fascist party (Alternative für Deutschland; AfD) preys on workers in the deindustrializing and low-wage former East, posing as a savior to those left behind.

In both the United States and Germany, two countries addressed in this book, worker standards are falling and have been for decades. Nationalist forces in both countries are claiming to be the "fighters for the working class." These forces are exploiting weakened, strike-averse trade unions and managerial-style political parties, the US Democrats and their closest equivalent in Germany, the SPD. In Germany, the current expression of fascism is the AfD party, and they talk a militant line in what remains of the big manufacturing plants. In the former East Germany, wage standards are 30 to 40 percent behind workers doing the same jobs but who live and work on the other side of what was the Berlin Wall, a full thirty years after it came down. This has resulted in a two-tiered nation, with the corrosive effects of a two-tiered contract spilling into their politics, not just their workplaces. In auto plants in the former East Germany, the AfD frequently blames unions and the state for failing to level the wage gap, and promises to use the strike weapon to win what those workers deserve.

The Clinton faction did the hard work of gutting the pro-union, pro-regulation elements of the Democratic Party, while the Koch Brothers built a vertically integrated empire to gut unions and regulations from state houses to Congress. In Germany, in the same period, unions agreed to shift to what was called the social partnership model, laying down the strike weapon and pulling up to the table with elite corporate and state actors. It's turned out that the "partnership" many German unions accepted as a replacement for strike readiness has more often than not shrunk to what "partners" means at Starbucks: it is in name only. As discussed in chapter 7, German employers can opt in and out of national sectoral agreements, they can subcontract workers and thus avoid the national standards altogether, and they use the threat of exit to their constant advantage.

Workers who have suffered decades of setbacks and losses, who are working harder for less in both countries, want to see someone "fighting for them." This is the genius of Trump; his chief campaign architect, Steve Bannon; and their top public relations hack, Tucker Carlson. As long as "sausage-making" is a secretive, behind-the-scenes process with few results, Trump and his ilk will succeed in dividing the working class by using fighting language and media theater while pretending to lead the battle for the working class—by which they exclusively mean white people. Donald Trump, Steve Bannon, and the AfD understand how to exploit this division far better than how the Democrats, the SPD, or most national unions in either country understand how to build the program of broad multiracial working-class unity that is needed to counter the Trumpian approach.

Politics is complicated, and no doubt messy, but it's not a roll of the dice or a shift in the weather. We should rarely be surprised by losses if we've not put in the work to assess what we're up against and then test whether we've built what we need to win. Having membership not only engaged in the process but taking ownership of it from bottom to top creates the real, measurable momentum needed to build power. And winning and enforcing transformative legislative change means we need to build a lot of it.

The examples discussed in this book of high-participation negotiations waged and won by workers point the way forward for making the kinds of gains workers desperately need in general, but especially as the world slowly and unevenly emerges from a catastrophic pandemic. During three years of COVID, the corporate elites around the globe—like those planted in the United States—showed how little they care about the people who earn them the profits, and how much there is to gain by bringing them and the politicians who represent them to heel.

The solidarity forged and thus the power built by workers in these case studies show that when workers are trusted to seriously engage in their own negotiations, they can achieve the commonly unthinkable: they can win against the odds. We propose that similar approaches to public policymaking could be just as successful in building more functioning societies, faced as we are with hard-working union busters of all kinds.

Whether you are a worker in Berlin or Boston, Lagos or Buenos Aires, the only way you win a decent life is by building enough measurable power to create a genuine crisis for the employer class. This is true at the negotiations table and on Capitol Hill. As the dominant political parties and the labor movement the world over move ahead from these major losses, amassing power needs to be front and center in our own efforts to build back better. Nothing less will do it.

We hope this book helps workers win more by challenging and changing how they conduct their negotiations. Proponents of democratic societies might also realize that to overcome the crises afflicting our politics, national unions and pro-worker politicians need to embrace the best of union negotiations and organizing strategies. This means understanding the direct relationship between workplace and civic democracy, and recognizing that the durable wins enabled by transparency and participation in union negotiations will only come in the political arena by adopting a similar, win-oriented approach to public policymaking. Good unions will be key to rebuilding a fairer country and world, and workers who have contracts expiring stand perhaps the best chance of creating the conditions necessary to fix our broken democracy (and to transform their ineffective unions in the process). If political leaders learn this too and seize the moment, we can win big. That's if unions will change from top-down and secret to transparent, big, and open, and if the political parties purporting to represent the multiracial working class will shift from a behind-the-scenes approach to conducting broad political education, backed by a well-organized mass working-class base, in all its diversity.

The stories in this book demonstrate success, and there's no time to waste. Now more than ever, as go unions, so goes democracy.

HANDY TERMS AND EXPLANATIONS

Anti-union campaign (also union avoidance; union busting): Umbrella terms for a variety of employer strategies and tactics to undermine workers' organizing rights by discouraging union membership and union activity, in particular during union recognition and contract campaigns. These include anti-union communications, captive audience meetings, retaliation against pro-union workers, and refusal to recognize or negotiate with the union, as well as contract proposals that would undermine a union standard. Too often, these activities are entirely permissible under current labor law, and companies frequently hire specialized consulting firms to provide instruction on how to avoid legal liability for interfering with worker organizing. In other cases, such as explicit retaliation, anti-union tactics may constitute unfair labor practices. Anti-union strategies sometimes produce short-term benefits for non-union workers, as when companies match union wages in order to discourage unionization. *Case studies: PASNAP; NewsGuild; MNA; UNITE HERE; ver.di*

Article checklist (also proposal tracker): An informational handout for workers attending negotiation sessions, listing each existing or proposed article in the collective bargaining agreement and providing updated information about the status of any proposals related to that article, including any tentative agreements reached and the names of union members working on particular articles. The article checklist should be updated and distributed to attendees for every negotiation session. *Case studies: PASNAP; NJEA*

Bargaining survey: A tool for developing and prioritizing issues through solicitation of input from all workers covered by the agreement. Participation in a bargaining survey may serve as a structure test in the lead-up to negotiations, and the negotiations committee should aim to gather responses from a supermajority of the bargaining unit. Bargaining survey results should also be shared back to members through meetings and/or a written report. *Case studies: PASNAP; NJEA; NewsGuild; MNA; ver.di*

Bargaining unit: In workplaces that are already unionized, or when workers are seeking to form a union, this term defines which types of workers and what job classifications are included or excluded by an existing or future union contract. Workers within a bargaining unit must possess certain elements of commonality, as defined by applicable labor law. Who is and isn't included in the bargaining unit is often highly contested between the employer and the union during a campaign to unionize. *Case studies: PASNAP; NewsGuild; MNA; ver.di*

Bargaining update (also negotiations bulletin; shop paper): A flyer, email, or other communication summarizing what occurred in a particular negotiation session, including any new proposals that were introduced, any progress made on existing proposals, any tentative agreements, any notable table talk, and any next steps. Bargaining updates should be drafted by the negotiations committee immediately after a negotiation session and distributed shortly thereafter. *Case studies: PASNAP; NewsGuild; MNA; UNITE HERE; ver.di*

Big negotiations: A form of collective bargaining that emphasizes having large numbers of workers present at negotiation sessions, in particular through the use of large negotiations committees. Big negotiations may also be open negotiations and vice versa; however, the two terms are not synonymous. *Case studies: PASNAP; NJEA; MNA; UNITE HERE; ver.di*

Biggest worst: The largest job classification, department, or area with the least union support and/or the strongest anti-union sentiment. An organizing campaign should focus on identifying and recruiting organic leaders in the biggest worst. *Case studies: NewsGuild; UNITE HERE*

Button up: A high-visibility structure test in which workers publicly wear a union button while at work on a set day or days. *Case studies: NewsGuild; UNITE HERE*

Captive audience meeting: An example of a union-busting tactic in which management holds mandatory meetings with workers in order to communicate management's opposition to unionization or other union activities. Workers cannot refuse to attend because they are on paid work time. *Case study: NewsGuild*

Card-check agreement: A binding agreement reached between an employer and a union through which the employer agrees to voluntarily recognize the union upon a showing of signed union cards from a majority of the bargaining unit rather than requiring an election to be held. The NLRB will then certify the workers as an official union. *Case study: UNITE HERE*

Caucus: A period in a negotiation session during which the union and the employer go into separate rooms in order to privately discuss proposals and formulate responses. Caucuses may range anywhere from a few minutes to several hours in length. Either party can call for a caucus, and the other must agree. *Case studies: PASNAP; NJEA; NewsGuild; MNA; UNITE HERE; ver.di*

Contract action team (also member action / member engagement team; mobilization/campaign/leadership committee): A committee of members who communicate bargaining updates and organize coworkers in their group to take part in structure tests and other coordinated actions around negotiations. *Case studies: PASNAP; NJEA; NewsGuild; UNITE HERE*

Delegation (also march on the boss): A planned but previously unannounced in-person visit by a group of workers to an employer representative or other person in a position of power in order to deliver a demand, petition, or other message. A delegation is an example of a structure test, with opportunities for workers to participate by attending or speaking on the delegation. *Case studies: MNA, UNITE HERE*

Direct dues: A form of dues payment in which union members directly authorize the union to charge monthly or yearly dues rather than relying on employer payroll deduction. Direct dues payment requires the union to obtain authorizations directly from individual members but removes the possibility that an employer can strategically terminate dues deduction in order to put pressure on the union during a labor dispute. An additional benefit of this approach is that only the union knows who is a member, complicating management's ability to run anti-union campaigns. *Case study: MNA*

Elected officers (also executive board / council / committee; unit council): Under a local union's bylaws or union constitution, the elected leadership of the local or a unit of the local. Depending on the union's bylaws and practice, elected officers may automatically serve on the negotiations committee. *Case studies: NJEA; NewsGuild; MNA; UNITE HERE*

Fact-finding: A dispute-resolution mechanism that may be required under public sector labor law if the union and the employer are unable to reach an agreement. During fact-finding a neutral third party reviews the negotiations situation, prepares a report, and makes a recommendation for reaching a settlement. *Case study: NJEA*

First contract: The first collective bargaining agreement reached following union recognition, in which the workers seek to establish core principles such as just cause and union jurisdiction. Under current labor law, workers often face similar union-busting tactics when negotiating a first contract as they do in seeking union recognition. First contract negotiations are often quite lengthy and may fail to result in an agreement. *Case studies: PASNAP; NewsGuild*

Going public: In an underground union organizing campaign, the act of publicly announcing that workers are organizing a union. Going public typically occurs only after the union has secured supermajority support and may coincide with a demand for voluntary recognition. Announcing the union campaign and the identities of union leaders provides some protection from employer retaliation and can help bolster public support for workers. *Case study: NewsGuild*

Ground rules: A set of rules proposed and agreed to at the outset of negotiations that impose restrictions on the behavior of the union and the employer during the bargaining process. Traditional ground rules often contain provisions that serve as barriers to big, open, or transparent bargaining by limiting who can attend negotiation sessions or limiting what information can be shared from negotiations. Under the National Labor Relations Act, ground rules are not a mandatory subject of bargaining; they are permissive, meaning a union may refuse to negotiate, agree to, or even discuss any ground rules without violating its duty to bargain in good faith. However, public sector or other applicable labor law may require that each side consider ground rules. *Case studies: PASNAP; NJEA; MNA*

Impasse: A formal declaration or finding that negotiations have ceased to progress. An impasse declaration allows an employer to implement its most recent offer in negotiations. In the public sector, an impasse finding may trigger mediation, fact-finding, contract arbitration, or all three. *Case studies: NJEA; MNA*

Information request: A formal request from the union to the employer for payroll data, hours of work, schedules, staffing, financial data, or other information that may affect the union's proposals and bargaining rationales. A benefit of the legal right to collective bargaining, the employer must comply. An employer that fails to do so commits an unfair labor practice. *Case studies: PASNAP; NewsGuild*

Jurisdiction: The scope of work that belongs to job classifications within the bargaining unit, as defined in the collective bargaining agreement. Strong jurisdictional language prevents the employer from undermining the union by assigning union work to non-union workers. *Case study: NewsGuild*

Just cause: As contrasted with the default of at-will employment, just cause requires basic due process before a worker can be fired and prevents an employer from firing a worker for no reason or a bad reason. Just cause is a fundamental protection in a collective bargaining agreement and is typically established in the first contract. *Case study: NewsGuild*

Local union (also local association/guild): An affiliate of a statewide, national, or international union consisting of one or more bargaining units in a particular geographic area or under a particular employer. A local union has its own bylaws and elected officials. *Case studies: NJEA; NewsGuild; UNITE HERE*

Lockout: As contrasted with a strike, an employer action to block workers from being able to work. *Case study: MNA*

Master agreement (also citywide agreement/contract): A standardized contract agreed to by union employers in a given industry in a particular city. A master agreement may be reached through negotiations between a union and an industry association acting on behalf of a group of employers, or achieved indirectly through the use of "Me Too agreements," or through individual negotiations in which workers insist on reaching an established union standard. *Case study: UNITE HERE*

Mediation: A process through which an impartial third party called a *mediator* helps the union and the employer reach an agreement by making suggestions for resolution of contested issues. Mediation may be voluntary or may be required under state or federal law following an impasse. *Case study: NJEA*

Me Too agreement: An agreement by an employer to accept the terms of a contract negotiated by the union with another employer or an industry representative. Me Too agreements can be used to establish or maintain a union standard in a given market. *Case study: UNITE HERE*

Negotiations committee (also bargaining committee/team; negotiations team): A group of workers, ideally elected by their coworkers, who take leadership in negotiations, including developing contract proposals, sitting at the negotiations table across from management, responding to company proposals, and reaching tentative agreements. Under union bylaws or tradition, the negotiations committee often includes designated elected officers or shop stewards. *Case studies: PASNAP; NJEA; NewsGuild; MNA; UNITE HERE; ver.di*

New organizing: Organizing among non-union workers aimed at achieving union recognition and a first contract. *Case studies: NewsGuild; UNITE HERE*

Ninety-ten rule: The employer-driven tradition that 90 percent of proposals in negotiations happen in the final 10 percent of negotiation sessions. *Case studies: NJEA; NewsGuild; MNA; UNITE HERE*

NLRB election: A process for proving majority support for unionization among workers in a bargaining unit through a secret election supervised by the National Labor Relations Board (NLRB). NLRB elections are often pursued after an employer refuses to voluntarily recognize the union despite a showing of majority support. *Case studies: PASNAP; NewsGuild*

Off-the-record (also sidebar): As contrasted with full negotiation sessions, during which everything said by either party is "on the record" and can be used as evidence for interpreting the contract in the future during disputes and arbitrations, off-the-records are more informal and potentially candid conversations between representatives from the union (typically the negotiator and members of the negotiations committee) and the employer about particular contract proposals. This allows both parties to explore settlement options outside of the legal framework of the negotiations room. *Case study: NJEA*

On-call: A scheduling system under which workers are given minimal advance notice of hours and must wait to be called into work, typically on that day. On-call systems place the risk of unexpected slowdowns in demand onto workers, allowing employers to save on labor costs. *Case studies: MNA; UNITE HERE*

One-on-one conversations (also structured organizing / targeted conversations): An approach to organizing centered on motivating worker participation through one-on-one relationship building and intentional discussion featuring open-ended questions, agitation, education, and concrete asks. *Case studies: PASNAP; NJEA; NewsGuild; MNA; UNITE HERE; ver.di*

Open negotiations: Negotiations in which sessions are open for all workers covered by the contract to attend. Open negotiations are not necessarily "big negotiations" because members may not automatically attend negotiations in large numbers. Open negotiations may additionally include union members from other bargaining units or members of the community. *Case studies: PASNAP; NJEA; NewsGuild; MNA; UNITE HERE*

Open-ended strike: A strike without a predefined end date. Contrasted with a short or defined strike, in which workers announce that they will strike only for a fixed period of time—for example, twenty-four hours. *Case studies: UNITE HERE; ver.di*

Organic leader: A respected worker who is able to move large numbers of coworkers to take action. Organic leaders are not necessarily pro-union, as contrasted with pro-union activists. Typically, they have no official title or position. *Case studies: PASNAP; NJEA; MNA; UNITE HERE; ver.di*

Organizing committee: A committee of workers formed for the purpose of organizing toward union recognition. To be effective, the committee is made up of organic leaders from each work area and shift. Standing organizing committees may also exist in already-unionized workplaces and serve a similar role to the contract action team in organizing around workplace issues and contract negotiations. *Case studies: NewsGuild*

Pay disparity: A marked difference in the wages or overall earnings between workers in the same job classification on the basis of gender, race, or ethnicity. Can also refer to a difference in the wages or overall earnings between two job classifications that cannot reasonably be attributed to differences in job responsibilities or required skills. *Case studies: NewsGuild; UNITE HERE; ver.di*

Payroll deduction: A method by which a union relies on the employer to collect dues, fees, and other authorized payments (including for strike or political action funds) directly from workers' paychecks and to remit them to the union on a negotiated, regular basis. Though efficient, employers may unilaterally terminate such deductions if the parties reach impasse in negotiations. Employers tend to require no-strike clauses in exchange for payroll deduction. One case study, MNA, presents the alternative: direct dues. *Case studies: MNA; UNITE HERE*

Picket duty: During a strike, a worker's assigned shift on the picket line, which may mirror their typical work schedule. Picket duty may be a requirement for collecting strike benefits from the union's strike fund. *Case study: UNITE HERE*

Poker face: A rule of the room instructing that workers attending negotiation sessions should not show visible anger, surprise, happiness, or other emotions in front of the employer unless the negotiations committee has planned for such a response. *Case studies: PASNAP; NJEA; MNA; UNITE HERE*

Power structure analysis: A means of evaluating how contract demands can be won by identifying possible points of leverage over the employer. Power structure analysis is grounded in an understanding of the power relationships held by workers in the bargaining unit as well as the employer's power relationships. *Case studies: NJEA; MNA; UNITE HERE; ver.di*

Ranking (also assessment): A process for evaluating workers' readiness to strike, or take other actions, based on one-on-one conversations and past participation in structure tests. *Case studies: NewsGuild; MNA*

Ratification vote: A process to formally approve or reject a new collective bargaining agreement through a vote by union members covered by the contract. Union bylaws or tradition may impose particular requirements for successful ratification. *Case studies: NJEA; NewsGuild; MNA; UNITE HERE; ver.di*

Rules of the room: A set of internal rules established by the negotiations committee that have been communicated and agreed to by all workers who attend negotiation sessions. Not to be confused with ground rules, which are negotiated with the employer and apply to both sides. Rules of the room should include poker face, negotiator as designated spokesperson, and a method for communicating with the negotiator during sessions, such as through passing notes. *Case studies: PASNAP; NJEA; MNA*

Safe staffing: As contrasted with *understaffing*, a term used in healthcare to refer to the number of nurses who should be scheduled in order to promote adequate workplace safety and patient care. The concept directly connects nurses' working conditions with the quality of care they are able to provide. *Case studies: MNA; ver.di*

Sectoral agreement: A collective bargaining agreement that is negotiated between one or more unions and an employer association that is binding on employers in a given sector. Under the German system of sectoral bargaining, participation in employer associations is voluntary. *Case study: ver.di*

Seniority: The amount of time that a worker has worked for a given employer or in a given job classification. Seniority is a mechanism to create fairness and constrain employer discretion, and applies to wage increases, layoffs, and opportunities for advancement, among other things. Workers, through the collective bargaining process, may decide that some benefits should be based on rotation instead of seniority, such as major holidays or vacation scheduling. *Case studies: MNA; UNITE HERE; ver.di*

Shop steward (also building representative; delegate): A union member who has formally taken responsibility for representing their coworkers in grievance proceedings and other union matters. Shop stewards may represent a particular job classification, department, spatial area, or shift within a workplace and may automatically serve on union leadership bodies such as a unit council or negotiations committee. These positions can be appointed or elected, and are typically filled by union activists. *Case studies: NJEA; NewsGuild; MNA; UNITE HERE*

Short strike (also defined strike): As contrasted with an open-ended strike, a strike whose duration is announced ahead of time to both workers and the employer.*Case studies: MNA; ver.di*

Staff organizer (also field/guild/union representative): An organizer paid by the members and who works for the local or state/national/international union. Staff organizers work to recruit new organic leaders and ensure majority and supermajority participation throughout the workplace. *Case studies: NJEA; NewsGuild; MNA; UNITE HERE; ver.di*

Strike authorization vote: A process for union members in a bargaining unit to vote to approve taking a strike action, often outlined in union bylaws. A strike authorization vote does not bind the union to actually going on strike but gives approval to the negotiations committee or another leadership body within the union to call for a strike. The decision to hold a strike authorization vote should be informed by past worker participation in structure tests and can itself serve as a structure test in building toward strike readiness. *Case studies: NewsGuild; MNA; UNITE HERE; ver.di*

Strike fund: A dedicated fund created through regular contributions by union members to provide for pay and additional hardship benefits during a strike. May be supplemented by outside contributions, typically collected from supporters during the strike itself. A healthy strike fund signals to an employer that a union can credibly embark on an open-ended strike. *Case study: UNITE HERE*

Strike pay: Payment from a union strike fund to striking workers to partially replace lost wages. May be contingent on worker participation in picket duty. *Case studies: UNITE HERE; ver.di*

Strike support: Financial or volunteer support for striking workers. May include roles outside of picket duty that strikers perform, including administration of hardship benefits, maintaining picket signs and equipment, and coordinating food and water for the picket lines. *Case study: UNITE HERE*

Structure test: A mass-participation action demonstrating majority support for the union or particular contract proposals or demands. A deliberate progression of structure tests that are increasingly public and have escalating stakes allows the union to gauge worker participation and readiness to strike. *Case studies: PASNAP; NJEA; NewsGuild; MNA; UNITE HERE; ver.di*

Table talk: On-the-record conversation at the bargaining table, which may later be introduced as evidence in contract interpretation disputes, including arbitrations. Excerpts from table talk may also be included in bargaining updates. *Case study: NewsGuild*

Tariff commission: The elected body within German trade unions that represents workers in collective bargaining and makes decisions at the negotiations table at both the sectoral and company level. Though the entire tariff commission may be present at negotiations, it is typical that a smaller negotiations committee is elected and attends on behalf of the commission as a whole. *Case study: ver.di*

Tentative agreement: An agreement reached between the union and the employer for language in a particular contract article or articles that is provisionally signed off on by both sides before there is agreement over the contract as a whole. Tentative agreements allow the parties to narrow the scope of negotiations over time. *Case studies: NJEA; NewsGuild; UNITE HERE*

Third-partying: A form of anti-union rhetoric that refers to the union as something that exists separate and apart from workers themselves. Third-partying undermines the idea that unions are collective and democratic organizations driven by their membership, casting them instead as outside service providers that represent workers in exchange for payment. Unions believe each workplace has two parties, workers and the employer, and the workers are the union. As such, there is no third party. *Case studies: NewsGuild; ver.di*

Transparent negotiations: A form of negotiations in which individual negotiation sessions may be open or closed but where the negotiations committee provides detailed and timely updates about what is happening, including the content and status of union and employer proposals, notable exchanges at the bargaining table, and when negotiations are next scheduled to occur. *Case studies: PASNAP; NJEA; NewsGuild; MNA; UNITE HERE; ver.di*

Two-tiering: A type of contract proposal that would establish multiple classes or "tiers" of workers within the bargaining unit, typically by distinguishing between the existing workforce and any future hires and providing lesser benefits to the second tier. Two-tiering is an employer strategy to divide workers by creating different standards within the workplace and to undermine worker solidarity over time. *Case studies: MNA; ver.di*

Underground organizing: The approach in a new organizing campaign of deliberately organizing quietly and out of sight of the employer until a certain threshold of support has been reached in order to delay triggering an anti-union campaign by the employer. During the underground phase of a new organizing drive, workers refrain from discussing the union outside of one-on-one organizing conversations. *Case study: NewsGuild*

Unfair labor practice (ULP): An act that violates a prohibition under applicable labor law and may result in successful charges against the employer (or the union). *Case studies: PASNAP; MNA*

Union activist: A union member who is an enthusiastic and ready union supporter but who does not effectively motivate or lead their coworkers to take action. Contrasted with an organic leader. *Case studies: PASNAP; UNITE HERE; ver.di*

Union density: A measure of how many workers within a given sector or industry in a given market or under a given employer are union represented. Union density is a rough proxy for union power, and higher union density corresponds with higher union standards. *Case studies: MNA; UNITE HERE; ver.di*

Union difference: The difference between the union standard and the wages and benefits for nonunion workers in the same industry and sector within the same labor market or employer. Employers may deliberately seek to eliminate elements of the union difference—particularly any wage gap—by attacking the union standard or by raising wages for its unrepresented employees in order to discourage unionization. *Case studies: MNA; UNITE HERE; ver.di*

Union leave: A right negotiated under a collective bargaining agreement for union members to take protected leave from their jobs in order to temporarily join the union organizing staff and gain additional organizing training and experience. *Case study: UNITE HERE*

Union orientation: A session led by shop stewards or other union leaders for newly hired workers conducted as part of the formal new-hire orientation. Depending on the strength of the collective bargaining agreement, these sessions may be employer-paid and mandatory for all employees. Union orientations have gained additional importance in light of the ongoing attack on unions' ability to collect dues because they provide an opportunity for new workers to learn about their rights and sign up as union members. *Case study: MNA*

Union standard: A baseline for wages and benefits shared across collective bargaining agreements within a given industry/sector and labor market. A union standard can be established and maintained through citywide contracts, Me Too agreements, or purely through the power of worker organizing. *Case studies: MNA; UNITE HERE; ver.di*

Warning strike: A short or defined-term strike that signals workers' readiness to embark on a future open-ended strike if an agreement is not reached on a new collective bargaining agreement. In Germany, such strikes have in practice become warning strikes in name only as they involve only brief symbolic demonstrations (such as a lunchtime rally) and do not lead to further escalations. *Case study: ver.di*

Whole worker organizing: An approach to organizing that recognizes that workers experience and are impacted by issues that intersect but extend beyond the workplace, such as access to quality education, housing, and healthcare, and forms of identity-based oppression. Whole worker organizing also rejects artificial distinctions between "workers" and "community" and seeks to use workers' roles in the community as sources of strategic power. *Case studies: PASNAP; MNA*

Work-to-rule: A structure test in which workers follow the existing collective bargaining agreement and other workplace policies or regulations to the letter, doing no more and no less than exactly what is required of them. This could entail a deliberate refusal to commit violations of workplace safety rules or to voluntarily take on additional work, even if such practices are commonplace or expected. *Case studies: NJEA; NewsGuild*

APPENDICES

Appendix 1: The Interview and Discussion Survey Tool

Collective Bargaining Survey

Name: **Title:**   **Union:**

I. Framework for Collective Bargaining

Do any of the written rules of your union apply to the collective bargaining process?

	Constitution	Bylaws	Other
IU/National Union			
State/Regional			
Local			

What do they say about how locals should collectively bargain?
Can you share a copy of relevant documents (constitutions/bylaws/policies/ best practices)?

In what circumstances do they apply?

Are bargaining practices consistent:

- Based on who the bargainer is?
- From contract to contract with the same employer?
- Across shops within the local?
- Across locals?
- Across union?
- For first contracts and successor contracts?

How does the union train bargainers and organizers/reps on collective bargaining and organizing for contract campaigns? Are there internal or external trainings/conferences/conventions which you participate in?

Has your union attempted to make changes to how you do collective bargaining in the last five years? What changes and how have you implemented them?

Can you share any written guidelines / best practices related to the implementation of this change?

II. Who Leads Contract Campaigns?

A. First Contract Campaigns

Who is on the campaign team for a first contract campaign?

Indicate # of people in each category and where they come from	Members on LOA/ Lost Time	Organizers/ Reps	Leads/ Directors	Bargainers	Other (research, comms, boycott, community, legal, etc.)
IU/National State/ Regional Local					

Is there a rank-and-file bargaining committee? ▫ Yes ▫ No
How many people are on the bargaining committee?
What is ratio of the bargaining committee members to number of workers in the bargaining unit?

Is it specific to the bargaining unit whose contract is being negotiated? ▫
Specific ▫ General
How are bargaining committee members selected?
▫ Elected by: _____ ▫ Appointed by: _____
Are there mechanisms for representation by work location/department/
unit? Race/gender/language? Other?

B. Successor Contracts

Who is on the campaign team for a successor contract? (Indicate #)

Indicate # of people in each category and where they come from	Members on LOA/ Lost Time	Organizers/ Reps	Leads/ Directors	Bargainers	Other
IU/National					
State/ Regional					
Local					

Is there a rank-and-file bargaining committee? ▫ Yes ▫ No
How many people are on the bargaining committee?
What is ratio of the bargaining committee members to number of
workers in the bargaining unit?
Is it specific to the bargaining unit whose contract is being negotiated?
▫ Specific ▫ General
How are bargaining committee members selected?
▫ Elected by: _____ ▫ Appointed by: _____
Are there mechanisms for representation by work location/department/
unit? Race/gender/language? Other?
Who is the bargainer?

Select title/ role	Level of Union Affiliation / Selection / Distance from Contract Being Negotiated			
	IU/National	*Regional/State*	*Local*	*Shop*
Elected Officer	President VP S-T Other	President VP S-T Other	President VP S-T Other	
Staff Member	Director Attorney Bargainer Organizer/rep Other	Director Attorney Bargainer Organizer/rep Other	Director Attorney Bargainer Organizer/rep Other	Organizer/ rep Other
Rank-and-File Member	E-Board Steward Barg. comm. Other	E-Board Steward Barg. comm. Other	E-Board Steward Barg. comm. Other	E-Board Steward Barg. comm. Other
Outside Consultant	Attorney Other	Attorney Other	Attorney Other	

How is the bargainer selected?

□ Elected by: □ Specific to contract   □ General

□ Appointed/hired by: _____   □ Specific to contract

□ General

III. How Do You Prepare for Bargaining?

Is there a unit-wide bargaining survey? □ Yes □ No

What, if any, are participation benchmarks relative to the size of the bargaining unit?

When is it circulated, and for how long?

Who compiles the results?

Are the results shared back with workers? When and how?

Can you share some recent examples of contract surveys + methodology (face-to-face or online)? Can you share results (# and % of workers who participated)?

Is there a meeting with members to set bargaining demands?

□ Open □ Closed

Who participates in the meeting, and what are their roles?

Participation in Meeting to Develop Bargaining Proposals							
	Bargaining Comm.	Bargaining Unit Members	Other Union Members	Principal Officer / E-Board	Union Staff	Lawyer	Community
Sets agenda							
Leads, facilitates, or presents							
Actively participates and weighs in on bargaining demands							
Participates, does not weigh in on bargaining demands							
Observes but does not participate							

How are proposals developed/drafted? Who drafts ?

Who reviews proposals?
- Bargaining unit
- Bargaining committee
- Campaign team
- Local union staff not on campaign team
- Lawyer
- Executive board
- Principal officer
- State/regional union officers/staff
- IU/national union officers/staff
- Community

Is there coordination
- Across shops/employers within the local?
- With other locals of the same union?
- With other unions?

Who signs off on proposals?
- Bargaining unit
- Bargaining committee
- Campaign team
- Local union staff not on campaign team
- Lawyer
- Executive board
- Principal officer
- State/regional union officers/staff
- IU/national union officers/staff
- Community

Is there a follow-up meeting with bargaining unit members to discuss/review/approve draft proposals? Open ▫ Closed

Participation in Meeting to Review Bargaining Proposals							
	Bargaining Comm.	Bargaining Unit Members	Other Union Members	Principal Officer / E-Board	Union Staff	Lawyer	Community
Sets agenda							
Leads, facilitates, or presents							
Actively participates and weighs in on proposals							
Participates, does not weigh in on proposals							
Observes but does not participate							

IV. What Happens in the Room during Bargaining?

A. Ground Rules

Do you agree to ground rules?
- Yes, always
- Depends on: _____
- Never

How often do you agree to the following types of ground rules (always/sometimes/never)?

Party Restricted	Restriction on Who Speaks at the Table	Restriction on Who Is at the Table	Restriction on Who Is in the Room	Restriction on Distribution of Proposals	Gag Order/ restriction on Reports Out
Bargaining unit members					
Other union members/ affiliates					
Community/ other external party					

B. Who Participates and How?

Is bargaining open or closed? ◻ Open ◻ Closed
How many people are on the union side of the table for bargaining?
_____Bargaining unit members
_____Bargaining committee members
_____Campaign team members
_____Local union staff not on campaign team
_____Lawyer
_____Executive board
_____Principal officer

_____State/regional union officers/staff
_____IU/national union officers/staff
_____Community
How are these people selected?
Are there limitations on who speaks at the table? ▫ Yes ▫ No

Who can attend bargaining sessions?
• Bargaining unit members
• Bargaining committee members
• Campaign team members
• Local union staff not on campaign team
• Lawyer
• Executive board
• Principal officer
• State/regional union officers/staff
• IU/national union officers/staff
• Community

How many workers total are in the room? _____ Is there an upper limit? ▫ Yes: _____ ▫ No
Are these numbers consistent throughout bargaining, or does it vary session by session? What determines how many members are in the room for a given session?
How do workers find out about bargaining sessions?
Where does bargaining take place? ▫ Shop ▫ Union Hall ▫ Other: _____
_____
When does bargaining take place? ▫ 9–5 M–F ▫ After 5 M–F ▫ Sat/Sun
Can workers attend on their breaks? ▫ Yes ▫ No
Can workers request PTO to attend bargaining? ▫ Yes – specific for union activities ▫ Yes — general ▫ No
Are materials presented by either side at the table distributed to everyone in the room? ▫ Yes ▫ No
Are materials distributed allowed to leave the room? ▫ Yes ▫ No
Are there accommodations available?

- Interpretation/translation
- Childcare
- Other: _____

C. Decision-Making

Who can call for a caucus?

- Bargainer
- Anyone at the table
- Anyone in the room
  What happens during caucuses?
  Who leads discussion? _____
  Who actively participates in discussions?
- People at the table
- Bargaining committee
- Everyone in the room
  Are there off-the-records? ◌ Yes ◌ No
   Who authorizes them?
   Who participates in them?
   What is the process for reaching tentative agreements?
- Decided at the table
- Decided in a caucus
- Decided in an open meeting outside of bargaining
- Decided in a closed meeting outside of bargaining

D. Coordination

Are there coordinated:

- National/statewide/regional/citywide tables with employers?
  o Multiple bargaining units?
  o Multiple locals?
- Multi-employer tables?
- Multi-union tables?

	Wages	Healthcare	Pension	Work Rules	Grievance Procedure	Union rights	Mgt. rights	Term	Other
Coordinated									
Localized									

How are decisions reached/coordinated within these tables?

V. What Happens between Bargaining Sessions?

Is information shared out from bargaining?
- Summary of what happened during the bargaining session
- Full text of employer proposals
- Full text of union proposals

How is information shared?
Are worker meetings held between bargaining sessions?
- Open – workers + community
- Open – workers only
- Bargaining committee only
- Other: _____

VI. How Is an Agreement Reached?

Who reviews an agreement before agreeing to a tentative settlement?

- Bargaining unit
- Bargaining committee
- Campaign team
- Local union staff not on campaign team
- Lawyer
- Executive board
- Principal officer
- State/regional union officers/staff
- IU/national union officers/staff
- Community

Is there a formalized process for ratification? ◻ Yes ◻ No
If codified somewhere, can you share?

Is there a ratification vote? ▢ Yes ▢ No
When/where does it happen?
How is the vote noticed?
Is the full contract available to workers prior to the vote? ▢ Full contract
▢ Partial summary ▢ Other
Who is allowed to vote?

- Everyone in bargaining unit
- Union members in bargaining unit
- Members in good standing in bargaining unit
- Other: _____

   What is the threshold for ratification? ▢ 50% + 1 of votes cast ▢ 2/3 of
   votes cast ▢ Other: _____

   Is the result of the vote binding? ▢ Yes ▢ No

VII. Follow-Up

Is there a recent (large-scale?) contract negotiation that has happened in
your union that is representative of your bargaining practice?

   Are there other folks at your union (IU/national/state/local level) that
are highly involved in bargaining or have had recent noteworthy bargaining experiences that I should talk to?

Appendix 2: PASNAP (Chapter 2)

Information Request for Negotiations

VIA FAX & Certified Mail

Barry Freedman, Chief Executive Officer
Einstein Healthcare Network
5501 Old York Road
Philadelphia, PA 19141

12 July, 2016

Dear Mr. Freedman:

Greetings. I will be serving as the chief negotiator for the collective negotiations process with Einstein Medical Center. We look forward to the opportunity to work together in the pursuit of excellence in quality healthcare and the professional development of the dedicated nursing staff. As I am sure you would agree, PASNAP has long understood that registered nurses are the heart, soul, and lynchpin of any hospital, indeed of our entire healthcare system.

We believe that the process of negotiating a collective bargaining agreement need not be a contentious affair. While we are not so naïve to believe that there won't develop differences over substantive issues between Einstein's leadership and the nurses, if the process we establish is grounded in a true mutual understanding and respect of one another's guiding philosophies, we will overcome such differences and reach satisfactory common ground. That is our objective in these negotiations.

Now that the NLRB has certified PASNAP as the representative of the registered nurses, this is a formal request for negotiations dates. Given the delays in this process, please consider that almost any date you provide me is one that I will do my best to be available. I'd like to propose negotiations every Wednesday starting August 3rd. I am open to adding more days/dates as needed.

After extensive engagement with the majority of Einstein nurses, including contract surveys filled in by over 65% of the nurses regarding their priorities, and to comprehensively prepare for the upcoming negotiations, we want to fully understand the successful medical center that Einstein has become. Therefore, we hereby request the following information. It is quite likely that this request for information will be supplemented during the ongoing process of negotiating this initial agreement.

1. A list of all current bargaining unit employees containing the following information. For *each individual* employee, please include the following information:
   a. name;
   b. address;
   c. cell phone number;
   d. email address;
   e. unit or department (by name);
   f. current wage rate, and if the employee is per diem, please indicate whether the wage provided includes any kind of per diem differential;
   g. status (full-time, part-time, per diem);
   h. cost center (including a listing of updated hospital cost centers)
   i. date of hire;
   j. number of years of relevant experience credited to the employee for the purposes of determining current wage levels;
   k. number of hours for which the employee received standby/on-call pay, and the rate of pay the employee received when called into work number of hours;
   l. the number of vacation, sick leave, and personal time hours used in the last fiscal year and the remaining balance currently existing in each category;
   m. the amount of tuition reimbursement paid to the employee since their date of hire;
   n. the number of continuing education hours paid to the employee in the last two (2) fiscal years;
   o. the amount of the child care subsidy paid to the employee in the last two (2) fiscal years;
   p. the specific dollar amounts contributed to the employee's 403(b) retirement plan by both the employer and the employee over the last three (3) fiscal years, and the current balance in such account(s);
   q. the amount of any recruitment bonuses awarded to the employee since their date of hire;
   r. the amount of any relocation bonuses awarded to the employee;

s. the amount of any certification bonuses awarded to the employee (and please distinguish how many different certification bonuses each employee receives);

t. the amount of committee work pay awarded to the employee;

u. if there are differences in remuneration for the categories described in sections "k" through "t" above because of which unit/department the employee works in, please explain such differences and the policy reasons guiding them;

v. all wage increases granted in the past three years, the dates on which they were granted and the reason for the increase (i.e., annual evaluation, across the board, merit, etc.)

w. the amount of any lump sum payments made to employee in lieu of an increase in hourly rate of pay; please indicate the percentage of the lump sum payment;

x. for each employee, the number of hours worked at the straight time hourly rate for the last three (3) fiscal years;

y. for each employee, the number of hours worked at the overtime rate for the last three (3) fiscal years;

z. number of hours worked in which employee qualified for a shift (night, evening, weekend, etc.) differential. Please specify the type and amount of the differential:

   aa. the number of hours employee was paid charge/relief supervisory differential (if you no longer offer this, when did such differential cease and why?);

   bb. the number of hours the employee was paid a preceptor pay differential (if you no longer offer this, what year did this differential cease and why?);

   cc. please describe whether any employee receives overtime payment in any other manner other than the statutory 40+ hours per week (for example, does any employee receive daily overtime after either 8, 10, or 12 hours in a day)

2. Copies of Plan Documents for any and all employee benefit plans that bargaining unit employees are eligible to participate in (health, defined benefit pension, 403(b), disability, severance, etc.) as well as the summary plan descriptions for each:

   a. A listing of all employees currently participating in such plans, including a breakdown of employee, employee/children, employee/

spouse, and employee/family coverage and the amount the employer and employee pay per month for each level of coverage;

b. A copy of the plan designs, including all co-payment, deductibles, co-insurance, etc. for all health plans offered to bargaining unit employees;

c. A copy of Form 5500s for all plans that are required to submit such forms

3. Copies of all current job descriptions for positions included within the bargaining unit;

4. A copy of all current work rules, policies, and procedures (including any and all employee handbooks, manuals, as well as any unit-based or unit-specific policies) that affect bargaining unit employees;

5. Staff turnover can impact patient care, staff morale, and working conditions. In order to bargain to improve employee retention, we request the following information:

a. The names, unit/department, wage rates, and years of relevant experience of all employees that worked in a bargaining unit–covered position who terminated their employment at Einstein any time in the last three fiscal years. Please provide the information for each year separately.

6. Quality patient care is very important to bargaining unit employees. In order to work with management to provide the highest level of patient care, we request copies and an explanation of the staffing patterns and acuity system for the medical center overall and, if applicable, for each unit/department. Please include the evaluation program or tools used to determine safe and/or adequate staffing for each unit and/or department. Additionally please provide copies of all Occurrence Reports submitted by employees in the last two fiscal years and the results of management's investigations of such reports.

7. In order to discuss how Einstein Medical Center's education affiliations impact bargaining unit employees, we request copies of all educational affiliation agreements the hospital has with outside educational institutions or agencies.

8. Please describe any existing nursing councils/committees, and include the following information:

a. A copy of the Shared Governance Bylaws;

b. A list of all current council members and participants, their job titles and departments;

c. Minutes of all meetings of any and all committees/councils with participation by bargaining unit employees held in the last 3 years;

d. A description of all nursing protocols, practices, and educational changes made in the last two (2) fiscal years as a result of the committee's recommendations;

e. A description of the Medical Center's Clinical Ladder program; and

f. A report on the status of Einstein Medical Center's Magnet application and plans for achieving Magnet recognition.

Please provide copies of the above requested information as soon as possible as we are excited to begin negotiations. We also respectfully request that the information be provided in an electronic format.

Finally, as PASNAP is now certified as the representative of the Registered Nurses, we make the following ongoing, continuous demand:

We hereby request to negotiate over *any and all* operational decisions of the employer, and the effects of such decisions, that would result in any changes to employees' terms and conditions of employment.

As I am sure you know, from this point going forward, any change to employees' terms and conditions of employment made without providing to PASNAP notice and the opportunity to bargain is considered a unilateral change in violation of Section 8(a)(5) of the National Labor Relations Act. So, for example, below is a (brief) list of the kinds of putative decisions/changes which we will insist not be made without providing notice and an opportunity to bargain over the decision and the effects of such decision:

• Job bidding and promotional opportunities, including positions outside the bargaining unit to the extent that such positions potentially impact the bargaining unit;

• Changes in employees' hours, shifts;

• Any and all discipline of employees;

- Any decision to impose discipline without affording employees the rights guaranteed by *Weingarten* and its progeny, which we hereby demand;
- Any decision to lay off or downsize employees, even for a single shift;
- Any decision to alter in any way the plan design of the health plan;
- Any decision to alter in any way the details of the defined benefit pension plan or the 403(b) plan;
- Any decision to reassign employees, including temporary reassignment, that may happen on a shift-by-shift, day-by-day basis;
- Any decision to introduce changes to the manner in which bargaining unit work is performed;
- Any decision to subcontract bargaining unit work, including the use of temporary agencies for short-, medium-, and long-term assignments; and
- Any decision to award, on a daily basis, extra shift and overtime opportunities to employees which could lead to employees earning more (or less) money in their bi-weekly paychecks.

We feel it is necessary to share our intentions on these important matters given that Einstein leadership has already initiated two appeals to the NLRB-conducted election. There exists the very real possibility that by continuing to refuse to negotiate with an NLRB-certified union, Einstein is voluntarily taking on the risk of substantial economic penalties.

We are sincerely hopeful that our relationship moves in the opposite direction, to one based on mutual understanding and respect, playing itself out at the negotiations table in a timely manner.

I thank you in advance for your cooperation in this matter. If you should have any questions regarding this letter, please do not hesitate to contact me.

Sincerely,
Jane F. McAlevey, PhD
Chief Negotiator
jmcalevey@law.harvard.edu
702-882-5555

CC: Registered Nurse Bargaining Unit, AEMC

Appendix 3: NJEA (Chapter 3)

NJEA Building Map

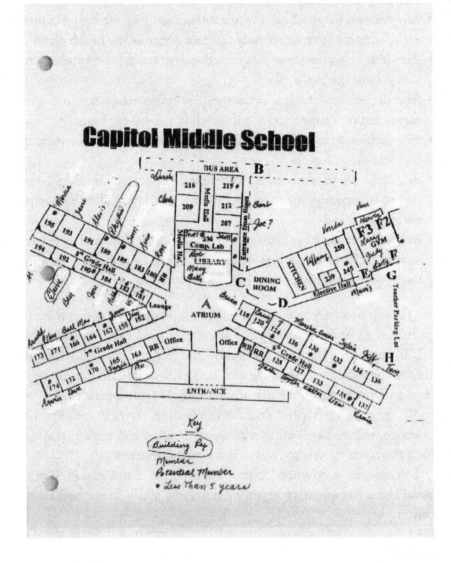

Appendix 4: NewsGuild-CWA (Chapter 4)

NewsGuild-CWA Bulletin on the Battle over Management Rights

Subject: FW: GUILD BARGAINING BULLETIN: A battle over 'management rights'
Attachments: management-rights-proposal.pdf

Date: Fri, Aug 23, 2019 at 11:32 AM
Subject: GUILD BARGAINING BULLETIN: A battle over 'management rights'
To: Guild Bargaining Committee

— The final battle over management rights looms
— Marathon session produces some language on freelancing, etc.
— T-shirt day on Tuesday!

Colleagues:

After a 12-hour bargaining session yesterday, we are now gearing up for a showdown over so-called "management rights." It's an arcane piece of language, but it will determine management's power to make major changes to our newsroom mid-contract without bargaining with us first.

Yesterday the bulk of the discussion centered on guardrails we want around the use of freelancers so the company can't replace us with a battalion of lower-paid non-staffers. It was a productive conversation (it helps to have the masthead at the table), and we believe we're close to a reasonable compromise.

But management rights remain a major sticking point.

We bargain again on Tuesday and Wednesday, and we will stay *as late as it takes.*

WHAT'S AT STAKE

A management rights clause is a list of ways that management could change the terms and conditions of our employment without bargaining, as it would ordinarily be obligated to do.

For each issue that's listed as a management right in our contract, it means we waive the right to bargain over that issue in the future.

Management will tell you that's not the case, because the company is still required to bargain over the *effects* of implementing each right, just not the decision to implement.

AN EXAMPLE OF HOW IT WORKS
Last summer, we engaged in effects bargaining over our move to El Segundo. We presented proposals that included moving stipends, commute subsidies and a more flexible work-from-home policy. The company declined them all and we moved anyway, getting nothing to ease the impact.

Basically, all that effects bargaining does is obligate management to listen to our concerns, but it gives us very little leverage to ensure that those concerns are actually addressed.

WHAT WE DON'T WANT
We've asked management to come to the table with specific proposals concerning anything they'd like to have the power to do over the life of our contract so that we can negotiate reasonable ways to safeguard our rights in each instance.

Instead, the company wants us to agree to broad waivers of our bargaining rights over some issues that we haven't discussed at the table, and that the company would ordinarily be required to bargain over, and other waivers that could conflict with terms we've bargained elsewhere in the contract.

Our legal counsel has advised us that giving management the broad right to do some of these things could undermine our protections under the law, as well as those we've already negotiated.

Here are examples from the company's most recent proposal:

WHAT IT SAYS MANAGEMENT CAN DO	WHAT IT COULD MEAN
"To determine what work will be performed by employees covered by this Agreement and the number of employees needed to perform such work; to determine the qualifications and responsibilities of employees"	Management could change employees' job descriptions without bargaining over the decision.
"To develop and implement performance evaluation and merit pay programs ... to set performance standards, goals or objectives for employees"	Management could set quotas — requiring reporters to file a minimum number of stories per day, for example, or to obtain a certain number of conversions — without bargaining. Managers would not rule out this possibility at the bargaining table.
"To subcontract work"	We are currently negotiating guardrails around subcontracting work in another area of our contract. This could permit management to circumvent those guardrails without bargaining over the decision.

You get the idea.

THE INDUSTRY STANDARD

The language proposed by the company goes beyond what's in many other Guild contracts.

For example, this is the management rights clause in the New York Times contract:

"All rights and discretion which ordinarily vest in management, and except those specifically modified herein, shall be the same as under the CBA."

Wall Street Journal contract:

"The Company reserves all rights customarily exercised by management except insofar as any such right may be specifically surrendered or abridged by express provision of this contract."

The L.A. Times' proposal is, by contrast, 500 words long. (Dying to read it? It's attached to this email.)

T-SHIRT DAY + MORE!!
Next week's sessions will be critical. The lawyers and management have indicated they are willing to stay late. And we're willing to stay *even later*.

Please show your support by wearing your banana shirts on Tuesday. It'd be great if the newsroom is a sea of yellow. Plus, the Campaign Committee will be in touch about other actions that will show the company that we are going to outlast them in this marathon.

Thank you all, as always, for all that you do.

Sincerely,
The Bargaining Committee

NewsGuild-CWA Bargaining Survey Report

Los Angeles Times Guild bargaining survey report
May 2018

Summary

The L.A. Times Guild's first bargaining survey confirmed what we already knew: Times staffers feel overworked and undervalued.

The survey was sent to 374 newsroom staffers March 19. Over about three weeks, we received 289 responses, or roughly 77% of members. We also conducted small group meetings led by delegates and bargaining committee members throughout March and April.

What we found was that staff attrition in recent years has forced many people to take on more day-to-day work while leaving them feeling more vulnerable to cuts. Increased job duties often do not mean an increase in pay, and across the newsroom wages have not kept up with the cost of living in Southern California. In fact, with the rising costs of healthcare and parking, as well as the elimination of benefits such as shift differentials and holiday pay, many Times employees feel their compensation has decreased over the years. The problem is worse for staffers of Times Community News, who report working second jobs or living with their parents to make ends meet.

While people generally report having positive relationships with their peers and direct supervisors, many do not feel respected by upper management. The pay disparities faced by women and people of color, in particular, are perceived as part of a company culture that does not value minority workers.

These are issues we organized around. The survey results demonstrate that the Guild has a mandate to address these issues with the company and develop a strong contract that would help keep people who are already here as well as make the newsroom a more attractive place to potential new employees.

Results

Job security

How secure do you feel in your job?
> Secure:18.9%
> Somewhat secure: 55.1%
> Somewhat insecure: 20%
> Insecure: 6%

How long do you plan to stay at The Times?
> Just a year or two: 1.8%
> Depends on what other opportunities come along: 35%
> For the foreseeable future: 38.2%
> I hope to retire from The Times: 25.1%

How important is establishing protections against layoffs?
> 88.7% of respondents said it was important (37.4%) or very important (51.3%)

Ranked benefits and protections in the event of layoffs:
> 1. Extra severance (2.45 average)
> 2. Extended healthcare (2.96 average)
> 3. Callback right (3.77 average)
> 4. Transfer rights (4.0 average)
> 5. Bridging service periods (4.86 average)
> 6. No NDAs (4.88 average)
> 7. Job training (4.9 average)

Sample comments:
- *"In the event of layoffs, it would be nice to have at least a month's notice so reporters can get their affairs in order/start looking for another job. It'd also be helpful to know how long our financial runways are. If I lose my job today, I am financially fucked. But if I know I have two more pay cycles before I lose my job, I can plan for that."*
- *"At TCN, job insecurity is directly linked to the health/future of our papers as a whole. We're more worried about our papers closing down than random LAT-wide layoffs that might include us."*
- *"As a metpro, job security isn't something that typically comes with the position. The only real security I feel stems from the fact that I know that myself and other fellows are the lowest paid employees in the newsroom."*

Summary: Job insecurity was a driving motivation behind supporting unionization. Older workers in particular feel targeted for layoffs and buyouts, while Metpros feel particularly vulnerable because they don't feel like full-time, permanent staffers. Workers in Times Community News fear those operations will be shut down entirely.

Wages and retirement benefits

Based on what you know about the job market, how do you feel your salary compares with others who perform similar jobs to yours at other news outlets?

> I make more 10.6%
> I make about the same 20.8%
> I make less 43%
> I don't know 25.7%

Do you feel affected by a wage gap in this newsroom?

> Yes: 40% total 58% women 21% men 34% white 66% non-white
> No: 24% total 11% women 40% men 65% white 35% non-white
> I don't know: 36% total 31% women 39% men 42% white 58% non-white

How important is it to have a starting minimum salary by position?

> 71% said "important" (37.1%) or "very important" (32.25%)

How important is it to have a clearly defined pay schedule/progression based on years of service with The Times?

> 78% said "important" (32.5%) or "very important" (45.5%)

How important are cost-of-living increases to you?

> 92.7% said "important" or "very important"

How important is an increase in the employer's 401(k) match?

> 79.2% said "important" (38.9%) or "very important" (40.3%)

Summary: The high cost of living in Southern California, the lack of raises in recent years and the rising costs of healthcare all contribute to financial insecurity. Metpros and Times Community News workers in particular bear this burden. Compensation is also believed to be a driving factor in our struggle to retain talent.

- *"Seeing my financial situation remain stagnant as all my other expenses rise year after year has got me looking for greener pastures."*
- *"I feel like I can just pay my bills/basic expenses every month, and that's not really sustainable in the long term."*

- *"My pay doesn't reflect my 14 years with TCN or my 22 years total experience of working in newspaper production. It has also utterly failed to stay anywhere near the cost of living in Southern California, especially my rent. Although I enjoy my job and the people I work with, in financial terms it's pointless."*

Healthcare benefits

What do you think of your plan at The Times?
Satisfied 65.6%   Very satisfied 9.3%   Not satisfied 25.1%

Tronc has said it is considering eliminating the Signature PPO plan. How important is preserving that plan (or a comparable one under Soon-Shiong's ownership)?
54.7% said "important" or "very important"

Selected comments:

- *"What I can afford, as a woman in my 30s, is essentially disaster insurance. And still, if something were to happen to me, I would be financially ruined because of the high deductible."*
- *"The Signature PPO plan is our best plan, yet many friends at other companies have far superior health benefits. Stronger health benefits package is an important part of opening contract."*
- *"As a foreign correspondent, there is no good health care plan for us. I end up never using my plan since its nearly impossible seeing a doctor abroad on the plan. Instead, I pay for all medical expenses out-of-pocket."*

Summary: Wages have stagnated, but healthcare costs keep rising. People are largely disappointed with current dental and vision benefits. The issue is even more difficult for foreign and national correspondents whose choices are more limited because they don't live in California.

Paid time off

For you personally, how fair is the flexible time off policy?
Fair: 49.7%   Unfair: 24.1%   I don't know: 26.2%

On the whole, how fair is the flexible time off policy?
Fair: 18.9%   Unfair: 40.6%   I don't know: 40.6%

How important do you consider restoring the policy of accrued time off?

4

57.4% said "important" (32.4%) or "very important" (25%)

How important is it for the company to provide paid parental leave and other types of leave?

87.3% said "important" (25.7%) or "very important" (60.8%)

Sample comments:

- *"I'm not opposed to flex time. But establishing guaranteed vacation/sick minimums on top of a flex schedule might help ensure no one is denied the opportunity to take time off. Or at least ensure those who are will be compensated."*
- *"The flexible time off policy in conjunction with key positions in my department remaining unfilled have meant significantly less time off for me -- plus regular work on days off without compensation -- than under the previous arrangement. There appears to be little interest among supervisors in ensuring a reasonable work-life balance."*
- *"Flexible time off depends on who's approving your time. My boss is understanding so I feel that the time off program is fair but it's not the program itself that's fair, it's the judgement of those who implement it. So I'd say it's not fair."*
- *"Our current parental leave policy -- or lack thereof -- is a straight-up joke, an insult to mothers and fathers and one of the key reasons why I wanted to unionize."*
- *"Research has shown that women come back to jobs after pregnancy if they're happy in their jobs. Additionally, research has shown that if paternity leave is offered and encouraged, the wage gap among men and women is less drastic. It's important that people feel like they can be parents and journalists and don't leave for less time-consuming jobs."*
- *"Under guild representation at a previous employer, comp time was recognized as actual overtime compensation. So it was formally recorded and recorded at time and a half. You cannot have a genuine comp time system that relies on random 'take some time off' comments from an editor. This is one of the most abused practices at The Times."*

Summary: Although people are largely personally happy with flexible time off, there are widespread concerns that the policy varies by department or manager and is vulnerable to abuse. Additionally, the company's parental leave policy is limited and confusing.

Quality-of-life and other issues

How important is it for the company to provide career development opportunities? (Examples include financial support for training, subsidies to attend professional conferences or to learn a new skill or language)

5

66.5% said "important" (34.1%) or "very important" (32.4%)

How important is it to stabilize the cost of parking?
74.9% said "important" (31.7%) or "very important" (43.2%)

Do you feel like you're being treated fairly at work?
Yes: 73.5%   No: 26.5%

How approachable is your supervisor?
Very approachable 56.1%
Approachable 31.2%
Somewhat approachable 9.8%
Not approachable 2.8%

What other benefits would you be interested in?
Lowered or tiered parking costs 166 (60.6%)
Comp time recognition 146 (53.3%)
Increased mileage reimbursement 108 (39.4%)
Increased commuter/transit benefits 94 (34.3%)
Night/early shift pay differential 94 (34.3%)
Childcare benefits 74 (27%)
Student loan repayment help 61 responses (22.3%)
Increased phone plan reimbursement 60 (21.9%)
Company cars 51 (18.6%)
Tuition help 45 (16.4%)

Selected comments
- *"Our newspaper talks a great deal about the importance of diversity but doesn't do a good job acting on it. It is absolutely vital that we hire more women and people of color to leadership positions and as reporters."*
- *"By my direct supervisors, I feel I am treated fairly. But coming out of the Metpro program, I feel my salary is artificially low and even after receiving some raises, I am stuck at a level below what people with similar experience are paid when they get hired in other ways."*
- *"I feel like a lack of a clear job description for my position has led to me inheriting numerous responsibilities that I consider above my pay grade as people have left the company."*

6

- *"Because of very tight staffing, I do feel an unfair burden of keeping things afloat. I do not take real vacations because no one else is available to write all the stories for my paper, and when I do take short trips (under 1 week) it is typical for me to "bank" stories the week before, or to do all my reporting before I leave and write stories on vacation, though I've been known to conduct interviews while on vacation."*

Summary: Most people feel respected and treated fairly by their co-workers and direct supervisors, but view upper management and the company much more negatively. This is particularly an issue among current and former Metpros but not limited to them. Understaffing and ill-defined job duties also contribute to making people feel overworked and underpaid.

Proposals

Common proposals:

- **Pay:** Resolve the pay equity issue and secure an across-the-board raise. Cost-of-living increases, separate from proposed annual step raises. Holiday pay and shift differentials. Increased pay for Times Community News employees.
- **Job security:** Advance notice of layoffs and mandatory buyout offers. Other proposals, by priority, include: Extra severance, extended healthcare, callback rights, transfer rights, bridging service periods, no NDAs and job training.
- **Healthcare:** Lower healthcare costs, maintain a PPO plan, LGBTQ-friendly plans.
- **Parking:** Lower or tiered parking fees. Additionally, employees in Sacramento and Fountain Valley don't pay for parking and want to ensure that this is maintained.
- **Career development:** Funding to attend conferences or take classes as well as tuition aid.
- **Retirement benefits:** Increase the 401(k) match. Some staffers have also suggested restoring the pension plan, though this appears to be a pretty small group.
- **Time off:** Returning to accrued time off appears to be largely preferred. Otherwise, establishing a consistent policy for approving flexible time off and requiring minimums to ensure people get time off.
- **Parental leave**
- **Metpro reform**

Other suggested proposals:

- Comp time recognition: a system that actually tracks comp time instead of it being between employees and supervisors off the books.

7

- Company cars or pool cars: People who already use company cars want that maintained. Pool cars -- kept at the office instead of driven home by individual employees -- would enable more reporters to use public transit to get to work without worrying about what they'd do if they got sent out on breaking news.
- Increased subsidies for public transit use
- A codified policy for working remotely
- Resale rights/licensing for photos
- Equipment -- photographers say they want to be able to keep certain gear, like cameras or lenses, when they leave through a buyout
- Student loan repayment help
- Priority for hiring internally when positions open up -- this proposal includes formalizing a path for TCN employees into the Times, whether it's through Metpro or priority when positions become vacant.
- Limits on time periods people can be interns or contract employees.
- Internal freelance and compensation for temporary assignments: Employees who perform work for other departments, like a copy editor who writes for another section, should be compensated for that work. Similarly, employees who take temporary assignments, such as TCN employees or editorial assistants being moved to fill vacancies in LAT departments or reporters filling in as editors, should be paid appropriately during that assignment.
- A mental healthcare advocate in the newsroom or counseling/therapy
- Hazardous duty pay, comp time, equipment
- HR hearing process for harassment or discrimination
- Skills training and professional development
- Increased cellphone stipend -- TCN employees say they're still using company-provided Blackberry phones and don't have a stipend option at all, which they'd prefer

Follow-up

Recommended for further surveying or clarification
Seniority: The biggest concern, predictably, is about how seniority will be used as a factor in layoffs. People are eager to talk about it, but they also need more information on what specific proposals could look like.

- *"This survey did not ask any questions about my stance on seniority as a method for determining layoffs. Why? I believe we should all be able to weigh in on such a decision. We were told repeatedly during the union drive that we would have the chance to pick and select and design a seniority policy that best fits what we all want. Was that true?"*

- *"The survey did not cover the seniority issue, which I think is extremely important. In the case of layoffs, a straight seniority clause (first one in, last one out) is extremely unfair and bad business for the paper."*
- *"Employees who have the most seniority and high productivity should be the last to be laid off."*

Merit-based raises: There appears to some confusion or concern that the union would do away with merit-based raises. We should improve our messaging on this.

- *"If you get scheduled increases, you may end up discouraging merit increases and just perpetuate the exodus of our best talent. There shouldn't be an agenda where everybody gets paid the same."*
- *"I don't have complaints about my pay per se. But I do want a recognition for bargaining purposes that it took 40 years to get to this pay, and it should not mean that I'm passed by for merit increases as I was in 2016. I started here making minimum wage, after all."*
- *"As long as I have the floor -- I do think merit pay has its place. If we try to take every tool out of management's hands, we'll look like the L.A. Unified teachers' union, coddling mediocrity. Similarly I think tenure and performance reports should both be considered in layoff decisions."*

Missing department group meeting notes:
Opinion
Sports
Politics
Metpro
D.C.

9

Appendix 5: MNA (Chapter 5)

MNA Bargaining Committee Letter

Cindy Russo, President
Baystate Franklin Medical Center
164 High St, Greenfield, MA 01301

Dear Cindy,

Recently you have written letters to the press, community and BFMC staff about our negotiations. We
have actually been *at* bargaining, as have been about half of all our RN co-workers who have witnessed
sessions for themselves. Respectfully, we are writing to say that, if you believe the descriptions of these
negotiations that have been published above your signature, then what you are being told about them by
your negotiators has been inaccurate.

1) It is uninformed and insulting to publish, as you have, "It appears that a larger MNA agenda is at
play, one that mirrors their tactics elsewhere…" Here's the reality: *We are* the MNA at BFMC, and
all our proposals come from the nurses at *this* hospital. The truth is that well over 90% of MNA
contracts are settled without picketing, 99% without strikes, the majority are settled at the bargaining
table without public mention of discord, and it is even more rare for MNA members to have to file
federal charges of overall bad faith bargaining.

In Western Mass., our contracts at Mercy Medical Center in Springfield and Providence Hospital in
Holyoke were settled before their expirations in *three sessions.* MNA members settled their contract
with Cooley Dickinson in January on time without discord. The same was true with our last round of
bargaining with the VNA & Hospice of Cooley Dickinson. MNA nurses at Smith College settled
their contract with no public fanfare. In February, our members' contract with Vibra Hospital in
Springfield was settled in *two* sessions. In Central Mass., in the past year our members at the
gigantic UMass Med Center Memorial Campus settled their contract ahead of expiration in
expedited bargaining, and members at their sister University Campus settled a few months later, with
neither party expressing negativity in public. In April we settled our Clinton Hospital contract
amicably. In 2016 we settled our contracts with the huge Tenet St. Vincent's Medical Center and with
Tenet Metro West in *two session.*

Our members' negotiations in 2013 with Noble Hospital actually fit the MNA "pattern," having been
settled without rancor. This round, though, there have been scores of sessions with limited progress
and public demonstrations. What changed? Nurses there have seen the more adversarial and less
organized negotiations from their hospital's new owner, Baystate.

2) It is just wrong to criticize RNs for fighting for best practices in patient care and not just focusing on
personal economic gain. In a better world, we would hope that Baystate executives would feel the
same urgency as we in moving toward best practices. Patients today are much sicker on average than
they were in the past, as treatment more often happens in an outpatient setting, resulting in the
hospitalized patient population being far more acutely ill than ever. We are working exhausted.

3) You sent a letter to our neighbors falsely stating our average annual base pay based on a "40 hour
work week." Did you decide that it didn't matter how infuriating it would be for your own staff to
read this, when we all know that approximately *two* staff nurses work 40 hours? As you know, the
majority of us are scheduled to work between 24 and 32 hours, a number work only 16 hours, and
one out of six work less than the 24 to 32 norm, as per diems without schedules and without benefits.

Continued ⟶

4) There is something that we did at the beginning of these negotiations which is *not* standard for the MNA: We made overtures, saying that there is no reason that we shouldn't be able to work together with Baystate on broad strategic goals, and we asked for an exchange of ideas on joint legislative and community goals. In the two prior years we also made an effort to change the relationship for the better by, among other things, working with management on the capital fundraising campaign to build the new surgery center. It would not be true to say our overtures went unanswered. They've been answered with hostility:

- A year ago management eliminated our "Gold" health Plan.
- In January, while in bargaining, management eliminated our "Silver" health plan.
- In January, management raised our premiums for the "Bronze" plan by about 26%.
- Management has said that it will not entertain any health care proposals except to maintain the substandard plans that management has forced on us. We work at a *hospital*, and we can't provide a decent health plan for our families.
- Management ordered all RNs who had worked every 3rd weekend to work every other.
- Management has refused to bargain over the basic issues of RN workload and safe patient limits. We can't get rest! We come in for 8 hour shifts, and often can't leave until we've worked 12 or 13 or more, because there are no longer staff to take over for us.
- We can't count on days off, because we're constantly called to come in. This is not the best practice for patient care, and it's been hurting our personal lives.
- Management even has refused our proposal that it will hire adequate staff so that it can comply with the contract and the law.
- We are working exhausted, and when we say we feel that this is becoming unsafe, and that we no longer have time for ourselves our families, it is cold hearted for management to describe our reality as "An Agenda."

We need to solve these problems together to make this hospital the best that it can be for the community, and to make it a decent place to work for the staff who are currently struggling.

Sincerely,

[handwritten signatures]

MNA Ratification Packet Cover Letter

May 30, 2018

Dear Fellow BFMC RNs,

Following 18 months of negotiations and a powerful effort to improve staffing and patient care, that included two strikes and tremendous solidarity, our bargaining committee has a reached a complete tentative agreement with management!

Our bargaining committee unanimously recommends it for your approval. There will be a secret ballot ratification vote on Monday, June 11 from 7AM until 7pm at BFMC in the Old Surgical Waiting Room.

We believe that this is a huge victory for Baystate Franklin patients, nurses and our entire community. The ultimate credit for this settlement goes to our 230 unified nurses and the Franklin County residents who joined with us.

A complete copy of all pages of the Tentative Agreement is attached. Here are some highlights:

- The hospital agrees not to diminish the current staffing grids as they relate to RNs.

- The hospital shall post and recruit positions to fill such positions that are necessary for the hospital to meet its contractual obligations.

- In the medical/surgical/telemetry units, the hospital will plan to have one charge nurse at all times without a patient assignment and one admissions nurse without a patient assignment from 11 a.m. to 11 p.m.

- On a daily basis in the medical/surgical/telemetry units, the charge nurse will have no patient assignment at the start of their shift. After two hours they may take up to two patient assignments in unplanned circumstances. In those circumstances, management will make all efforts to make available an RN who can take the transfer of the charge nurse's patient assignment.

- In the OR, charge nurses are not given a patient assignment.

- MHU: So that RNs are not required to perform MHC work, a 3rd MHC will be scheduled at 14 patients. Also: There will be an assigned Charge / Admissions RN at all times.

- The hospital agrees to reinstate the Silver health insurance plan (which management took away before negotiations began) effective September 1. And an agreement to "maintenance of benefits" language assuring that there will be no cuts to the benefits to or increase to the Silver health plan co-pays or other out of pocket costs through 2021.

- The hospital withdrew proposals to reduce nurses' earned time and holidays.

- Wages: Improvements which will help recruit, retain and better compensate:
  - Ratification bonus: Nurses will receive $0.50 for every hour paid in 2017 up to the first full pay period after ratification.
  - 2.5% across-the-board increase the first full pay period after ratification.
  - 1.4% effective Jan. 1, 2019
  - 1.5% effective Jan. 1, 2020
  - 2% effective Jan. 1, 2021
  - Increased differential pay for on-call, CNL/Charge, evening, nights, weekends, advanced degree nurses (BSN & MSN) , and precepting.
  - Quality & Risk Management/Case Management RNs move up from paygrade 26 to 27.
  - Improved tuition reimbursement.
- Improved retirement language, locking down the details of the plan benefits,
- New workplace violence prevention agreements.
- Floating language and the creation of a new float pool to improve staffing and patient care.
- Language affirming compliance with a) Mass. Meal Break law, b) Mass Earned Sick Time (which also provides per diems with up to 40 hours of sick time per year), c) the ICU patient care law, and d) language saying that the Patient Safety Act, when passed, will be effective in the hospital 7/1/2020.
- Limited Duty Nurse (per diem) language that makes clear that per diems work as needed without a regular schedule. (The implication being that if a PD is being regularly scheduled to a particular department, then a position should be posted).
- Discipline: Any negative notes placed in an RN's file will be provided to the RN, and, in addition to the right to file a grievance, one has the right to place a rebuttal statement in one's own file.
- Increasing or decreasing hours: New improved language.
- Redefined "Emergency" as it is used in the contract (which had been used over-broadly in the past by some managers) to be "An unforeseen event that could not be prudently planned for or anticipated by a hospital and affects patient safety in the hospital and where there is a government declaration of emergency, catastrophic event or hospital emergency declared by the president of the hospital."
- LOAs: Improved language for military leave and education leave (so RNs can more easily stay employed while enrolled in school to advance their skills).
- Improved vacancy/job bidding language and leave language.

Please join us after the vote for a gathering to express appreciation to each other and supporters at Hawks and Reeds starting at 7pm!

In Solidarity,

Your BFMC MNA Bargaining Committee

Appendix 6: UNITE HERE (Chapter 6)

UNITE HERE Bargaining Newsletter with Structure Test

Marriott wants to make our jobs worse. This week at bargaining Marriott management said they want to change our contract. They want to:

Make it easier to discipline and fire us!

Make it easier to cut our hours!

Make it easier to not pay us overtime!

Force housekeepers to do more rooms!

Be able to open NON-UNION restaurants and bars!

We told them NO! We gave the company our petition in support of our demands. **This petition was signed by over 70% of Marriott workers.** We told the company we will do WHATEVER IT TAKES to win.

Then, housekeepers from every Marriott hotel told management that they are DISRESPECTING us and NOT LISTENING to us. They explained that we worked hard on our demands. **They told Marriott that these negotiations are different: we will not settle until we get what we deserve!**

Now we take the fight into our hotels. Talk to your bargaining committee members about the plan! Get ready to stand up and shout until Marriott management listens to us!

UNITE HERE Power Structure Letter

STRIKE UPDATE

OCTOBER 30, 2018

Powerful Local and State Politicians
Support Our Strike!

Local leaders delegated Marriott management with this letter signed by 30 local and state politicians calling for meaningful negotiations that make sure ONE JOB IS ENOUGH!

October 29th, 2018

Arne Sorenson
President and CEO
Marriott International
10400 Fernwood Road
Bethesda, MD 20817

RE: Marriott Strike in Boston

Dear Mr. Sorenson:

We write to express our concern with the ongoing strike of Marriott hotel workers in Boston and to voice support for our constituents' desire to provide for themselves and their families with fair earnings and benefits from one job.

Your employees who belong to UNITE HERE Local 26 are ambassadors for the Greater Boston area. Like all workers, they deserve to be paid a living wage and enjoy basic protections from unfair scheduling practices, sexual harassment, and other workplace abuses.

We urge you to negotiate in good faith with the representing union, UNITE HERE Local 26, to reach a fair compromise that will end the strike and allow both parties to move forward amicably as soon as possible.

We appreciate your attention to this important matter and look forward to a resolution in the very near future.

Sincerely,

Senator Elizabeth Warren   Senator Edward Markey

Congressman Stephen Lynch   Congresswoman-elect Ayanna Pressley

Senator Joseph Boncore   Senator Nick Collins   Senator Sal N. DiDomenico
First Suffolk and Middlesex   First Suffolk   Middlesex and Suffolk

Representative Adrian Madaro   Representative-Elect Liz Miranda   Representative Elizabeth A. Malia
1st Suffolk   5th Suffolk   11th Suffolk

Representative Dan Ryan   Representative Chynah Tyler   Representative Daniel Cullinane
2nd Suffolk   7th Suffolk   12th Suffolk

Representative Aaron Michlewitz   Representative Jay Livingstone   Representative Daniel Hunt
3rd Suffolk   8th Suffolk   13th Suffolk

Representative-Elect David Biele   Democratic Representative-elect   Representative Kevin G. Honan
4th Suffolk   Jon Santiago 9th Suffolk   17th Suffolk

Michael Flaherty   Edward Flynn   Matt O'Malley
Boston City Council   Boston City Council   Boston City Council
At-Large   District 2   District 6

Annissa Essaibi George   Frank Baker   Kim Janey
Boston City Council   Boston City Council   Boston City Council
At-Large   District 3   District 7

Michelle Wu   Andrea Campbell   Josh Zakim
Boston City Council   Boston City Council   Boston City Council
At-Large   District 4   District 8

Lydia Edwards   Timothy McCarthy
Boston City Council   Boston City Council
District 1   District 5

UNITE HERE Bargaining Newsletter in Three Languages

STRIKE UPDATE

NOVEMBER 4, 2018

Smart Negotiations:

After two days of local bargaining and three days of national negotiations with Marriott, we have made significant progress on our key demands.

Hours and Overtime:

We've won major changes in our contract that will allow union members to get more hours. These are:
- Strict limits on managers doing our work.
- Real, understandable, scheduling language that will help more workers have more regular schedules with more hours.
- Guarantees that if you are on the schedule you stay on the schedule. No more getting called out the night before!
- Layoff language that allows workers to tell Marriott not to call them during a week. This will make it easier to collect unemployment and plan our lives.

Technology:

We have won real protections from the introduction of new technologies in our hotels this is the best contract language of its kind in the country. It includes:
- A negotiations process that makes Marriott tell us about new technology in advance, gives us a say in how and when technology is introduced, and guarantees that new jobs created by technology will be union.
- Guaranteed severance pay and extension of benefits if a union member is laid off because of technology.
- Funding for education if workers need to be retrained to take new jobs created by technological innovation.

Food and Beverage Job Security:

We have won real job security for existing food and beverage workers. This includes:
- The right to strike if Marriott wants to change, re-concept, convert, or overhaul our F & B outlets and we don't agree.
- A guarantee that Marriott will not open any subcontracted non-union restaurants or bars in our hotels
- A pilot program to open ONE new F & B outlet in Boston. This outlet will be union. It cannot replace an existing F & B outlet. It will open with the company health plan and will come in to the union pension after a year. All other wages and job descriptions need to be agreed upon by the union.

We have also been engaged in productive discussion with Marriott on our other major demands. They have shown an openness to resolve green choice, increasing our income (banquet gratuity, bell/door wage scale, other housekeeping workload reduction, etc.), retiree health coverage, and health care for casual workers.

President Lang and the bargaining committee are continuing to have discussions with the company this week. While these talks are ongoing, we must keep our strike strong.

We will continue to win by staying united!

STRIKE UPDATE

NOVEMBER 4, 2018

Negociaciones Eficientes:

Luego de dos días de negociaciones locales y tres jornadas de sesiones negociadoras a nivel nacional con Marriott, hemos logrado progresos importantes en nuestras exigencias principales:

Horas de Trabajo y Tiempo Extra:

Ganamos grandes cambios en nuestro contrato que permitirán a los afiliados recibir más horas de trabajo. Son estos:

- Límites estrictos a que los gerentes hagan nuestro trabajo.
- Cláusulas reales y comprensibles que ayudarán a más trabajadores a tener horarios más regulares y con más horas.
- Garantías para que si un empleado tiene su horario seguirá con ese horario. ¡No más avisos en la noche para no ir a trabajar al día siguiente!
- Cláusulas sobre ceses temporales que permiten a los trabajadores pedir a Marriott no ser llamados a trabajar durante una semana entera. Eso nos permitirá pedir pago por desempleo y planificarnos mejor.

Tecnología:

Hemos logrado protecciones reales sobre la introducción de nuevas tecnologías en nuestros hoteles. Ahora tendremos las mejores cláusulas de este tipo en todo el país. El contrato incluirá:

- Un proceso de negociación que exigirá a Marriott informarnos con antelación de las nuevas tecnologías, nos permitirá opinar sobre cómo y cuándo se introducirá la tecnología y garantizará que los nuevos puestos creados por la nueva tecnología tengan Unión.
- Pago por despido garantizado y extensión de los beneficios si se despide a un empleado a causa de la nueva tecnología.
- Fondos para educación si los empleados necesitan nuevos entrenamientos para desempeñar los nuevos puestos creados por la innovación tecnológica.

Seguridad Laboral para Empleados de Comidas y Bebidas (F & B):

También logramos seguridad real para los trabajadores actuales de F & B, que incluye:

- El derecho de ir a la huelga si Marriott quiere cambiar, reformar el concepto, convertir o traspasar nuestros centros de F & B y nosotros no estamos de acuerdo.
- La garantía de que Marriott no abrirá ningún restaurante o bar subcontratado sin Unión en nuestros hoteles.
- Un programa piloto para abrir UN nuevo centro de F & B en Boston, que tendrá Unión y no podrá sustituir a ningún otro F & B actual. Los empleados tendrán desde el principio el plan de salud de la compañía y entrarán en el plan de pensiones de la Unión luego de un año. Todos los demás salarios y descripciones de puestos deben ser aceptados por la Unión.

Además, tuvimos conversaciones productivas con Marriott acerca de las demás exigencias importantes. Se mostraron abiertos a resolver el problema de Green Choice, a aumentar nuestras ganancias (propinas por banquetes, escala salarial para botones/porteros, otras reducciones en la carga de trabajo de limpieza, etc.), y también hablamos del seguro médico en la jubilación y para los trabajadores ocasionales.

El Presidente Lang y el comité negociador seguirán discutiendo asuntos con la Compañía esta semana. Mientras continúen estas conversaciones, nosotros debemos mantener fuerte nuestra huelga.

¡Continuaremos ganando si nos mantenemos unidos!

STRIKE UPDATE

2018年11月4日

智慧的谈判：

与万豪经过两天的当地谈判和三天的全国谈判，我们在关键需求方面取得了重大进展。

工时和加班：我们已经赢得了合约中的一些重大变化，这将使工会成员能够获得更多的工作时间。这些是：

- 严格限制管理人员做我们的工作。
- 一个真实和可理解的时间表安排语言，可以帮助更多的工人有更多的工作间。
- 保证当你的名字出现在工作时间表上你便会按时间表上班，以后再也不会前一晚通知你不用上班！
- 设定裁员语言允许工人告诉万豪不要在一星期内打电话给他们。这将使它更容易领取失业金和规划我们的生活。

技术：我们在酒店引入新技术上赢得了真正的保护，这是全国最好的酒店合约语言。 这包括：

- 一个让万豪提前告诉我们新技术的谈判过程，让我们对如何以及何时引入技术发表意见，并保证技术创造的新工作将会受工会保护。
- 保证如果工会成员因技术而被解雇，则会支付遣散费和延长福利。
- 如果工人需要接受再培训以获得技术创新创造的新工作，就可以为教育提供资金。
- 如果工人需要接受再培训以获得技术创新创造的新工作，就可以为教育提供资金。
- 提供教育基金让工人在需要接受再培训以获得技术创新创造的新工作。

食品和饮料工作保障：我们为现有的食品和饮料工人赢得了真正的工作保障。 这包括：

- 若万豪希望改变，重新构思，转换或改革我们的餐饮店但我们不同意的情况下有权利进行罢工。
- 万豪保证不会在我们的酒店开设任何分包的非工会餐厅或酒吧。
- 在波士顿开设一家新的餐饮店的试点项目。而这间餐饮店将会是工会制。它无法取代现有的餐饮店。它将与公司医疗保险一起开放，并将在一年后拥有工会养老金资格。所有其他工资和工作描述需要与工会商定。

我们还与万豪就其他主要需求进行了有成效的商讨。 他们表现出开放态度去解决绿色选择，增加收入（宴会小费，开门/行李运送工资水平，其他房务员工作量减少等），退休工人医疗保险和临时工的医疗保险。

工会主席布莱恩朗连同我们的谈判委员会在这星期会继续与酒店方商讨条款。在这些谈判正在进行的同时，我们必须保持进行强有力的罢工活动。

我们将继续通过团结一致来赢得胜利！

UNITE HERE Strike Pledge

ONE JOB SHOULD —BE— ENOUGH

TO LIVE WHERE WE WORK
TO RAISE OUR FAMILIES
TO RETIRE WITH DIGNITY

YES, I WILL STRIKE

NAME _____

HOTEL _____

POSITION_____

CELL PHONE _____

COLLECTED BY _____

By providing your contact information, you agree to receive
text messages from UNITE HERE. Standard rates may apply.
To OPT-OUT, circle here.

I authorize UNITE HERE Local 26 or its designees to use my
photo in its materials.

BOSTON'S LOCAL 26

ONE JOB SHOULD —BE— ENOUGH

TO LIVE WHERE WE WORK
TO RAISE OUR FAMILIES
TO RETIRE WITH DIGNITY

YES, I WILL STRIKE

NAME _____

HOTEL _____

POSITION_____

CELL PHONE _____

COLLECTED BY _____

By providing your contact information, you agree to receive
text messages from UNITE HERE. Standard rates may apply.
To OPT-OUT, circle here.

I authorize UNITE HERE Local 26 or its designees to use my
photo in its materials.

BOSTON'S LOCAL 26

ACKNOWLEDGMENTS

This is a book about what high participation makes possible—and would not itself have been possible without the significant contributions of workers, staff, and community supporters from PASNAP, NJEA, NewsGuild, MNA, UNITE HERE, and ver.di. It cannot be overlooked that most of these contributions took place against the backdrop of a pandemic that created life-or-death risk and unprecedented strain for healthcare workers, educators, frontline journalists, and hospitality workers. The new demands of work under COVID, and the economic devastation of the travel industry, created existential challenges for the unions featured, and all were engaged in serious organizing to secure workplace safety protections and recall rights, maintain their contract standards, and support members struggling with sickness, loss, and un-employment. A second volume could be written about how practicing the skills of high-participation negotiations prepared workers for this crisis and were employed in response. For now, the chapter on ver.di may give you some idea.

The participants in this project were ready teachers because they were also ready learners. Throughout our research, workers drew on common touchstones—past campaigns within their own unions: Jane McAlevey's book, *No Shortcuts: Organizing for Power in the New Gilded Age*; and her domestic and global training programs—for building both their awareness of high-participation negotiations and their organizing muscles for carrying out big, open, and transparent campaigns. We would have had nothing to write about without these past efforts and the people who made them possible. Nor would this book exist without workers' immediate buy-in to the project of unpacking their own campaigns to help future workers win.

This book began as a research project, initiated and developed by Jane McAlevey, who then hired Abby Lawlor as a graduate student researcher to help get the effort done! Some parts of it were previously published by the University of California, Berkeley Labor Center under the title "Turning the Tables." Ken Jacobs, Brenda Munoz, and Danielle Mahones in particular, and the entire UC-Berkeley Labor Center, were unswerving in their commitment to the project from start to finish, providing financial, intellectual, and creative resources spanning two and a half years.

Practitioners immediately began to put the report to good use, and we thought we were done, mission accomplished. But then renowned sociologist Jeff Goodwin, a professor at New York University, relentlessly insisted it be expanded—both in terms of its theoretical argument as well as the number of cases—and made into a book. Thank you, Jeff!

In addition to the individuals named throughout, we gained invaluable assistance and important insights into the campaigns featured from Carlos Aramayo, William Lee, Tim Graumann, Paul Henzel, Max Manzey, Ingo Singe, Oskar Stolz, and Luigi Wolf. We also learned from several campaigns that ultimately have not appeared in print. For that, we give great thanks to Fabiola Benavides, Ian Lewis, Anand Singh, Kate Baker, Matt Hilton, Casey Parr, Kasey Zimmer-Stucky, and Stacy Chamberlain.

Early encouragement from Kate Bronfenbrenner, Barry Eidlin, and Rebecca Givan convinced us that the task of seriously chronicling how unions negotiate would be a worthwhile undertaking. Along with Dave Graham-Squire, Kate also provided valuable insights on survey methods.

Larry Alcoff, Kyle Arnone, Mark Brenner, John Lacny, Gordon Lafer, and Barbara Madeloni provided great guidance in our early days of casting about for examples of big and open negotiations and confirmed our hunch that examples of high-participation campaigns were out there, but were hard to find.

Everline Aketch, Adriana Rosenzvaig, Alan Sable, Federico West Ocampo, and Luigi Wolf were our guides to understanding the relevance (and irrelevance) of formal legal structures for shaping worker participation in their respective regions of the world. Once again, our final chapter on ver.di may spark interest in this regard.

Patrick DeDauw, a fantastically smart PhD student at the CUNY Graduate Center, provided his sharp intellect and feedback, and even sharper copy editing as the final deadline approached.

The vast majority of interviews for this book were conducted in English, which created an additional ask for our interview subjects from UNITE HERE Local 26 and ver.di, for whom English was a second (or third or fourth) language. They gamely tolerated the discomfort and occasional frustration of telling their stories without their full choice of words, and were brilliant nonetheless. For other interviews, we relied on skillful interpretation from Francisco Meza and Ingo Singe.

James Cook was amazing as editor of *No Shortcuts, Organizing for Power in the New Gilded Age*. Likewise, it was a total pleasure going from concept through peer review and onto him accepting the final copy for *Rules to Win By*. Once a manuscript has been accepted, a team of extraordinary talent gets to work turning our thoughts and words into the book in your hands. This team includes Amy Whitmer, diligently overseeing the entire process with grace and efficiency. Sarah Ebel facilitated more than we know, including helping to move the contract and cover design. The cover design was produced by Brady McNamara. Wonderful copy editing was completed by Bob Land. And finally, the indexer Ken Hassman did a heck of a job with little time! We deeply appreciate everyone at Oxford University Press for this incredible effort.

—Jane McAlevey and Abby Lawlor

The research that became this book was an unexpected pandemic project and would not have happened without the loving acquiescence of my spouse, Josh. When I first told Josh I wanted to take on a half-time

research job at the Berkeley Labor Center in January 2020, just a semester into my first year of law school, he was unwaveringly supportive,
even as it threatened to swallow what already scant time we had together.
What we didn't know was that we'd actually be spending quite a lot
of time (physically) together over the life of this research. As I began
interviewing workers that COVID spring, Josh was just on the other side
of our tiny Berkeley apartment. And he was there for nearly every one of
the interviews that followed, tolerating the endless loop of background
noise and helping debrief each of dozens and dozens of conversations with
patience and insight. I am so grateful for his presence in my life and for
the family and friends who populated Friday Zoom calls, weekend bike
rides, and sporadic email and text threads over the course of this work.

Talking with workers about their negotiations has provided ample opportunity to reflect on my own experiences negotiating and the people
who shaped them. I am thankful to the organizers and coworkers who
turned me out to negotiation sessions and trusted me with a seat at the
table—especially my Magic City committee and my UUHS comrades.
I learned so much, too, from long days and nights of deliberations in
hotel banquet rooms with the indominable members and staff of UNITE
HERE Local 8.

Over the last several years, the steady, strategic organizing of my
union siblings in UAW 2865, SRU-UAW, and UAW 5810 brought personal urgency to the question of how to pull off high-participation
negotiations on a mass scale. Summer gaps in this research were filled
by formative experiences at PowerSwitch Action, whose work highlights
the opportunities all around us to make democratic demands, and at
Weinberg, Roger & Rosenfeld, whose attorneys have shown me the best
of what labor lawyering can be.

—Abby Lawlor

Once we decided to turn our research report into a book, life kept
interrupting in ways familiar to tens of millions during this pandemic,
where housing and health stability were disrupted and complex life issues arose. Facilitating my ability to work throughout was a great team of
longtime friends and family, starting with my sister Bri and her husband,

Scott, and my brother Mitch and his wife, Suzee. Additional friends who jumped into the fray, including Cori Valentine, Laura Pandapas, Marne Brady, KB Brower, Lisa Bruce, Dominique Nispernos, Bronwyn Dubchuckland, Catherine Banghart, Susan Wray and her husband, Chris, and Janice Fine and her husband, David. My life functions so much better because of my entire large family, whose names would fill a chapter, along with an equally big list of friends and mentors.

The people who are most responsible for teaching me about negotiations and power are names that regularly show up in the acknowledgments section in all of my books, and there's no reason to stop thanking them now, certainly not when it comes to the book in your hands. The two people who taught me the most about what a workers' "art of the deal" flows from are Jerry Brown and Larry Fox, who together with many thousands more helped found and develop the still powerhouse District 1199NE, now a part of SEIU, but still retaining the best of what the US labor movement can be, leading by example and teaching so many. Once I had hired the incredibly dream graduate student researcher, Abby Lawlor, she become a summer intern at the same law firm that contributed the next most to my understanding of labor law and how it relates to negotiations and strikes: Weinberg, Roger & Rosenfeld. David Rosenfeld and Bill Sokol each played helpful roles in my development as a union negotiator specifically. Deep gratitude to all of you for your patience and support.

—Jane F. McAlevey

NOTES

Introduction

1. Phil Satre is what Thomas R. Colosi, Arthur Eliot Berkeley, and the American Mediation Association refer to a "mediator avec baguette" in their book *Collective Bargaining: How it Works and Why*, 3rd ed. (Huntington, NY: Juris Publishing, 2006), 125.

2. Theda Skocpol, *Diminished Democracy: From Membership to Management in American Civic Life* (Norman: University of Oklahoma Press, 2004); Robert Putnam, *Bowling Alone: The Collapse of American Community* (New York: Simon and Schuster, 2000).

3. *Knox v. SEIU* (2012), *Harris v. Quinn* (2014), *Janus v. AFSCME* (2018), and *Epic Systems Corp. v. Lewis* (2018; this case consolidated two other related cases dealing with forced arbitration clauses used to gut workers' rights to class action lawsuits, among other egregious implications).

4. Elijah Chiland, "Boyle Heights Mariachis Agree to 14 Percent Rent Hike but Win New Leases Ending Months-Long Strike," Curbed Los Angeles, February 16, 2018 (https://la.curbed.com/2018/2/16/17018298/boyle-heights-mariachi-gentrification-rent-strike); See Tracy Rosenthal and Leonardo Vilchis, *Abolish Rent* (London: Verso, forthcoming [2023]).

5. Ed Pilkington, "Governor's Islamist Terrorist Comparison Shocks Protestors," the Guardian, Feb. 27, 2015 https://www.theguardian.com/us-news/2015/feb/27/wisconsin-protests-scott-walker-islamic-terrorism-cpac

6. Jane McAlevey, *No Shortcuts, Organizing for Power in the New Gilded Age* (New York: Oxford University Press, 2016).

7. Jane McAlevey, *A Collective Bargain: Unions, Organizing and the Fight for Democracy* (New York: Harper Collins, 2020).

8. See Frances Fox Piven, *Challenging Authority: How Ordinary People Can Change America,* Polemics (Lanham, MD: Rowman and Littlefield, 2006).

9. See, for example, Matt Witt and Rand Wilson, "The Teamsters' UPS Strike of 1997: Building a New Labor Movement," *Labor Studies Journal* 24, no. 1 (1999): 58–72; Karen Beckwith, "Hinges in Collective Action: Strategic Innovation in the Pittston Coal Strike," *Mobilization: An International Journal* 5, no. 2 (2000): 179–199.

10. Roger Fisher, William L. Ury, and Bruce Patton, *Getting to Yes: Negotiating Agreement without Giving In* (New York: Penguin, 2011).

11. Robert Mnookin, *Bargaining with the Devil: When to Negotiate and When to Fight* (New York: Simon and Schuster, 2010).

12. Chris Voss with Tahl Raz, *Never Split the Difference: Negotiating as If Your Life Depended on It* (New York: HarperCollins, 2016).

13. See Michael Carrell and Christina Heavrin, *Labor Relations and Collective Bargaining: Private and Public Sectors*, 10th ed. (New York: Pearson, 2012).

14. Harry Katz, Thomas Kochan and Alexander Colvin, *An Introduction to Collective Bargaining and Labor Relations* (Ithaca, NY: Cornell University Press, 2017).

15. John W. Budd, *Labor Relations: Striking a Balance*, 4th ed. (New York: McGraw-Hill Education, 2012).

16. Colosi, Berkeley, and American Mediation Association, *Collective Bargaining*, 136–137.

17. Robert Michels, *Political Parties: A Sociological Study of the Oligarchical Tendencies of Modern Democracies* (1911; repr. New York: Free Press, 1962) (originally published in German).

18. See Tony Huzzard and Hans Björkman, "Trade Unions and Action Research," *Work, Employment and Society* 26, no. 1 (2012): 161–171.

19. Giovanni Radaelli, Marco Guerci, Stefano Cirella, and Abraham B. (Rami) Shani, "Intervention Research as Management Research in Practice: Learning from a Case in the Fashion Design Industry," *British Journal of Management* 25, no. 2 (2014): 335–351.

20. Susan McGrath-Champ, Mihajla Gavin, Meghan Stacey, and Rachel Wilson, "Collaborating for Policy Impact: Academic-Practitioner Collaboration in Industrial Relations Research," *Journal of Industrial Relations* 64 (May 2022): 1–26.

21. Ruth Wilson Gilmore, "Scholar-Activists in the Mix: The Role of Geography in Public Debate," *Progress in Human Geography* 29, no. 2 (2005): 179.

22. McAlevey, *No Shortcuts*, 16–20.

23. Kim Moody, "Reversing the 'Model': Thoughts on Jane McAlevey's Plan for Union Power," *Spectre Journal* 1, no. 2 (2020): 61–75.

24. See the "Clean Slate" report, or Kate Andrias and Benjamin J. Sachs, "Constructing Countervailing Power: Law and Organizing in an Era of Political Inequality," *Yale Law Journal* 130, no. 3 (January 2021): 546–635.

Chapter 1

1. Ihna Mangundayao and Celine McNicholas, "Congress Should Boost NLRB Funding to Protect Workers'

Well-Being," Economic Policy Institute, Working Economics Blog, February 28, 2022, https://www.epi.org/blog/congress-should-boost-nlrb-funding-to-protect-workers-well-being/.

2. Jane McAlevey, *A Collective Bargain: Unions, Organizing and the Fight for Democracy* (New York: HarperCollins, 2020).

3. Thomas R. Colosi and Arthur Eliot Berkeley, *Collective Bargaining: How It Works and Why*, 2nd ed. (New York: American Arbitration Association, 1994).

4. Joseph McCartin, *Collision Course: Ronald Reagan, the Air Traffic Controllers, and the Strike That Changed America* (New York: Oxford University Press, 2011).

5. Kate Bronfenbrenner and Tom Juravich, "It Takes More Than House Calls: Organizing to Win with a Comprehensive Union-Building Strategy," Cornell University ILR School, 1998, https://core.ac.uk/download/pdf/5129458.pdf.

6. Jane McAlevey, *No Shortcuts: Organizing for Power in the New Gilded Age* (New York: Oxford University Press, 2016), 12–16.

7. Jane McAlevey, *Raising Expectations (and Raising Hell)* (New York: Verso, 2012).

8. McAlevey, *No Shortcuts*.

9. McAlevey, *No Shortcuts*, 1–70.

10. Michael R. Carrell and Christina Heavrin, *Labor Relations and Collective Bargaining, Cases, Practice and Law*, 8th ed. (New York: Pearson-Prentice Hall, 2007), 216–219; John W. Budd, *Labor Relations: Strike a Balance*, 4th ed. (New York: McGraw-Hill Irvin, 2013), 236–237; Harry C. Katz, Thomas A. Kochan, and Alexander J. S. Colvin, *An Introduction to Collective Bargaining and Industrial Relations*, 4th ed. (New York: McGraw-Hill Irvin, 2008), 202–204.,

11. Jane McAlevey, "The Strike as the Ultimate Structure Test," *Catalyst: A Journal of Theory and Strategy* 2, no. 3 (Fall 2018): 122–135.

12. If the setting is a one in which strikes are officially outlawed, as for too many public sector workers, a negotiations committee can wield plenty of other leverage, such as the union negotiator knowing that several moves by the extended power structure are already lined up, combined with big-direction actions by the workers that will force a favorable settlement soon enough. For concrete examples of what this looks like, see chapter six in McAlevey's book, *Raising Expectations (and Raising Hell)*, by Verso Press.

13. These visuals, and this method, developed by brilliant community organizer Anthony Thigpenn, SCOPE (Strategic Concepts in Organization Policy and Education), https://scopela.org.

Chapter 2

1. Dan Clawson, *The Next Upsurge: Unions and the New Social Movements* (Ithaca, NY: Cornell University Press, 2003), 14, 106, 110–124, 189–190; see also Janice Fine, "Building Community Unions, in Stamford, CT,

Organizers Are Putting the Movement Back into Labor," *The Nation*, December 14, 2000.

2. Jane McAlevey, *A Collective Bargain: Unions, Organizing and the Fight for Democracy* (New York: HarperCollins, 2020), 155–196.
3. McAlevey, *A Collective Bargain*.
4. Unlawful, according to Celine McNicholas, Margaret Poydock, Julia Wolfe, Ben Zipperer, Gordon Lafer, and Lola Loustaunau, "U.S. Employers Are Charged with Violating Federal Law in 41.5% of All Union Election Campaigns," Economic Policy Institute, December 11, 2019, https://www.epi.org/publication/unlawful-employer-opposition-to-union-election-campaigns/.
5. Case No. 04-RC-170989, in the matter of Albert Einstein Medical Center, employer and the petitioner, Pennsylvania Association of Staff Nurses and Allied Professionals. All legal documents in possession of the authors.
6. Case No. 04-RC-170989, in the matter of Albert Einstein Medical Center, employer and the petitioner, Pennsylvania Association of Staff Nurses and Allied Professionals. All legal documents in possession of the authors.
7. A short four-minute fundraising video about the 150th campaign appears at EinsteinHealth, "Einstein Healthcare Network: 150 Years of More Than Medicine," January 26, 2016, https://www.youtube.com/watch?v=NeSdhkbgvQ8.
8. Philip Rucker and Robert Costa, "Bannon Vows a Daily Fight for 'Deconstruction of the Administrative State,' " *Washington Post*, February 23, 2017, https://www.washingtonpost.com/politics/top-wh-strategist-vows-a-daily-fight-for-deconstruction-of-the-administrative-state/2017/02/23/03f6b8da-f9ea-11e6-bf01-d47f8cf9b643_story.html.
9. Marne Payne, interview with author, April 2, 2017.
10. Elizabeth Miller, interview with author, June 2017.
11. https://www.inquirer.com/news/anti-union-busting-employers-report-20191211.html

Also https://www.epi.org/publication/unlawful-employer-opposition-to-union-election-campaigns/

Chapter 3

1. Lyndsey Layton, "Chris Christie to Teachers Union: You Deserve a Punch in the Face," *Washington Post*, August 3, 2015, https://www.washingtonpost.com/local/education/chris-christie-to-teachers-union-you-deserve-a-punch-in-the-face/2015/08/03/86358c2c-39de-11e5-8e98-115a3cf7d7ae_story.html. Christie was speaking specifically of the American Federation of Teachers, but his remarks could have just as easily applied to the National Education Association–affiliated NJEA, who had directly experienced the brunt of Christie's attack on public education over the previous four years.
2. For the text of the act, see https://www.njleg.state.nj.us/2010/Bills/PL11/78_.HTM.

3. Kate Zernike, "Pensions Haunt Christie 4 Years after Being 'Fixed,' "
     New York Times, February 25, 2015, https://www.nytimes.com/2015/02/25/
     nyregion/chris-christie-of-new-jersey-budget-address.html.
4. Zernike, "Pensions Haunt Christie"; Martin Z. Braun, "New Jersey
     Tops Illinois as State with Worst-Off Pension System," Bloomberg,
     November 2, 2016, https://www.bloomberg.com/news/articles/2016-11-02/
     new-jersey-tops-illinois-as-state-with-worst-off-pension-system.
5. Nancy Solomon, "A Republican Star Fallen, Chris Christie Leaves
     Office," National Public Radio, January 15, 2018, https://www.npr.
     org/2018/01/15/577650714/a-republican-star-fallen-chris-christie-leaves-
     office.

Chapter 5

1. Greenfield Historical Society, Collection Area: Greenfield Tap &
     Die, accessed November 17, 2022, http://chc.library.umass.edu/
     greenfield-historical/category/greenfield-tap-die/.
2. Tom Goldscheider, "At Sword's Point: The United Electrical Workers
     Union and the Greenfield Tap & Die Company," *Historical Journal
     of Massachusetts* (Winter 2019): 32–75, http://www.westfield.ma.edu/
     historical-journal/wp-content/uploads/2020/01/At-Swords-Point-final.pdf.
3. Rebecca Ducharme, "Greenfield Tap & Die: Economic and Historical
     Analysis," *Historical Journal of Massachusetts* 34, no. 2 (Summer 2006): 132–
     148, https://www.westfield.ma.edu/historical-journal/wp-content/
     uploads/2018/06/Ducharme-summer-2006-combined.pdf.
4. Franklin County, MA: Business Development Profile, accessed
     November 17, 2022, https://frcog.org/wp-content/uploads/2014/02/2016_
     BusinesDevelopmentProfile.pdf.
5. https://www.baystatehealth.org/-/media/files/baystate-health-fast-
     facts-2022.pdf.
6. Baystate Franklin Medical Center, "Community Health Needs
     Assessment: Adopted by the Baystate Health Board of Trustees on
     September 10, 2019," https://www.baystatehealth.org/-/media/files/
     about-us/community-programs/community-benefits/2019-community-
     health-needs-assessments/baystate-franklin-2019-chna-report-final-web.
     pdf?la=en.

Chapter 8

1. C-SPAN, October 25, 2021, Vice President Harris talking with
     the media about the status of climate legislation. An actual
     statement from White House records appears at https://www.
     whitehouse.gov/briefing-room/speeches-remarks/2021/10/25/
     remarks-by-vice-president-harris-during-a-meeting-on-climate-change/.
2. Ipsos, "President Biden Continues to Lose Ground with the American
     Public on a Range of Issues," January 30, 2022, https://www.ipsos.com/
     en-us/news-polls/president-biden-continues-lose-ground-american-public.

3. Michael Carrell and Christina Heavrin, *Labor Relations and Collective Bargaining: Private and Public Sectors*, 10th ed. (New York: Pearson, 2012), 213.
4. For a full account of this contract campaign, read Jane McAlevey, *A Collective Bargain: Unions, Organizing and the Fight for Democracy* (New York: Harper Collins, 2020), chapter XX.

REFERENCES AND INTERVIEWS

BOOKS AND ARTICLES

Andrias, Kate, and Benjamin J. Sachs. 2020–2021. "Constructing Countervailing Power: Law and Organizing in an Era of Political Inequality." *Yale Law Journal* 130, no. 3: 546–635.

Block, Sharon, and Benjamin Sachs. 2020. "Clean Slate for Worker Power: Building a Just Economy and Democracy." Harvard Law School Report, Labor and Worklife Program.

Bronfenbrenner, Kate. 1997. "The Role of Union Strategies in NLRB Certification Elections." *Industrial and Labor Relations Review* 50, no. 2: 195–212.

Bronfenbrenner, Kate. 2009. "No Holds Barred: The Intensification of Employer Opposition to Organizing." Economic Policy Institute Briefing Paper 235.

Budd, John W. 2013. *Labor Relations: Striking a Balance*. 4th edition. New York: McGraw-Hill Irwin.

Carrell, Michael R., and Christina Heavrin. 2007. *Labor Relations and Collective Bargaining: Cases, Practices and the Law*. 8th edition. Hoboken, NJ: Pearson-Prentice Hall.

Colsi, Thomas R., and Arthur Eliot Berkeley. 1994. *Collective Bargaining: How It Works and Why*. New York: American Arbitration Association.

Fiorito, Jack, and Wallace Hendricks. 1987. "Union Characteristics and Bargaining Outcomes." *Industrial and Labor Relations Review* 40, no. 4: 569–584.

Fisher, Roger, and William Ury. 1981. *Getting to Yes*. New York: Houghton Mifflin.

Gilmore, Ruth Wilson. 2005. "Scholar-Activists in the Mix: The Role of Geography in Public Debate." *Progress in Human Geography* 29, no. 2: 165–193.

Grannis, Rick, David A. Smith, and Judith Stepan-Norris, 2008. "Working Connections: Shop Floor Networks and Union Leadership." *Sociological Perspectives* 51, no. 3: 649–672.

Hertel-Fernandez, Alexander, William Kimball, and Thomas Kochan. 2020. "What Forms of Representation Do American Workers Want? Implications for Theory, Policy, and Practice." *Industrial and Labor Relations Review* 75, no. 2: 267–294, https://journals.sagepub.com/doi/abs/10.1177/0019793920959049.

Hodgkinson, Gerard P., and Denise M. Rousseau. 2009. "Bridging the Rigour-Relevance Gap in Management Research: It's Already Happening!" *Journal of Management Studies* 46, no. 3: 534–546.

Huzzard, Tony, and Hans Björkman. 2012. "Trade Unions and Action Research." *Work, Employment and Society* 26, no. 1: 161–171.

Hyde, Alan. 1984. "Democracy in Collective Bargaining." *Yale Law Journal* 93, no. 9: 793–856.

Katz, Harry C., Thomas A. Kochan, and Alexander J. S. Colvin. 2008. *An Introduction to Collective Bargaining & Industrial Relations*. 4th edition. New York: McGraw-Hill Irwin.

Kieser, Alfred, and Lars Leiner. 2009. "Why the Rigour-Relevance Gap in Management Research Is Unbridgeable." *Journal of Management Studies* 46, no. 3: 516–533.

McGrath-Champ, Susan, Mihajla Gavin, Meghan Stacey, and Rachel Wilson. 2022. "Collaborating for Policy Impact: Academic-Practitioner Collaboration in Industrial Relations Research." *Journal of Industrial Relations* 64 (May): 1–26.

McAlevey, Jane. 2012. *Raising Expectations (and Raising Hell)*. New York: Verso.

McAlevey, Jane. 2020. *A Collective Bargain: Unions, Organizing and the Fight for Democracy*. New York: ECCO/HarperCollins.

Michels, Robert. 1962 [1911]. *Political Parties: A Sociological Study of the Oligarchical Tendencies of Modern Democracies*. New York: Free Press. (Originally published in German)

Mnookin, Robert H. 2010. *Bargaining with the Devil: When to Negotiate, When to Fight*. New York: Simon & Schuster.

Radaelli, Giovanni, Marco Guerci, Stefano Cirella, and Abraham B. (Rami) Shani. 2014. "Intervention Research as Management Research in Practice: Learning from a Case in the Fashion Design Industry." *British Journal of Management* 25, no. 2: 335–351.

Rosenfeld, David. 1995. "Offensive Bargaining," Institute for the Study of Labor Organizations. https://books.google.com/books/about/Offensive_Bargaining. html?id=FaxXAAAAYAAJ.

Stepan-Norris, Judith, and Maurice Zeitlin. 1995. "Union Democracy, Radical Leadership, and the Hegemony of Capital." *American Sociological Review* 60, no. 6: 829–850.

Ury, William. 2007. *Getting Past No*. New York: Bantam.

Voss, Christopher, and Tahl Raz. 2016. *Never Split the Difference: Negotiating as If Your Life Depended on It*. New York: HarperCollins.

Chapter 2
- Patricia Eakin, Founding President, PASNAP
- Patrick Kelly, Vice President, PASNAP
- Liz Miller, Member, PASNAP
- Marne Payne, Nurse Practitioner, (formerly Einstein), Philadelphia
- Peg Lawson, President, Einstein Chapter

Chapter 3
- Karen Burke, Member, Mercer County Special Services Education and Therapeutic Association
- Alexander DeVicaris, UniServ Field Representative, NJEA
- Kenneth Karnas, President, Watchung Hills Regional Education Association
- Jennifer Larsen, UniServ Field Representative, NJEA
- Kevin Meyer, President, Readington Township Education Association
- Leah Pray, President, Mercer County Special Services Education and Therapeutic Association
- Marisa Walsh, Member, Watchung Hills Regional Education Association
- Keith Whitacre, Retiree, Mercer County Special Services Education and Therapeutic Association

Chapter 4
- Judith Atkins, Community Member, Franklin County, MA
- David Cohen, Community Member, Franklin County, MA
- Suzanne Love, Member, MNA
- Rudy Renaud, Staff Director, MNA
- Dana Simon, Staff Director, MNA
- Donna Stern, Board of Directors, MNA

Chapter 5
- Stewart Bishop, Member, Law360 Union
- Kristina Bui, Member, L.A. Times Guild
- Braden Campbell, Member, Law360 Union
- Jody Godoy, Member, Law360 Union/Executive Committee, NewsGuild of New York
- Carolina Miranda, Member, L.A. Times Guild
- Matt Pearce, Member, L.A. Times Guild
- Anthony Pesce, Member, L.A. Times Guild
- Juan Carlos Rodriguez, Member, Law360 Union/Executive Committee, NewsGuild of New York
- Jon Schleuss, President, NewsGuild-CWA
- Danielle Smith, Member, Law360 Union/Executive Committee, NewsGuild of New York
- Alex Wigglesworth, Member, L.A. Times Guild

Chapter 6

- Richie Aliferis, Executive Board Member, UNITE HERE Local 26
- Carlos Aramayo, President, UNITE HERE Local 26
- Saihua Deng, Member, UNITE HERE Local 26
- Juan Eusebio, Member, UNITE HERE Local 26
- John Flannery, Member, UNITE HERE Local 26
- Alganesh Gebrilibanos, Member, UNITE HERE Local 26
- William Lee, Staff Organizer, UNITE HERE Local 26
- Courtney Leonard, Staff Organizer, UNITE HERE Local 26
- Ian Seale, Member, UNITE HERE Local 26
- Maryann Silva, Member, UNITE HERE Local 26
- Ye Qing Wei, Staff Organizer, UNITE HERE Local 26

Chapter 7

- Rowena Filzmaier, Member, ver.di
- Tim Graumann, Union Secretary, ver.di
- Silvia Habekost, Member, ver.di
- Paul Heinzel, Political Organizer, Organizi.ng
- Denise Klein-Allerman, Member, ver.di
- Kim Lenzen, Member, ver.di
- Dana Lütkzendorf, President for Health, Social Services, Welfare and Churches, ver.di
- Max Manzey, Organizer, Organizi.ng
- Stella Merendino, Member, ver.di
- Ingo Singe, Researcher, Center for Labor and Politics at the University of Bremen
- Lynn Stephainski, Member, ver.di
- Oskar Stolz, Staff Organizer, Organizi.ng
- Anja Voigt, Member, ver.di
- David Wetzel, Member, ver.di
- Luigi Wolf, Director, Organizi.ng

INDEX

For the benefit of digital users, indexed terms that span two pages (e.g., 52–53) may, on occasion, appear on only one of those pages.